THE FACTS ON FILE

DICTIONARY OF 20TH-CENTURY ALLUSIONS

THE FACTS ON FILE
DICTIONARY OF 20TH-CENTURY ALLUSIONS

From Abbott and Costello to Ziegfeld Girls

Sylvia Cole
Abraham H. Lass

Facts On File

The Facts On File Dictionary of 20th-Century Allusions

Copyright © 1991 by Sylvia Cole and Abraham H. Lass

Facts on File, Inc.
460 Park Avenue South
New York NY 10016
USA

Library of Congress Cataloging-in-Publication Data

Cole. Sylvia.
    The Facts On File dictionary of 20th-century allusions: from
  Abbott and Costello to Ziegfeld girls/Sylvia Cole, Abraham H. Lass.
      p. cm.
  Includes index.
  ISBN 0-8160-1915-0
  1. Allusions—Dictionaries. I. Lass, Abraham Harold, 1907–
II. Title.
  AG5.C7234 1990
  031.02—dc20   90-41796

A British CIP catalogue record for this book is available from the British Library.

Facts On File books are available at special discounts when purchased in bulk quantities for businesses, associations, institutions or sales promotions. Please call our Special Sales Department in New York at 212/683-2244 (dial 800/322-8755 except in NY, AK or HI) or in Oxford at 865/728399.

Text design by Donna Sinisgalli
Jacket design by Ellie Nigretto
Composition by Facts On File, Inc.
Manufactured by Maple-Vail Book Manufacturing Group

Printed in the United States of America

10 9 8 7 6 5 4 3 2

This book is printed on acid-free paper.

CONTENTS

To
Stephen and Jonathan

INTRODUCTION

The reader of an editorial exhorting a New York City mayor to clean out the Augean stables of his city can consult any number of readily available reference books to clarify the meaning of this classical allusion to one of the labors of Hercules. Every day we read in newspapers, books and periodicals or hear on radio and TV allusions to a senator's Achilles' heel or to a candidate's steering between Scylla and Charybdis or to the hailing of a civil rights advocate as an Antigone. All of these classical allusions have been assembled for the reader's quick enlightenment.

But there is no handy reference for clarifying the meaning of 20th-century allusions. And yet, allusions are constantly entering and enriching our vocabulary, some of them as timely as Chernobyl, meltdown, Tiananmen Square and Lebanon.

Imagine a *gung-ho* sales manager *making a pitch* to his sales staff. "O.K. fellas, this is it! *D-Day!* Let's get out there and *blitz* the competition. *Give 'em hell!* Now we've planned our strategy down to the last T. No *Maginot Line* here! And oh, we want no *Quislings* on our team. The last thing we need in this outfit is a *Fifth Column.* On the other hand, give yourselves room to maneuver. Don't get into any *Catch-22* situation. Promise them anything: a *New Deal*, a *Fair Deal*, a *Square Deal.* Make the first sale and the rest will follow like the *domino effect.* The *bottom line* is sell, sell, sell!"

With the substitution of "Win, win, win!" in the last line, we can imagine an almost identical pitch by an eager-beaver coach to his football team in a pregame harangue. The allusions taken from war are adaptable to almost any competitive arena, from business and politics to sports.

Before July 19, 1969, nobody had ever heard of Chappaquiddick except the handful of people who lived near that tiny island in Massachusetts. After Ted Kennedy's fateful accident there, Chappaquiddick became a household word. Everybody knew how his car had plunged over the little bridge into the water, how he had extricated himself but could not do the same for his young companion of the evening, Mary Jo Kopechne, how he had waited hours before notifying the police. Everybody now knows that the events at Chappaquiddick cost Kennedy the chance to run for president of the United States. Chappaquiddick is no longer a place but now a set of circumstances.

When one has said all of this, most people respond with: Oh, yes, his Waterloo! True, Waterloo is a 19th-century allusion to the defeat of Napoleon and to speak of any person's Waterloo is to allude to his downfall. But every word has its special significance. Implicit in Chappaquiddick is defeat not by superior force, as at Waterloo, but by a tragic flaw, a failure of character, a hint of scandal in an otherwise powerful and even, for the most part, good person. So when one says, "Senator Gary Hart's brief fling with Donna Rice proved to be his Chappaquiddick," we recognize the full force of this 20th-century allusion.

Chappaquiddick has become a metaphor capable of being used in a context different from its original context, but with similar meaning. And we have been present at the birth and development of a 20th-century allusion.

Let's look at the birth of another 20th-century allusion, catch-22. Joseph Heller's immensely popular satirical novel *Catch-22* (1961) tells the story of Yossarian, a bombardier in World War II, who is not particularly interested in furthering his fanatical commander's ambition to advance his own career at the expense of his squadron. Yossarian's limited ambition is to get out of the Air Force and out of the war with his skin intact. Yet his efforts toward this end are constantly foiled by arbitrary bureaucratic regulations, among them catch-22. As a last desperate measure, Yossarian feigns madness, but, say the bureaucrats, if you are sane enough to try to get out of the war, you can't be insane enough to be dismissed from the war. In former times, when every educated person was acquainted with classical allusions, one might have described Yossarian's plight as being caught between Scylla and Charybdis, two equally ferocious monsters blocking the passage of Odysseus through a strait. Today, anybody trying to get out of a paradoxical bind is said to be, like Yossarian, in a catch-22 situation. The specific has become generalized and metaphorical.

One more: teflon. Teflon is a chemical originally applied to machines to reduce friction. It is a very slippery substance. A smart entrepreneur coated pots and pans with teflon to prevent food from sticking and burning. In the 1980s we began to read descriptions of President Ronald Reagan as the "teflon President." Some magic slippery substance, of personality or maybe luck, made him impervious to blame. Although all around him his aides and appointees were being tarnished with shady allegations, and even legal convictions, nothing stuck to Reagan. Pretty soon we began to read about a teflon attorney general (Ed Meese) and a teflon electorate, etc., etc. The word for a chemical substance had turned into a 20th-century allusion.

This book documents more than nine hundred such transformations in our century. In every realm of experience we come across the names of people, places, things and events that have traveled the road from mere reference to metaphorical allusion. These names become shorthand for extensive descriptions or explanations. For example, when we read: "Bush is Jimmy Stewart after Reagan's John Wayne," we get in a few words what it would take paragraphs to explain. But we have to know the personae of Jimmy Stewart and John Wayne, the images projected by their movie roles, in order to decode the shorthand. In this book we provide the key to unlock the code.

We are not concerned here with John Wayne as a person born in a particular place on a particular day. We are not concerned with his biography. We are concerned only with the image of strong, laconic, macho maleness projected by all of his movie roles. A John Wayne is a Marlboro Man, another 20th-century allusion. He has become his characters. To be more exact: If we say that John Wayne played the principal role in *True Grit*, then John Wayne in that sentence is used to state a fact; but if we say that Ronald Reagan was a John Wayne president, we are using John Wayne as an allusion.

An allusion, then, as we use the word, is not a mere reference. It is a reference transformed through use into a metaphor, into a word or phrase that stands for something.

Similarly, the names of artists have entered our vocabulary. The name is identified with the work. The name, itself, has become shorthand for whatever mood, situation, character or image in real life reminds us of the work of the artist. We look out of the window of an airplane upon the grid of the city below and say to our companion, "Look, a Mondrian!" And if our companion shares our vocabulary, there will be instant communication between us. We pass a luncheonette, and through its grimy window we see a lone coffee drinker at the counter. "That's a Hopper," we say, subsuming within the one word all the loneliness, the shabbiness, the longing and the mystery evoked by an Edward Hopper canvas. We encounter a human being and immediately sum up our first impression by labeling that person a Modigliani, a Giacometti, a Lachaise or a Renoir. It is not just that life imitates art, but that art names life and defines life for us. The artist's name enters our vocabulary as shorthand to sum up a complex vision of life.

This is true, too, of the names of writers, who give us a literary vision of life. The one word Faulknerian calls up a complex pattern of Southern social castes, racial violence, religiosity, obsession with the antebellum past, morbid sexuality, alienation, hallucinatory and rhapsodic language, as well as rambunctious humor. Quite a freight for one word!

At the same time, the names of certain literary characters created by these authors also enter the language as prototypes. We recognize the Snopes among us as a seedy, rapacious opportunist; a Dilsey as a woman who, through strong faith and compassion, patiently and quietly endures.

In every age certain names have taken on significance. Among classical allusions, Hercules stands for strength; Venus for beauty; Juno for regal stature; Antigone for heroic resistance to tyranny. From the Bible, Solomon stands for wisdom; Cain and Judas for betrayal; Herod for tyranny.

The 20th century has its own icons. A Mother Teresa is saintly; an Einstein is brilliant; a Rockefeller is rich; a Schweitzer has reverence for life. The 20th century, unlike other eras, also borrows heavily from popular culture for its mythology. Thus a Rambo or a Superman is our Hercules; a Monroe or a Garbo is our Aphrodite; a Darth Vader is our Iago; a Jackie Gleason is our Falstaff.

We have gathered more than 900 20th-century allusions. We have taken them from all walks of contemporary life: literature, art, movies, radio and TV, comics, politics, war, the Holocaust, science, social customs, psychology, crime, people and places, religion, sports. For each we have provided the original context; that is, the history of its birth and development. And for each we have given its present meaning and application. Wherever possible, we have provided examples of its use in today's newspapers, periodicals and books.

Will any of these endure? Will they stand the test of time? Will Chappaquiddick last as an allusion for more than 2,000 years, as Achilles' heel and nemesis have lasted? Will it live for almost 200 years as Waterloo has? Ted Kennedy is not the hero of a Homeric epic nor the central character in world events on the magnitude of the Napoleonic wars. But the 20th century has had its share of epic events and epic tales and epic visions. Or, if not epic, then at least epochal. Surely Kafkaesque will endure as a certain vision of life; Molly Bloom as an archetype of womanly sensuality; Hitler as a symbol of man's potential for evil.

We have caught allusions on the wing. Some will stay; some will disappear. Some, we are sure, got away. For now we have set them down, for the record, so to speak. We hope that the reader will find as much excitement in discovering these allusions as we have had in tracking them down.

S.C.
A.H.L.

Abbott and Costello   Bud Abbott (the tall, debonair one) and Lou Costello (the short, explosive one) were the top money-making comedy team in movies of the 1940s, then became the most watched, most syndicated TV performers (1951–1953). The critics hated them and the show itself. The audiences loved them and the show itself.

Essentially, Abbott (1895–1974) and Costello (1906–1959) were reusing material that they had been using on stage and in film since the 1930s. The Abbott and Costello show consisted largely (the critics maintained *exclusively*) of lowbrow slapstick; outrageous puns; knockabout, physical, "prat fall" comedy routines; contrived, improbable situations; frenzied, unrelated sights and gags. Nonetheless, out of this mad, hilarious melange came such classic routines as "Who's on First?"

Abie, the Agent   The "portly, pop-eyed, mustached" central character of Harry Hershfield's ethnic comic strip, which first appeared on February 2, 1914. *Abie, the Agent* (full name Abe Mendel Kabibble shortened to Abe Kabibble) was not the first ethnic comic strip. It had been preceded by *Happy Hooligan* (Irish) and the *Katzenjammer Kids* or *The Captain and the Kids* (German). It was, however, the first ethnic comic strip to deal sympathetically with its characters.

Abie, the Agent reflects some of the essential quality of urban life among the lower-middle classes circa 1920.

Hershfield handles his characters with great warmth, compassion and good humor.

1

according to Hoyle   Edward Hoyle (1672–1769) was a British authority on card games, especially whist. His compilation of the rules governing these card games achieved worldwide acceptance.

Hoyle's name has entered the language in the phrase "according to Hoyle." By extension, it has come to mean behaving honorably, fairly, following the rules faithfully.

Use: "Gentlemen, we're undertaking a very important project. The company's survival may very well depend on how well we do our job. Everyone will be watching us. I want everything done according to Hoyle, no sharp practices, no corner- cutting."

Adams, Ansel   Photographer (1902–1984) famous for his wide-angle American West landscapes of towering, snowcapped mountains and great trees. His pictures, which have been reproduced in more than 35 books, helped to establish photography as a legitimate art form with its own way of seeing.

Addams, Charles   American cartoonist (1912–1988) who for 50 years contributed his outrageously macabre humor to the *New Yorker.* He created an Addams family, an Addams house and Addams situations that are all ghoulish. In one well-known cartoon he shows a slinky, witch-like family on the roof of their haunted-looking Victorian house. It is Christmas and they are about to pour upon the carolers below a cauldron-full of boiling oil. In another cartoon Addams depicts a weird-looking man waiting outside a delivery room. The nurse is saying, "Congratulations! It's a baby!" His spooky, archetypical work antedated and paved the way for "black humor."

A Charles Addams is any weird person, house or situation that suggests a macabre sense of humor, a topsy-turvy sense of values.

Adler, Polly   As practitioner and entrepreneur in prostitution, the "oldest profession," Polly Adler (1900–1962) was widely known as "the last of the great madams" and her establishment as "New York's most famous bordello."

In her autobiography, *A House Is Not a Home,* Polly Adler boasts of "a clientele culled not only from *Who's Who* and *The Social Register*—but from *Burke's Peerage* and *The Almanac de Gotha.* " Her "guests" also included politicians, gangsters (Dutch Schultz, Frank Costello, Lucky Luciano), writers, etc. She and her "girls" worked out of fashionable, lavishly decorated apartments equipped with bars and dining rooms.

After a highly colorful career, Polly Adler retired from her "business" in 1944 to write her autobiography and to pursue other, non-"business" activities.

Use: In 1986, the book *Mayflower Madam* appeared, an account of how Sydney Biddle Barrows, whose ancestors arrived in America on the *Mayflower*, started and ran a successful, slick, elegant, modern "call girl" enterprise called Cachet. When the police finally "busted" her for running what in an older parlance was called a "disorderly house," Miss Barrows was widely described as another Polly Adler, though her business methods and entrepreneurial skills differed somewhat from Miss Adler's.

Adlerian   In accordance with psychoanalytical theories and treatment formulated by Alfred Adler (1870–1937). Adler started out as a disciple of Freud but broke away from the Master because he rejected Freud's emphasis on sex. To Adler the individual's drive for power, his desire for superiority, often to compensate for feelings of inadequacy, was at the heart of neurosis.

Adler coined the phrases "inferiority complex" and "superiority complex."

Afghanistan   In December 1979, Soviet troops invaded the small central Asian country of Afghanistan in order to prop up their unpopular communist puppet regime in Kabul. For 10 years they were unable to prevail against the Afghan Mujahedeen, Islamic guerrilla warriors who controlled the mountain passes with arms supplied mostly by the United States, West Germany and Japan. In spite of almost universal condemnation by the United Nations, the loss of thousands of lives and the drain on their resources, the Soviet Union did not pull out its forces until 1989. The fire that Leonid Brezhnev started was finally put out by Mikhail Gorbachev.

Afghanistan is to the Soviet Union what Vietnam is to the United States, a humiliating defeat of a great power by a tiny country.

Use: "[Russia's] armies had just suffered a stunning defeat in the Crimean War, which proved to be an 'Afghanistan' many times over, sapping Russian morale and sense of mission." (*New York Times*, July 29, 1989)

Alcatraz   In 1868, the United States War Department established a prison for deserters on Alcatraz, an island in San Francisco harbor. In 1934 Alcatraz was taken over by the Department of Justice as a "super-prison for super criminals" who couldn't be contained in the regular federal prisons.

The warden, James A. Johnston, ruled "The Rock" (as Alcatraz was known) with an iron hand. Under his stern, unsentimental administration, Alcatraz became known as America's Devil's Island, characterized by maximum security, minimum privileges, a rule of silence, prisoners locked up 14 hours a day, no trustee system, bad behavior punished by beatings and special handcuffs, straitjackets and solitary confinement ("the hole").

Some inmates tried to escape. None succeeded. Some tried suicide. Others became insane. The infamous Al Capone, master criminal, was sent here. He was paroled in 1939, suffering from advanced syphilis. Widespread criticism of Alcatraz's methods led to its closing in 1963.

Alcatraz has become a symbol for escape-proof, harsh, cruel prisons.

Alger, Horatio, Jr.   American writer (1832–1899) of 119 boys' books, in which the heroes begin as poor newsboys or bootblacks and rise to great wealth and influence. He encapsulated in each book the American dream of rags to riches.

Use: *"The Ragman's Son* is an American myth wrapped inside an American myth. Horatio Alger with a Russian-Jewish accent. The poor immigrant's kid who becomes a millionaire movie star." (Susan Stamberg reviewing the autobiography of Kirk Douglas; *New York Times*, August 14, 1988)

Alibi Ike   Main character and title of a 1924 short story by RING LARDNER (1885–1933). Later, a comic strip.

An Alibi Ike is a person who always has a ready excuse.

All-American   Originally, an honor conferred on the outstanding football players at each team position. In 1889, the first All-American team was chosen by the famous football player, coach and authority, Walter Camp, for the magazine *Weeks' Sports.* Today, All-American athletes are chosen in many other sports.

All-American now stands for general, all-around excellence.

Use: "Bill's a clean-cut, all-American boy."

all animals are equal, but some animals are more equal than others From George Orwell's satirical fable *Animal Farm* (1945). The animals on Mr. Jones's farm stage a revolution against their human masters and drive them out. The pigs, under their leader Napoleon, take over. Corrupted by power, they in turn become tyrannical and rationalize their hegemony with the above slogan.

Used cynically or satirically to demolish the hypocrisy of claims to absolute equality in the face of a privileged elite.

Allen, Woody United States film director, writer, actor, comedian (1935–). Uses autobiographical material, especially his own soul-searching for meaning in the universe. A Woody Allen movie is usually funny, philosophical, cerebral, satirical, with a New York City, middle-class Jewish milieu. His films include *Sleeper* (1973), *Bananas* (1971), *Annie Hall* (1977), *Manhattan* (1979), *Hannah and Her Sisters* (1986) and *Radio Days* (1987).

"Allen's Alley" Radio show starring Fred Allen. Allen's Alley was a street with odd characters, and Fred Allen was its man on the street. Every Sunday, Allen, as a weary pollster, knocked on doors and posed his "tiny questions" to radio's most hilarious interviewees.

"All in the Family" This TV sitcom made its revolutionary debut on January 12, 1971. It changed the face of the TV situation-comedy. For the first time, TV audiences found themselves watching and listening to a different kind of "relevance." "All in the Family" confronted formerly taboo issues and subjects with new openness and humor. Race, color, feminism, homosexuality, menopause etc. had come out of the closet.

"All in the Family" introduced a new type of comedy, with shouting, ethnic jokes and epithets. The audiences loved seeing the characters having at each other with an intensity and abandon that they were witnessing for the first time.

The central character, Archie Bunker, is the quintessential racist and bigot. Perhaps because he is made to overplay his role, he remains the audience's favorite butt.

all quiet on the western front   Phrase used in military communiqués and newspapers during World War I to indicate no dramatic action, only the usual attrition in the trenches. Erich Maria Remarque used the phrase with irony and bitterness in his 1929 novel *All Quiet on the Western Front*, about the German infantry in World War I, because men were still suffering and dying when it was "all quiet on the western front."

The phrase has been used in nonmilitary situations, but always with irony, as when tensions in a school over certain incidents are hushed up and someone mordantly observes, "all's quiet on the western front."

Use: A newspaper headline, "All Is Far From Quiet on The Western Front," covers a story about opposition to Mortimer Zuckerman's development plans for the western arc of Columbus Circle in New York City and for Donald Trump's West Side project, Television City. (*New York Times*, October 11, 1987)

Alphonse and Gaston   A super-polite team of Frenchmen created by the gifted cartoonist Fred Opper for Hearst's Sunday papers in the early 1900s. Flamboyantly dressed as 19th-century French dandies, they observed a code of highly artificial good manners:

> "You first, my dear Alphonse."
> "No-no-you first, my dear Gaston."

They were universally understood as "symbols of excessive politeness."

American Dream   A vision of America as a land of opportunity, a land in which every individual may achieve his innate potential regardless of sex, color, religion, class, circumstances of birth etc. The dream drew millions of immigrants to the United States and propelled them across a continent. The dream is often corrupted to mean a mere drive for materialistic values. The tragic toll taken by the pursuit of the American Dream has been portrayed in such utterly different novels as *Giants in the Earth* (1924) by Ole Rölvaag, *An American Tragedy* (1925) by Theodore Dreiser and *The Great Gatsby* (1925) by F. Scott Fitzgerald.

Use: "Talk about the American Dream! Here is the most seductive, the most magical, the cushiest and dreamiest American dream of them all—winning the capitalist jackpot, the whole damn thing just dropping into your lap out of nowhere. Only for Senator Quayle it isn't a dream—to him this looks like reality. No wonder that of all the performers in the '88 election, he alone plays his role to perfection." (Philip Roth on Op-Ed page, *New York Times*, September 19, 1988.)

American Gothic   Painting by American regionalist Grant Wood (1892–1942). The 1930 canvas is filled with a closeup of an American farm couple posed stiffly against their house. The couple looms almost as large as the house, which has a Gothic, arched attic window. They are immaculately and precisely dressed in farm clothing, the man in a jacket and overalls and carrying a pitchfork; the woman in a cover-all apron over a Peter Pan-collared dress. Their expression is determined, dour, even fierce. The artist's treatment of them seems double-edged—half epic, half ironic.

The popular use of the term American Gothic certainly is meant to indicate satirically stiff, upright, precise and correct.

American Legion   National organization of military service veterans chartered by Congress in 1919, with posts throughout the country and a strong lobby in Washington, D.C. Associated with veterans advocacy, super-patriotism, flag-waving and parades, and fervid opposition to communism.

An American Tragedy   Novel published in 1925 by Theodore Dreiser (1876–1945), based on the Chester Gillette–Grace Brown murder case of 1906. The protagonist, Clyde Griffiths, is ashamed of his poverty-stricken, street evangelist parents. He yearns for the wealth, the easy living, the mobility of the world he first encounters as a bellhop in a hotel. At his uncle's home in upper New York State, he comes in contact with high society. His ambitions flare, especially when he senses the possibility of marrying the very wealthy Sondra Finchley. Unfortunately, he has already impregnated a poor factory girl, Roberta, who refuses an abortion. Faced with this dilemma, Clyde daydreams of murdering Roberta. Matters are taken out of his hands after Roberta accidentally drowns when their rowboat capsizes. Clyde is arrested, tried and sentenced to death. Dreiser, through the defense attorney, indicts society for the crime, for filling youthful heads with false, tawdry, glittering illusions. Dreiser exposes the shoddy American dream of success based on materialistic values.

America's Sweetheart   Nickname given to Mary Pickford (born Gladys Smith, 1893–1979), for 23 years the most popular screen star in the world. Pickford invariably played Little Mary, the pure, innocent but self-reliant girl with the long blonde curls and the sweet smile, just on the verge of womanhood. She appeared in many films, including *Poor Little Rich Girl, Daddy Long Legs*, and *The Little American*. The marriage of America's Sweetheart to Douglas Fairbanks, the all-American male, represented in real life a kind of epiphany of movie dreamland.

Now used tongue-in-cheek for a too-sweet, too-pure, too-popular girl.

"Amos 'N' Andy"   A "blackface" radio comedy created by Freeman Gosden (Amos) and Charles Correll (Andy), it appeared in 1929 on NBC, sponsored by Pepsodent. It was an immediate, overwhelming success, one of the first truly original creations of early radio. A vast audience was charmed by its wit and warmth.

In 1950, "Amos 'N' Andy" moved into television—only to discover that a new era had come into being, demanding an end to "blackface" comedy. All black characters henceforth were to be played by black actors.

With superb actors, directors and writers, "Amos 'N' Andy" continued to charm its new audience. But the growing civil rights movement found the depiction of blacks in "Amos 'N' Andy" offensive and damaging to the image of blacks in America. Continued pressure led to the withdrawal of "Amos 'N' Andy" from syndication in 1966.

Despite the critical acclaim, it was held that "one of the finest ensemble casts of any color" still tended to perpetuate black stereotypes.

angry young man   Expression applied to certain British playwrights and novelists of the 1950s and to the characters they created. Their heroes were usually lower-middle-class, anti-establishment rebels. Outstanding examples are: John Osborne in *Look Back in Anger* (1956 play); Kingsley Amis in *Lucky Jim* (1954, novel); and Alan

Sillitoe in *The Loneliness of the Long Distance Runner* (1959, novello).

Annie Oakley   In baseball, a free ticket to a game. So named by American League president Ban Johnson because complimentary tickets to a baseball game have holes punched in them. So they look like the playing cards that the legendary sharpshooter Annie Oakley shot full of holes in Buffalo Bill's Wild West shows in the 1880s.

By extension an Annie Oakley has come to mean any free ticket, such as a pass to a theater.

Antonioni, Michelangelo   Italian film director (1912–). Antonioni created strangely haunting landscapes against which indolent Monica Vitti women drift in an atmosphere of melancholy ambiguity tainted with corruption. Antonioni achieved international recognition with his trilogy: *L'Avventura* (1960), *La Notte* (1961) and *L'Eclisse* (1962). His 1967 film *Blow-Up* explored Antonioni's obsession with illusion and appearance. His photographer hero, spying on a couple making love in a London park, fails to see an extraordinary thing, which shows up only in the blow-up of his pictures—the corpse of a murdered woman among the trees. Seeing, like beauty, is in the eyes of the beholder. Antonioni's cinematography has suggestive power. Out of a sequence of everyday images he projects mystery, solitude, alienation and despair.

Appalachia   A region in the Appalachian Mountains of the United States associated with poverty, backwardness and ignorance. Home of the hillbillies. Its people were depicted with sensitivity in the photographs of Walker Evans and in the poetic prose of James Agee in *Let Us Now Praise Famous Men.*

apparatchik   Russian word for a member of an organization or existing power structure, especially in a communist country (1940– 45). Bureaucrat.

Use: "This [Iran-Contra hearings] is no mere joust between Congress and the executive; nor is it a national soap opera about a telegenic marine colonel, his wife Betsy and their perils at the hands of cruel Congressional inquisitors and White House apparatchiks who would suddenly throw the handsome hero to the criminal winds." (Carl Bernstein, *New York Times* Op-Ed, July 4, 1987)

apple pie   Traditionally regarded as the quintessential American dish. Now expanded to apply to a situation or circumstance embodying American values.

Use: "He's a true American. What he's advocating in the Senate is as American as apple pie."

Appointment in Samarra   Title of a 1934 novel by the American writer John O'Hara. Although the novel is about the tragic life of Julian English, the head of a Cadillac agency in Gibbsville, Pennsylvania, the exotic title comes from a legend felicitously narrated by Somerset Maugham. This legend is used as a kind of epigraph and parable for the book. It is called "Death Speaks" and tells of a servant who was jostled by Death in a Baghdad market. Terrified, he jumped on his master's horse and galloped away to Samarra, where Death would not find him. The master asked Death why he had threatened his servant. Death replied, "That was not a threatening gesture...it was only a start of surprise. I was astonished to see him in Baghdad, for I had an appointment with him tonight in Samarra."

Thus an appointment in Samarra is an inescapable rendezvous with death.

April is the cruelest month   Opening words of T.S. Eliot's *The Waste Land* (1922).

> April is the cruelest month, breeding
> Lilacs out of the dead land, mixing
> Memory and desire, stirring
> Dull roots with spring rain.

Often used superciliously with mock sensitivity to the stirrings of spring.

Use: In an editorial in the *New York Times* (March 2, 1989) headlined "Farewell, Cruel Feberrery," we see a spoof of the expression:

"Of twelve adults adept at polysyllabic discourse who were polled recently, only three declared they could say February correctly, that is, to pronounce the first as well as the second r...So February, not April, is the cruelest month. Thank Heaven it's now March."

arbeit macht frei   German for "work makes you free," the motto inscribed over the entrance gates to the Nazi concentration camps at

Auschwitz (Oswiecim, Poland); cynical, in view of the forced labor, starvation and almost certain death that awaited the inmates.

Used sarcastically today when imposing an unwelcome chore or task. (See also AUSCHWITZ.)

Arbuckle, "Fatty"   Roscoe Arbuckle, a former plumber's helper, he became one of Mack Sennett's original Keystone Kops, a grotesque, slapstick but popular silent film comedian. A grossly fat person.

Archie   First appearing in 1941, it quickly became one of the most widely-read comics; "the consummate American humor feature," it dealt with the teenagers of the day as seen through adult eyes: Archie Andrews, the quintessential high school student; Jug Head, whose passion for hamburgers exceeded his passion for girls; Reggie, Archie's black-haired rival; and Betty and Veronica, Archie's girlfriends and rivals for his attentions. Though rooted in the mores of another era, *Archie* remains one of the most popular comic books; at its peak, it was selling over 1,000,000 copies a month.

Archie, like *Batman, Superman* and a small handful of others has transcended comic books and become pure Americana.

armchair quarterback   See MONDAY MORNING QUARTERBACK.

Armstrong, Louis Henry "Satchmo"   Jazz trumpeter (1900–1971). His friends called him "Satchelmouth" because his mouth was unusually large. Later, they abbreviated his name to "Satchmo." To millions the world over, he was a living legend. The critics lavished praise on him: "The greatest of the early jazz trumpeters...a showman of genius...an exuberant extrovert...one of the most popular singers of the 20th century...a prodigious improvisor...great innovator in improvising, he pushed back the technical boundaries of the trumpet...broke the traditional rhythmic patterns...."

Henry Pleasants is quite sure that "almost everything we have heard in the past 40 years in jazz...short of folk and rock...derives from Armstrong."

Equally certain is Leonard Feather that "Americans, unknowingly, live part of every day in the house that Satch built."

Satchmo had no imitators. He was, in fact, not imitable. His distinctive, gravelly voice was immediately recognizable. He made music for its own sake because, as he once said, "I'm just glad."

Arno, Peter   American cartoonist (1904–1968) for the *New Yorker* magazine. Born Curtis Arnoux Peters, of a prominent family in Rye, New York, Arno was educated at Hotchkiss Preparatory School and at Yale University. Oddly enough, he chose to delineate in his cartoons low-life characters such as might have crashed one of Jay Gatsby's bizarre parties: half-naked flappers, exotic dancers, speakeasy types, boors and drunks.

Use: Jack Kroll, in a review of *Jerome Robbins' Broadway* in *Newsweek* (March 6, 1989), writes: "Comedy is one of Robbins's greatest talents and this show exhibits some masterpieces in this vein. The 'Charleston' from *Billion Dollar Baby* (1945) whips the entire jazz-age 20's into a whirligig of flouncing flappers, boozing socialites, collegiates in pink raccoon coats, mobsters and bootleggers; it's like a giant Peter Arno cartoon brought to life!"

Arrow collar man   In 1924, the Arrow Collar ad that made the Arrow Collar Man the most popular of contemporary male icons. Perfectly clad in Arrow shirts, square-jawed, pink-cheeked, clean shaven, elegantly groomed, young and handsome by any standard, he fluttered female pulses throughout the land.

Arrowsmith, Martin   The protagonist of Sinclair Lewis' novel *Arrowsmith* (1924). A young doctor and medical researcher, he must fight all along life's way various temptations to abandon his ideals in exchange for wealth and fame. In his struggle to maintain his integrity he is influenced by his mentor and idol, Dr. Max Gottlieb, a German-Jewish refugee dedicated to science. In the end Arrowsmith, together with his friend Terry Wickett, retires to a quiet place in Vermont to devote himself to pure research. The novel is a kind of *Pilgrim's Progress* for the medical profession and has been the prototype for others in the genre, e.g., *The Citadel* by A.J. Cronin.

Arsenal of democracy   President Franklin Delano Roosevelt's description of the United States as it undertook to supply the Allies with the weaponry and material needed to fight the Axis countries of Germany and Italy, before the United States (and Japan) entered World War II. This was initially called a "lend-lease" program. By the end of the war, the United States had supplied $48.5 billion worth of military equipment to 42 countries.

Ash Can School   Twentieth-century art movement. Ugly subjects can make beautiful paintings, if the technique is lively and emphatic. So taught Robert Henri (1865–1929), an American artist who was the spokesman and the leader of a group of painters who came to be known as the Ash Can School. They included William Glackens (1870–1938), George Luks (1867–1933), John Sloan (1871–1951), Everett Shinn (1876–1953), George Bellows (1882–1925) and Henri himself. They flourished just prior to World War I. Akin to the naturalists in literature (Zola, Dreiser), they based their art on the observation of the seamy side of American urban life: Bowery bums, prizefighters, bored office workers, prostitutes, subway commuters, tenement dwellers, scrubwomen, breadlines, overflowing garbage cans and dirty slums. Their style derived from their original experience as illustrators. In England their counterparts led by John Bratby were called the Kitchen Sink School.

Thus we refer to certain obsessions with ugly, realistic subjects in books, printing or real life as belonging to the Ash Can School.

Ashley, Lady Brett   Heroine of *The Sun Also Rises* (1926), a novel by Ernest Hemingway. She is a beautiful, abandoned Englishwoman in love with Jake Barnes, the hero; but because he has been rendered sexually impotent by war wounds, she engages promiscuously in a series of love affairs with Jake's friends in Paris. In Pamplona, where the group has gone for the bull-running, she seduces Pedro Romero, a star torero. In the end, she gives Romero up for his own good, thus achieving in renunciation the feminine counterpart of the Hemingway hero code.

ask not what your country can do for you; ask what you can do for your country   These memorable words were spoken by President John F. Kennedy at his inauguration on January 20, 1961. They were an inspiring call to Americans to rededicate themselves to the ideals upon which the nation had been founded.

They are often used today by politicians, but also by those who simply substitute another word for "country." For example, "Ask not what your mother can do for you; ask what you can do for your mother."

assembly line   Moving belt used by Henry Ford in the manufacture of the Model T automobile. It made mass production quick, easy and cheap, each worker contributing a single maneuver as the object on the moving line went by him. It also made for boredom on the part of the worker.

Today the assembly line idea seems to be used not only in industry but in human affairs as well. The trend in health services, for example, is toward assembly line medicine, as the patient is passed from one "specialist" to another.

Astaire, Fred   Born Fred Austerlitz (1899–1987) in Omaha, Nebraska, he became what many people believe to be America's greatest dancer. Slim, graceful and stylish, Astaire was sophisticated perfection in white tie and tails. Together with his best partner, Ginger Rogers, with whom he appeared in nine movie musicals between 1933 and 1939, he made routines of dazzling bravura seem effortless. His films include: *Top Hat, Shall We Dance, The Gay Divorcee, Flying Down to Rio, Roberta,* and *The Story of Vernon and Irene Castle.*

Synonymous with elegant male sophistication and debonair grace on the dance floor and off.

Use: In a 1984 election campaign, George Cunningham disparagingly called his opponent, Senator Larry Pressler, "a flash-dancing Fred Astaire type, blow-dried, cellophane-wrapped representative who deals more with public relations than with public policy."

Atlas, Charles   In his early years, Atlas (1894–1972) was a poor physical specimen: anemic, lacking in strength, listless, underweight. Depressed by his physical condition, he set about building himself up with his own regimen, which he called "dynamic tension." In time, he won the title of "The World's Most Perfectly Developed Man." He opened his own gym where he worked up his original physical development system, which he offered by mail order. His potent advertising campaign drew tens of thousands of responses yearly from individuals who wanted to do something quick and dramatic about their physical plight. They all saw themselves as the "80 lb. weakling" that Atlas depicted himself as having been— before he developed into the magnificent persona that dominated every ad. They fervently believed that he would rescue them from a life of weakness and inferiority.

atom bomb   Awesome explosive weapon deriving its power from splitting the atom (atomic fission); used radioactive uranium for its production. First tested and exploded on July 16, 1945, at Alamogordo, New Mexico. The First bomb was dropped in wartime on August 6, 1945, on Hiroshima, Japan, with greater power than 20,000 tons of TNT. The second bomb was dropped on August 9, 1945, on Nagasaki, Japan. So ruinous was the effect of these bombs, that Japan surrendered on August 14, 1945. The United States had a monopoly on the manufacture of the atom bomb until the U.S.S.R. exploded one in 1949. Then Great Britain, France, Communist China and India tested bombs of their own. The ultimate weapon; the ultimate threat; destructive power.

Use: "Kirk B. Johnson, general counsel of the Medical Association, expressed disappointment today that the Court had allowed 'The atom bomb of the anti-trust laws' to be used against peer review panels..." (*New York Times*, May 19, 1988)

attention must be paid   Phrase spoken by Linda, the wife of WILLY LOMAN in *Death of a Salesman* (1949) by Arthur Miller. She has discovered evidence that Willy is planning suicide. Willy is an embittered man, a failure as a provider and especially as a father. She says to Biff the estranged son who has failed to live up to Willy's expectations: "I don't say he's a great man. Willy Loman never made a lot of money. His name was never in the paper. He's not the finest character that ever lived. But he's a human being, and a terrible thing is happening to him. So attention must be paid. He's not to be allowed to fall into his grave like an old dog. Attention, attention must be finally paid to such a person..."

Attica   A maximum security prison in New York state. On September 9, 1971, the prisoners mounted what was said to be the most violent prison riot in American history. It involved about 1,000 inmates who seized part of the compound and held 30 guards and civilian workers as hostages.

Negotiations continued for almost a week between inmates and an "observers' committee" consisting of representatives of government, newspapers etc. Russell G. Oswald, state commissioner of correction, accepted most of the prisoners' demands. He rejected their demand for no reprisals and total amnesty for the rioters. The inmates answered Oswald by displaying a number of hostages with knives at their throats. The assault on the prison followed. State troopers, prison guards and 1,500 sheriffs' deputies finally smashed the revolt.

Twenty-eight prisoners and nine guards were killed. Attica left a stain on the administration of New York state's penal system.

Attica has become synonymous with extreme brutality and misguided zeal in the handling of prisons and prisoners.

Use: In his letter to the governor, the warden wrote, "Unless we change our present prison procedures, we are sure to have another Attica on our hands."

Auschwitz   Nazi death camp in southwest Poland. Between 1942 and 1944 about two million Jews were exterminated at Auschwitz (Oswiecim, in Polish), gassed in gas chambers and their bodies burned in adjacent crematoria. Terrorized by brutal SS guards and dogs, convoys of newly-arrived Jews were lined up for "selection": those who were to die immediately and those who were to live for awhile. Everything of conceivable value was confiscated and used: clothing, possessions, gold fillings, hair, even the ashes. The camp was liberated by Soviet troops on January 27, 1945.

Auschwitz is synonymous with ultimate, premeditated horror, with man's inhumanity in its most brutal and deadly form, carried out with mechanistic efficiency. (See also DACHAU.)

Axis   Term coined by Italy's Benito Mussolini in 1936 after signing an agreement with Hitler. He said that Berlin and Rome would form "an axis around which all European states can assemble." Actually, the Axis in World War II comprised only Germany, Italy and Japan, with a little help from Bulgaria, Hungary and Rumania. An "axis" is an alliance of two or more states for coordinating foreign and military affairs. Today, it's any alliance, as in Senator Bentsen's statement upon learning he had been chosen to run as vice presidential candidate on the Democratic ticket in 1988: "The Massachusetts and the Texas axis was good for the country and good for the Democratic Party in 1960 and it's going to be a real winner in November of '88."

ayatollah   Among Shiite Muslims, a religious leader who has achieved great understanding of Islamic laws. The word became well known in the Western world after Ayatollah Khomeini succeeded in ousting the shah of Iran and in imposing his fundamentalist government on his country. Now it stands for any highly repressive, punitive, rigidly fundamentalist person; a theocratic despot.

Use: "In Puritan Massachusetts there was a staunchly independent Congregationalist minister, John Wheelwright, who supported his famously independent sister-in-law, Anne Hutchinson; because of his own mental freedom he was also banished from godly Boston by the ayatollahs of the day." (Alfred Kazin, *New York Times Book Review*, March 12, 1989)

B

Babbitt, George F.   Main character in Sinclair Lewis's satirical novel *Babbitt* (1922). His name has added a word to the English language. A Babbitt is a "typical" American midwesterner. He is a standardized man, a product of 20th-century mass production, with a standardized family, a standardized house and car and other appurtenances of the materialistic life. He is a conformist, a joiner, a booster, a philistine, a man of conventional morality and conservative politics who "thinks" in clichés and platitudes. If ever he questions the worth of his own mode of life, his attempt to wander results in cheap, tawdry, futile affairs, such as that of George Babbitt and Janis Judique, and he is glad to return to the haven of middle America.

Baby M   Infant girl born in 1986 to surrogate mother Mary Beth Whitehead and the natural father William Stern. After the baby's birth, Mrs. Whitehead reneged on her contract to give up the baby to Mr. and Mrs. Stern for a payment of $10,000. She rejected the money and fought to retain the child. After a long, complicated battle fought in the courts, the media and every household, Judge Harvey R. Sorkow in March 1987 awarded the baby to Mr. and Mrs. Stern and presided over the adoption of the child by Mrs. Elizabeth Stern. Baby M became Melissa Elizabeth Stern.

On February 3, 1988, however, the New Jersey Supreme Court ruled that surrogate motherhood contracts involving an exchange of money violated the law against the sale of children. It ruled, too, that Baby M would be reared by the Sterns but that Mrs. Whitehead

18

retained full parental rights, including visitation. The adoption of Baby M by Mrs. Stern was voided.

Baby M has become a catchword for legal and ethical problems arising out of surrogate parenting.

back street   From the novel of the same name (1931) about a married man and his mistress who carry on a longstanding secret affair in one of the "back streets" of town. Written by Fannie Hurst (1889–1968).

Back street refers to the non-respectable part of town where illicit affairs and illegal transactions are hidden from public view.

Use: "For the sake of winning, not for any deeper reason, [George Bush] is willing to deprive 1.5 million American women every year of safe legal abortions and make them return to the back streets." (*New York Times* Op-Ed page, November 6, 1988)

Balanchine, George   Choreographer (1904–1983). Born Georgi Militonovich Balanchinadze in St. Petersburg, Russia. In the 1920s, after training at the Petrograd Imperial Ballet Company, Balanchine became the chief choreographer for Diaghilev's Ballets Russes. He formed a friendship with Igor Stravinsky, whose music inspired him to his best innovative ballets for the rest of his life. In 1934, he came to New York at the invitation of Lincoln Kirstein. There he founded the School of American Ballet and in 1948, the New York City Ballet, with its permanent headquarters since 1964 at the State Theater in Lincoln Center. Balanchine grafted the tradition of Russian classical ballet onto American soil, but he went on to create a new, spare style with plotless ballets and long-legged ballerinas in leotards.

balkanize   From the Balkan Peninsula, made up of Albania, Bulgaria, Greece, Rumania, Yugoslavia and the European part of Turkey. These small, contentious states (and their predecessor states) engaged in the First and Second Balkan Wars in 1912 and 1913. In 1914, the assassination of Archduke Francis Ferdinand of Austria-Hungary by a Serbian nationalist in Austrian-held Sarajevo was the immediate cause of World War I.

To balkanize now means to divide and conquer; to divide groups or areas into small, contending and ineffectual factions—that is, to prevent minorities from exercising political power by "balkanizing" them, one against the other.

Use: "At the same time the field [sociology] became balkanized as schools began offering degrees in competing disciplines like black studies, Jewish studies and women's studies." (Joseph Berger, "Sociology's Long Decade in the Wilderness," (*New York Times*, May 28, 1989)

Ball, Lucille   See I LOVE LUCY

ball game   Originally applied to sports, as in baseball or football. Now extended to mean a set of circumstances, conditions etc. involving two or more contenders or opponents.
Use: "Gorbachev's tactics have brought about a new Soviet-American ball game."

banality of evil   See EICHMANN, ADOLPH.

Band-Aid   Trademark for a small strip of adhesive bandage with gauze in the center; used to cover or protect minor cuts, wounds, abrasions. Invented by Earle Dickson and commercially launched by Johnson & Johnson in 1921. Has come to mean a temporary solution that does not meet long-range, basic needs; limited or makeshift help; a temporary, stop-gap remedy.
Use: "Our Band-Aid approach to economic development must be changed..." (*New York Times* Op-Ed page, July 29, 1989)

Bara, Theda   Born Theodosia Goodman (1890–1955). Dark-haired beauty of the silent movie era, she played the evil vamp (short for vampire) who lures men, ruins them and tosses them aside. "Kiss Me, My Fool," a line from her 1914 film *A Fool There Was*, is still quoted satirically.

Barbie Doll   Trade name of a very popular, blue-eyed, blonde, teenaged doll with a stylish wardrobe. Named after Barbie Handler, daughter of the owners of the Mattel Toy Company, it first went on the market in 1958. Today it is a term applied to a bland, saccharine, mindless person.
Use: "Our Barbie Doll president with his Barbie Doll wife." (Hunter S. Thompson), referring to Ronald and Nancy Reagan.

Barnes, Jake   Central character in Ernest Hemingway's novel *The Sun Also Rises* (1926). An American journalist, sexually impotent because of war wounds, he is in love with the beautiful and promiscuous Lady Brett Ashley. Deeply frustrated, he moves in a circle of aimlessly drifting expatriates in Paris. With them he is drawn to wherever he can find excitement, as to Pamplona for the bull-running festival.

Jake Barnes is a prototype for those who try to overcome psychological wounds in pointless drinking, drifting, cynicism. He is representative of the "lost generation."

Barney Google   The creation of cartoonist Billy DeBeck, Barney Google appeared in a daily comic strip sequence called *Take Barney Google, For Instance* (June 17, 1919). The American public took Barney to itself immediately. It couldn't resist Barney, his wife Lizzie (three times his size), his horse Spark Plug (a carefully draped blanket covered his knock-knees) and their dizzyingly varied adventures. He won and lost fortunes, wooed heiresses, got involved in murders, hijackings, secret trips to Cuba and Europe. For 15 years, the feisty, top-hatted, diminutive Barney enjoyed America's unbounded affection.

Barrymore   Stage name of an American theatrical dynasty, the "royal family of the American stage." Their real name, never legally changed, was Blythe.

Maurice Barrymore married Georgianna Drew, the daughter of John and Louisa Drew (both well-known actors). Maurice and Georgianna had three children: Lionel Barrymore (1878–1954); Ethel Barrymore (1879–1859); and John Barrymore (1882–1942). These three were outstanding in classical as well as modern roles, in tragedy as well as comedy, on the stage as well as on the screen. Lionel is remembered for his annual Christmas interpretation on radio of Ebenezer Scrooge in Dickens' "The Christmas Carol." John Barrymore, after his brilliant performance as Hamlet in 1922, was considered the greatest Shakespearean actor of his day. The Barrymores were all very handsome people, but especially John, who acquired the nickname of "the Great Profile," because of his aquiline nose. The name Barrymore is the standard against which all other acting performances are measured.

basket case   Term probably originated during World War I to refer to young soldiers who had lost all their limbs, becoming quadriplegic and thus totally incapable of getting around on their own or doing anything for themselves. Dalton Trumbo's harrowing novel *Johnny Got His Gun* (1939) tells the story of one such "basket case." Today, a basket case refers dismissively to any person or even nation considered so inept as to be utterly helpless and hopeless.

Use: On the CBS TV program "60 minutes" (April 30, 1989) Richard Miller, an FBI agent convicted of espionage for the Soviet Union, was asked by Mike Wallace why he had confessed if, as he now claimed, he was innocent. He replied, "I was falling apart, physically, mentally, spiritually. I was a basket case."

Bataan   Battle in the Philippines lost in 1942 by the American and Filipino forces under General Douglas MacArthur. After having been ordered to escape by President Franklin D. Roosevelt and upon his arrival in Australia, MacArthur announced the now famously prophetic words: "I shall return."

Bataan is notorious for the "Death March" and for other brutalities to which the Japanese victors subjected their prisoners of war.

Use: "The unbroken sound of our footsteps was beginning to feel ominous like the Bataan death march." (Ella Leffland, *Rumors of Peace*)

Batman   In May 1939, Batman made his debut in *Detective Comics*. By day, Batman is Bruce Wayne who has inherited a great fortune. Orphaned when his parents were killed in a street holdup, he devotes his life to fighting crime or, occasionally, to "one-man vigilante justice."

By night, Wayne becomes Batman, "self-trained strong man, gymnast, acrobat"—the scourge of criminals whom he pursues with relentless zeal. As Batman, he wears a bat-like cape and cowl.

Batman has no superpowers. He catches criminals by employing his superior intelligence. Despite some of his unsavory, questionable behavior, Batman has maintained his hold on his vast audience for a half-century. His crime-plagued readers still find security and solace in his swift if occasionally crude and unconstitutional treatment of criminals.

Use: "Only a total recasting of the edifice [the New York City school system] from top to bottom and a new structuring of priorities from discipline to values—will do the trick. I'd make *Batman* even money, but Joe Fernandez (the new Chancellor)? Strictly a long shot." (Ray Kerrison, *New York Times*, September 27, 1989)

bat a thousand   In baseball, to achieve a perfect record, to get a hit every time at bat—an obvious impossibility. This expression has come instead to mean compiling an outstanding, extraordinary record.

In popular use, to bat a thousand is to be highly successful, very popular.

batting average   In baseball, a number expressing a player's batting performance or ability. It is arrived at by dividing the number of hits by the number of times at bat—and carrying the result to three decimal places.

Batting average now applies to any measure of achievement.

Use: Among the salesmen in The Eastern division, Garfield has the best batting average.

Battle of the Bulge   December 1944, when a dent about 60 miles deep was created by the German counterattack against the Allied line in Belgium-Luxembourg. When American General Anthony McAuliffe received an ultimatum from the Germans to surrender, he answered with the now-famous, laconic "Nuts!" In January 1945 the Allies advanced and straightened the bulge. Now applied humorously to heroic efforts at dieting to reduce bulges—of the flesh.

Bauhaus   Influential school of design founded in 1919 in Weimar, Germany, by the architect Walter Gropius (1883–1969). Its original faculty included Wassily Kandinsky, Paul Klee, Lyonel Feininger, Marcel Breuer, Herbert Boyer and, after 1923, Laszlo Moholy-Nagy. In 1926 it moved to Dessau. In 1928, Mies Van Der Rohe, the German architect, became its head. In 1933, because of Nazi hostility, it was dissolved. Its staff was dispersed and its influence spread throughout the world.

The Bauhaus philosophy was encapsulated in the tenet: "Form follows function." All design, whether of a building, a household object like a chair or a lamp, an industrial machine or an entire city, should be based strictly on the function and needs of that entity and upon a close scrutiny of the nature of the materials used. The Bauhaus stressed the importance of the craftsman-designer in the manufacture of mass-produced objects. Its style was clean, unadorned, severe, refined.

The Bauhaus had a beneficial influence in calling attention to the need for beauty in everyday objects, and to the use of modern materials and techniques in their manufacture. The Museum of Modern Art in New York City has a special department for award-winning industrial design based on Bauhaus principles.

Bauhaus refers to anything—glass buildings or pots and pans or chairs—that shows refinement of line and shape coming from economy of means and an understanding of the materials of construction.

Use: "Perish the slavish Bauhaus born black and white. In the loft's dining/living room savvy color accelerates the warming trend—with gray-brown carpeting, aqua sofa covers and glowing hardwood floors." (*Metropolitan Home*, April 1989)

Bay of Pigs   Site of the April 25, 1961, invasion of Cuba by anti-Castro Cuban exiles living in the United States. This counterrevolutionary attempt, supported by President John F. Kennedy, was easily repulsed by the Cuban military.

Now used as an example of an ill-conceived, badly managed, disastrous military adventure, a fiasco.

Use: Asked whether U.S. troops should be in Central America, one of the respondents said, "No. It's like doing the Bay of Pigs again. America should let other countries solve their own problems." (*New York Post*, March 18, 1988)

beast of Buchenwald   Ilse Koch, wife of the commandant of the Buchenwald concentration camp (near Weimar, Germany), infamous for having lampshades made out of the skin of her victims. She committed suicide in September 1967, while serving a life sentence for atrocities that even SS officers deemed excessive.

beat generation   From "beat," meaning worn-out, pooped, exhausted, plus "beatitude," meaning bliss. Members of the beat generation hoped to achieve out of the lowest depths of despair that spiritual illumination that leads to the peace that passeth understanding. The Beats represented a Bohemian revolution against the mores and values of a corrupt, materialistic, military-minded society. They adopted unconventional modes of dress and behavior. They sought release from moral restriction in hallucinogenic drugs, alcohol, sexual experimentation and poverty.

The term was first applied in the 1950s to the poets who gathered at the City Lights Book Store in San Francisco: Allen Ginsberg, Gregory Corso, Lawrence Ferlinghetti and, later, Gary Snyder; and to the prose writers Jack Kerouac and William Burroughs. (See also THE BEST MINDS OF MY GENERATION.

Beatles   British Rock and Roll Quartet; John Lennon (1940–1980); [James] Paul McCartney (1942–); George Harrison (1943–); Ringo Starr [Richard Starkey] (1940–).

In 1961, this popular singing group burst out of Liverpool, England, to conquer the world and alter the style and substance of a segment of popular music. Discovered by manager Brian Epstein, they made musical history.

In the 1960s the Beatles' albums sold over 250,000,000 copies—a musical milestone. Lennon and McCartney wrote most of the songs. Lennon added complexity and a heightened social consciousness to the lyrics. McCartney wrote the immensely appealing melodies. The Beatles' distinctive hair-do "made long hair a token of disaffection."

beatnik   Member of the BEAT GENERATION.

beat to the punch   In boxing, the boxer who lands a punch before or faster than his opponent is said to beat him to the punch. In general, to act faster, to get an advantage over a competitor.

Use: "Carrel seemed to be the best man for the job. But he never got it. Bradley beat him to the punch."

behind the eight-ball   In the game of pocket billiards the players must pocket all the other numbered balls before pocketing the eight-ball—a black ball with a small white circle in the center. To be positioned behind the eight-ball makes it impossible for the player to strike any other ball without striking the eight-ball first. Therefore he is in danger of losing the match, if by chance he pockets the eight-ball before all the other balls have been put into the pockets.

"Behind the eight-ball" has come to mean being in a difficult, awkward, unpleasant, untenable position.

Use: "Because he hadn't anticipated the opposition's strategy, he found the entrance blocked. He was behind the eight-ball."

Beirut   Capital of Lebanon.
Use: "The project was 'once a good place to live' Now, however, it's a small-scale Beirut, where rival drug-selling gangs use guns and razors in a vicious struggle to monopolize sales."
"Reclaim Housing from Drug Lords," *New York Times* editorial, June 16, 1989) (See also LEBANON.)

Belmondo, Jean-Paul   French film star (1933–). Played existential, tough guy anti-hero in Jean Luc Godard's *Breathless* (1960), appealing to disaffected youth. Continued his career in popular modern swashbuckler roles.

bench   In baseball, the bench is where the players sit when they are not playing in a game. To bench a player means to keep him out of the game for poor performance, injury etc.
Use: Blake was benched until his fellow-salesmen were able to regain the confidence of his customers.

bench warmer   In sports, a player who seldom plays. Generally a substitute, he sits on the bench and "warms" it. By extension, anyone who does not play an active role in any enterprise, job etc.

benign neglect   Phrase used by Senator Daniel Patrick Moynihan (then a counsellor to President Nixon): "The time may have come when the issue of race could benefit from a period of 'benign neglect.'"—in a March 2, 1970, memo leaked to the *New York Times*. Moynihan was misunderstood and excoriated by blacks, who passed over "benign" and emphasized "neglect."
Use: "It is time for a period of benign neglect...to let Gorbachev be Gorbachev." (Michael Ruby, "The Benefits of Benign Neglect," *U.S. News & World Report*, July 31, 1989)

Benny, Jack   Born Benjamin Kubelsky (1894–1974). One of the finest comedians of radio and television, "a comedian's comedian," a master of timing and inflection, and the "pregnant pause"—best illustrated in one of his famous routines:
He is held up on a dark street. A nervous robber threatens him: "Your money or your life, mister."
Benny makes no move to comply. He is silent—for a long, long fraction of a minute.

The by-now frightened robber:
"Hurry up, mister. Your money—or your life."
Benny's slightly impatient reply: "I'm thinking! I'm thinking!"
Benny projected a unique comic persona: pathologically stingy (he kept his money in a vault); the butt of insults and humiliations from lesser characters; his below-par violin playing; his pose of elegant inadequacy; his special relationship with Eddie Rochester, his sardonic, gravel-voiced valet.
Use: "Bosco greets this news with the deadest of pans, blank-faced and unblinking and he sustains this for what seems like light years. The 'take' is so long, in fact, it would have given Jack Benny pause, if not flop-sweat..."(Monty Arnold, from *Playbill* article on actor Philip Bosco, June 1989.)

Benton, Thomas Hart   American regionalist painter (1889–1975) from Missouri who used only American themes, most of them rural. Benton depicted in muralist style the landscape and farm workers of the Midwest. His figures are sculptural and are endowed with energy and vitality. He rejected foreign influences, modernist aesthetics and urban culture as decadent. He aimed to create an authentic American epic style based on themes from American life and history. *Cradling Wheat* (1938) is typical of his style. Benton is associated with the epic treatment of American rural life.

Bergen, Edgar and Charlie McCarthy   Edgar Bergen (1903–1978), a deft, sophisticated ventriloquist, and Charlie McCarthy, his fresh, master-of-back-talk dummy, were among radio's most listened to, pre-television pair. Bergen's understated, witty thrusts and Charlie's irreverent retorts and equally irreverent comments about institutions and people delighted audiences everywhere. Later in the program Bergen added Mortimer Snerd, a dull simpleton, often capable of unexpectedly fey repartee.
When Bergen decided that his performing days were over, he donated Charlie to the Smithsonian Institution.
Use: "I like it. It's as good a way out as any, maybe the best. You got this kid up there, you gotta do something with him, so why not make him out a dummy? He fits—a regular Charlie McCarthy." (*The Last Hurrah* by Edward O'Connor)

Bergman, Ingmar   Swedish film director (1918–) who gathered about him a company of exceedingly gifted actors (Liv Ullmann, Bibi

Andersson, Max von Sydow), cameramen (Sven Nykvist and Gunnar Fischer) and technicians, whom he used with stunning effect in all his pictures. His masterpieces are dark, brooding meditations upon large themes: the silence of God; the nature of appearance and reality; the terrible isolation of man; the ambiguity of evil; the absence of faith and love; the duality of the artist in society; the intensely erotic psychosexuality of women in confined environments. Although he has tried his hand at comedy, it is as a tragic visionary that he has set his stamp upon the cinema. His films include: *The Seventh Seal* (1956), *Wild Strawberries* (1957), *Persona* (1966), *Cries and Whispers* (1972), *Scenes from a Marriage* (1974) and *Autumn Sonata* (1978).

Bergman, Ingrid   Swedish-born film actress (1915–1982) whose films include: *Intermezzo* (1939) *Casablanca* (1943) *For Whom the Bell Tolls* (1943), *Spellbound* (1945), *Notorious* (1946) and *Autumn Sonata* (1978). Her image of radiant natural beauty and wholesomeness was tarnished when she had an extra-marital affair with Italian movie director Roberto Rossellini and gave birth to his child. The world was scandalized at the time and Bergman was ostracized. Sexual mores changed, however, and eventually Bergman's transgression was forgiven and she continued her interrupted career.

Berkeley, Busby   American film choreographer (1895–1976) who created dazzling effects of "patterned drill" in the Hollywood musicals of the 30s. In such movies as *42nd Street, Gold Diggers of 1933* and *Footlight Parade,* he thrilled audiences with seemingly perfect kaleidoscopic patterns made with huge companies of beautiful chorus girls.
    Use: "Fifteen different models for the Coliseum site were submitted to the city by May 1, 1985. Two of the proposed buildings were more than 130 stories high...architecture critics heaped scorn on almost every one. Even Mayor Koch poked fun at some of the designs, calling one the 'Flash Gordon Building,' another the 'Busby Berkeley Tower,' and a third the 'King Kong Building.'" (*New York Magazine,* September 28, 1987)

Berle, Milton   A pioneer of the television variety show, Milton Berle (1908–) made his raucous debut on June 9, 1948, as host of the Texaco Star Theater. A graduate of the vaudeville and burlesque circuits, Berle brought with him the gags and routines he had mastered: rowdy, off-color, sure-fire and played for belly-laughs.

The new television audiences found Berle's clowning and irreverent humor irresistible. Before long he became the first television superstar, affectionately dubbed *Uncle Miltie* and *Mr. Television*. In a sense, Berle was the one who really popularized the new medium.

Berle's antics are synonymous with noisy, low-brow, occasionally tasteless comedy. He is uniquely American.

Berlin wall   A concrete wall replacing a barbed wire fence first strung up on August 13, 1961, by armed East German soldiers to stop the exodus of East German refugees to the West. A confrontation between U.S. and Soviet tanks on either side of the wall threatened for a time the uneasy peace of the Cold War. The wall came down in November 1989.

The Berlin wall was a symbol of the ideological intransigence between East and West. (See also COLD WAR; IRON CURTAIN.)

Use: "The dark side for the congressional camp is the hectoring and badgering of presidential initiatives, the Berlin Wall of Boland amendments built around administration policy." (Max Lerner, *New York Post*, July 18, 1987)

Bernhardt, Sarah   Great French tragedienne (1844–1923) who came to be known as "the Divine Sarah" and mockingly, among lesser mortals, as "Sarah Heartburn." Her acting technique, unlike the more natural bent of her most famous rival, Eleanora Duse, was operatic, exaggerated, mannered. She was famous for her long death scenes and her equally long-drawn-out murder scenes, as in *Phedre* by Racine and in *La Dame Aux Camellias* by Dumas, in which latter play she made her American debut. She even played men's parts, like Hamlet and L'Aiglon.

Born Henriette Rosine Bernhard in Paris, the illegitimate child of a Dutch Jewish mother and an Amsterdam merchant father, she was baptized as a Roman Catholic and educated in a convent school. She studied at the Paris Conservatoire and in 1862 made her debut at the Comedie Francaise in *Iphigenie en Aulide* by Racine. Beautiful, graceful, with a magnificent speaking voice, she became a star among stars and eventually an actress-manager in her own theater. In 1914 one of her legs was amputated, but she continued her career. Her talent for showmanship and her much advertised love affairs entranced the public of two continents.

Today if a child has a tantrum or if a woman seems to be self-dramatizing, somebody is sure to say, "Look at Sarah Bernhardt" or "Look, Sarah Heartburn." Her name has come to stand for over-acting.

Berraisms (also Yogi-isms)   Linguistic mutilations attributed to the great Yankee catcher Yogi Berra (1925–). As with GOLDWYNISMS, questions have been raised about the authenticity of some of these Berraisms:

- Sometimes you can observe a lot by watching.
- It ain't over till it's over.
- No wonder nobody comes here—it's too crowded.
- A nickel ain't worth a dime anymore.
- Even Napoleon had his Watergate.
- I want to thank all the people who made this night necessary.
- Why don't you pair them up in threes?
- Ninety percent of this game is half mental.
- Half the lies they tell me ain't true.

The best lack all conviction, while the worst are full of passionate intensity   These lines close the first stanza of "The Second Coming," a poem by William Butler Yeats (1865–1939), the Irish poet and playwright. The stanza conveys the disorder, the chaos threatening to swamp the world in a tide of anarchy. In the lines above, Yeats refers to well-meaning people who are no longer sure of their values and to the ideologues and fanatics who are all too sure of theirs, being ready to kill for them.

These lines are often quoted and applied to the newest demagogues, authoritarians and despots, as well as to those like Hitler, Stalin, Mussolini et al., who have disappeared but have left their horrible mark on the world.

best minds of my generation   From the opening line of Allen Ginsberg's poem "Howl" (1956), which denounces the mechanistic dehumanization of a society whose God is Moloch, a god that demands human sacrifice. Ginsberg sees the most sensitive young men of his generation "destroyed by madness, starving hysterical naked/dragging themselves through the negro streets at dawn looking for an angry fix,/ angelheaded hipsters..." Ginsberg is their spokesman in this incantatory Jeremiad, the opening salvo of the BEAT GENERATION.

Bhopal   A city of about 200,000 inhabitants in India where, on December 3, 1984, a deadly leak of methyl isocyanate gas from an insecticide plant owned by Union Carbide killed over 2,000 people. Thousands more were hospitalized with symptoms of choking, vomiting, dizziness, sore throat and burning eyes. Many were blinded. Those who could, fled to escape the noxious fumes. Union Carbide was sued for $15 billion and eventually a settlement was reached. In an age in which environmental concerns have reached the forefront of international attention, Bhopal stands for man-made industrial catastrophe on a huge scale. It is equaled, perhaps, only by the meltdown at CHERNOBYL in the Soviet Union.

Bible Belt   Areas in the South and Midwest of the United States where religious fundamentalism is a powerful political force. Publishers of textbooks, for example, must consider how their treatment of evolution will go over in the Bible Belt. Librarians are often pressured to remove from their shelves certain books that are offensive to the mentality of some Bible Belt readers, and politicians are often judged by their position on single-issue causes fanatically held by Bible Belt voters.

Big Bang   Generally accepted theory of the origin of the universe in a single big explosion of a highly compacted bit of matter. That happened abut 15 billion years ago, and the universe has ever since been expanding outward from the center of the initial explosion.

Big Bertha   Huge siege cannon used by the Germans in World War I. Said to be named after Bertha Krupp, a member of the German armsmaker family.

Large, amply endowed women used to be referred to as Big Berthas—uncharitably.

Big Brother   In George Orwell's *1984* (1949), the despotic "leader" of Oceania, whose ubiquitous portrait stares out of countless posters that bear the caption "Big Brother is watching you." He represents the pervasive presence of totalitarian rule, the invasion of privacy.

Use: In an article about the use of satellites to keep tabs on big trucks: "Truckers have mixed feelings about being monitored. 'The downside is that Big Brother is watching you.'...The Big Brother aspects of the technology may become even more apparent when...companies introduce pocket-size versions in the 1990s." (*U.S. News & World Report*, March 21, 1988)

big enchilada   Phrase coined by White House aide John Ehrlichman in referring to Attorney General John Mitchell, on the Nixon tapes, connected with WATERGATE. Ehrlichman, a gourmet cook, was fond of making enchiladas, filled tortillas topped with cheese and chili sauce. The big enchilada was simply the big cheese, the top man. The "whole enchilada" means the whole world or the whole situation.

Big Lie   Technique used by the Nazi propaganda machine under Goebbels. If the lie was big enough, outrageous enough, how could people fail to give it credence even though it contradicted all the evidence? After all, who could invent so big a lie? One of the biggest lies that the Nazis succeeded in getting accepted was the story that the deportation of Jews to Eastern European concentration camps and extermination centers was just a "resettlement" program. Another was to depict as "sub- humans" the Jews whom they had systematically dehumanized through brutality, intimidation, starvation, imprisonment and murder.

In the spring of 1989 the Chinese government tried to use the Big Lie after they fired indiscriminately at crowds of unarmed students and workers demonstrating for democracy in Tiananmen Square, Beijing. The presence of TV cameras and satellite broadcasting made the Big Lie more difficult to get away with.

Use: "China's old men are cynically rewriting history every day, hoping the Big Lie can hide savagery seen by the whole world." (*U.S. News & World Report*, June 26, 1989)

big stick   From the maxim coined by President Theodore Roosevelt in 1901 to describe his interventionist policies in Latin America: "Speak softly and carry a big stick, and you will go far." A big stick is the threat of force to achieve one's way.

Birth of a Nation, The   Landmark silent film directed by David Wark Griffith in 1915, based on Thomas Dixon's novel *The Clansman* (1905). Its three-hour-long dramatization of the events leading up to and through the Civil War and the Reconstruction that followed established the film medium as an art form. It is notable for its realistic and spectacular battle scenes. However, it has become an extremely controversial film because of the anti-Negro bias in the Reconstruction scenes, when the hero, an aristocratic Confederate veteran, joins the newly formed Ku Klux Klan.

Use: "I've tried to produce a synthesis between the traditional view of Reconstruction—the old *Birth of a Nation* image—and the revisionist view, the continued hold of racism and federalism." (Eric Foner, quoted by Herbert Mitgang in the *New York Times Book Review*, May 22, 1988)

Bitburg   To commemorate the 40th anniversary of the end of World War II, President Ronald Reagan planned to lay a wreath on the graves of German soldiers in Bitburg, Germany, where Nazi SS troops were also buried. This created a furor in the United States. To make matters worse, Reagan said that the Bitburg dead were just as much victims of Nazism as the ones who died in concentration camps. Reagan had put his foot in his mouth. To do Reagan justice, this was more a mark of stupidity than malice. Elie Wiesel took the president to task in an eloquent and impassioned talk. But Reagan, for political reasons, had to keep his commitment to the German chancellor to visit the site.

Bitburg implies a faux pas of a certain magnitude.

black belt   A rating of "expert" in various arts of self-defense (judo, karate, etc.).

In informal use, someone who is expert in any field.

Use: "In a highly competitive field, Jerry Barat has been judged a black belt by his peers."

blackboard jungle   From a 1955 movie based on a novel of the same name by Evan Hunter, telling of a teacher's harrowing experiences with a gang of kids in a New York City school. The term has become a metaphor for the terror, chaos and mayhem in many inner city schools.

black hole   A black hole in astronomy is not strictly speaking a hole at all, but a mass of such great density that nothing can escape its gravitational pull, not even light rays, which it absorbs (hence, *black* hole). The theory is that black holes originated in the explosions of very dense stars at a time when the universe was very young.

The term is used figuratively in everyday layman's language to connote a deep hole from which one cannot extricate oneself. It is always depressing.

Use: "We are a family of very modest economic means, and I wasn't about to embark on a campaign that would have led us into a financial black hole." (Senator Paul Laxalt upon withdrawing from the presidential race; *New York Times*, August 27, 1987)

Black Monday   Monday, October 19, 1987, when the Dow Jones average on Wall Street fell about 500 points and set off fears of a 1929-type Crash and Depression.

Refers generally to a collapse or wildly fluctuating prices on Wall Street.

blackout   The practice of extinguishing all lights or covering windows at night during the London Blitz of World War II. Now used for blackout of news, or power blackout as a result of heavy use of electricity.

blimp   Originally a B-limp type of airship, meaning of a British, World War I, non-rigid design. These were used mostly for coastal patrol. Now a blimp is a fat person with the shape of a dirigible.

blitzkrieg (or blitz)   German for "lightning war." Unlike the slow, holding technique of trench warfare in World War I, the German technique in World War II was the blitzkrieg. This involved the element of sudden surprise attack, softening the target with air strikes, and the use of swift motorized units to surround and cut off resistance. Thus was Poland, Denmark, Norway, Belgium, the Netherlands, France, Yugoslavia and Greece each conquered within a few days or weeks. The shortened form "blitz" described the bombing strikes on civilian populations, as in the London blitz. Frequently used today in the phrase "media blitz," to denote an intensive advertising promotion or political campaign.

Use: "The liberals raised enormous amounts of money to mount an anti-Bork [nominee for Supreme Court justice] 'blitz' of full-page ads, television spots and direct lobbying of uncommitted senators." (*New York Post*, Norman Podhoretz, October 6, 1987.)

blockbuster   Four-ton bombs dropped by the RAF in 1942; called blockbusters because they could destroy an entire city block. By the end of the war the Allies were dropping bombs of up to 11-tons on enemy cities. Now a blockbuster is anything gigantic, effective, impressive or having wide popular or financial success; e.g., a movie or a sales campaign can be a blockbuster.

Blondie   One of the most famous comic strip characters. Blondie, a "hare-brained flapper," is pursued by DAGWOOD BUMSTEAD, the playboy son of a tycoon. In 1933, Dagwood is married to Blondie and promptly disinherited by his father.

Blondie, now head of the household, becomes a devoted, affectionate, level-headed wife, getting Dagwood out of his many misadventures. The family is in a state of constant agitation. Yet they are happy and optimistic.

Blondie has been translated into many languages. Once its readers numbered in the hundreds of millions.

blood, toil, tears and sweat   "I have nothing to offer but blood, toil, tears and sweat," declared Winston Churchill on May 10, 1940, in his first address to the House of Commons as prime minister of Britain. Churchill was referring to the task of fighting Hitler in World War II. This phrase has been shortened generally to "blood, sweat and tears" and is used to suggest nothing but sacrifice in a prospective task or relationship.

Bloom, Molly   The epitome of female sensuality, she is married to Leopold Bloom, the main character in *Ulysses* (1922) by James Joyce. Her lengthy, unpunctuated, erotic stream of consciousness as she lies in bed at the end of the day—the day on which the entire action of the novel takes place, June 16, 1904—waiting to receive her husband from whom she has been estranged, closes the novel and is undoubtedly the most famous interior monologue in literature. Her last word is "yes," an affirmation of love and life and experience. Molly, in the Homeric scheme of the novel, represents Penelope, but a lusty one.

Molly was modeled on Joyce's wife, Nora Barnacle.

Bloomsday   June 16, 1904, the day on which all the events of James Joyce's *Ulysses* take place. Joyce is said to have picked this date for his novel to commemorate the anniversary of his first walk with Nora Barnacle who was to become his wife. Every June 16 people who have a passion for *Ulysses* celebrate "Bloomsday" by following the route taken by Leopold Bloom through Dublin (if they are in Ireland) or by a non-stop, oral reading of the entire novel.

blue bird of happiness   The object of a search by the woodcutter's children Tyltyl and Mytyl in Maurice Maeterlinck's drama *The Blue Bird* (1909). Used symbolically today for elusive happiness.

boat people   Refugees from South Vietnam who tried to escape the communist takeover at the end of the Vietnam War by piling into flimsy vessels of every description and heading for neighboring territories. Many drowned; many were turned into a seemingly endless odyssey through pirate-infested coastal waters. It is estimated that 1.5 million Vietnamese and other Indo-Chinese have fled from their homelands since 1975. The phrase "boat people" has come to stand for refugees desperate to find safe harbor from oppression.

body count   Term used by the U.S. Department of Defense during the Vietnam War to indicate the number of Vietcong soldiers killed in action. American and South Vietnamese troops could lose a battle and yet take gruesome consolation from the higher body count of the enemy dead. The body count became a grisly item on nightly television.

Bogart, Humphrey   American star (1900–1957) of such film classics as *The Petrified Forest* (1934), *The Maltese Falcon* (1941), *Casablanca* (1942), *The Treasure of Sierra Madre* (1948) and *The African Queen* (1951).
   Nicknamed Bogey, he played a lean and tough guy with narrowed eyes made narrower from the smoke of a cigarette clenched between his teeth. He hid idealistic values beneath a seemingly impenetrable veneer of cynicism.

Bolshevik Member or adherent of one of the two main branches of Russian socialism. Vladimir Ilyich Lenin gained a brief majority for this radical branch in 1903; established as a separate party in 1912. In 1917, after 11 years of exile, Lenin returned to Petrograd (now Leningrad) after the abdication of Czar Nicholas II. On November 7, 1917, the Bolshevik Party, organized into workers' councils, overthrew the moderate provisional government of Alexander Kerensky and seized power. The first thing the new Marxist government did was to start peace negotiations with Germany. The Russians had already lost 3.7 million people in World War I. The Bolsheviks (under Lenin and Trotsky) were on their way to establishing a "dictatorship of the proletariat."

Bolshevik, in general parlance, denotes a fiery radical with Marxist ideology.

Bond, James Agent 007, super-spy played originally by Sean Connery, and later by David Niven, George Lazenby, Roger Moore and Timothy Dalton in films based on the novels of Ian Fleming, including *Dr. No* (1962), *Goldfinger* (1964), *From Russia With Love* (1963), *You Only Live Twice* (1967). Always involved in foreign intrigue, Bond is good-looking, suave, irresistible to women, pleasure-loving, equipped with the latest gadgetry for destruction, expert in the martial arts. He always plays his part with tongue-in-cheek bravado.

Bonnie and Clyde American film (1967) with Faye Dunaway and Warren Beatty, based on two real-life outlaws, both in their twenties, Texans Bonnie Parker and Clyde Barrow. Their four-year spree of violence, bank hold-ups and 12 murders throughout the Southwest of the early 1930s ended in their being ambushed and riddled with bullets by a posse of Texas Rangers. The film romanticized them and turned them into folk heroes.

booby trap In World War II, a hidden explosive designed to go off on contact, or when detonated by some remote control device; designed to harass or kill enemy forces.

Now a booby trap has come to mean a seemingly harmless ploy or arrangement that conceals trouble for an opponent in business or, perhaps, for an adversary in an argument.

Use: "Don't debate Harmon. His speech is usually full of booby traps."

boondocks   An uninhabited backwoods or marsh. Now any remote area far from the activities of big city life. For example, in trying to save their children from the dangers and temptations of Manhattan, the Lewises moved to Queens, which, as far as they could see, might just as well have been out in the boondocks.

borscht belt   A string of hotels, boarding houses and rooming houses in the Catskill Mountains of New York catering to mostly Jewish vacationers. It was named by *Variety* editor Abel Green after the cold beet soup popular with Jewish gourmets. The borscht belt hotels were famous not only for their superabundant food but also as the testing ground for such well known stand-up comics as Milton Berle, Buddy Hackett, Danny Kaye, Mel Brooks, Jackie Mason, Lenny Bruce and many, many others.

Boston Strangler   Between June 1962 and January 1964, 13 women were murdered in Boston, all elderly, all living alone, all sexually assaulted, all strangled. When caught, Albert H. de Salvo (1933–1973), the Boston Strangler, confessed, furnishing details of the murders that only he could have known. Sentenced to life imprisonment, he was stabbed to death by one or more of his fellow inmates.
   Use: The rash of murders of women led the police to believe that a new Boston Strangler was on the loose.

bottom line   Originally, the line at the bottom of a financial state-ment. It indicates either a net profit or a net loss. The use of the term has been extended to cover the end result of any dealings, practices, theories, emotions etc., or to identify the crux, the essential point involved in them. It has been further extended to suggest practicality, a concern with profit.
   [Schenck v. United States] was "The case that set the bottom line on freedom of speech...." The Court ruled that falsely shouting fire in a crowded theater could not be protected under the free speech guarantee of the First Amendment. "An Incomplete Education" by Judy Jones & William Wilson.

Bow, Clara   See IT GIRL.

Bowery   Street in Manhattan, once associated with flop houses, derelicts, drunks and vagrants; often the last stop on the way down.

For example, George Hurstwood, a tragic character in SISTER CARRIE (1900), a novel by Theodore Dreiser, ends his life on the Bowery. He has fallen from prosperity and a stable family life to joblessness, penury, drunkenness and despair.

The Bowery was New York City's SKID ROW.

boy next door   The 1930s stereotype of the nice, wholesome, ideal boyfriend or sweetheart. This quintessentially sweet, kind, wholly loving and lovable character is enshrined in Hugh Martin and Ralph Blane's song, "The Boy Next Door," sung by Judy Garland in the movie *Meet Me in St. Louis* (1944).

Use: "Everybody's favorite 'Guy next door' has some very adult projects on the horizon. "(*McCalls*, July 1989, article on Michael J. Fox.)

Boy Scout   Member of the Boy Scouts of America, founded in 1910 by William Boyce, a wealthy Chicago publisher, and modeled on the British Boy Scouts, started in 1908 by Colonel Robert Baden-Powell with the motto "Be Prepared." A quasi- military organization with "troops" and uniforms, it proposed to build skills and develop character, self-sufficiency, courage, courtesy, citizenship, in every boy who joined. A boy could advance from level to level, all the way to the top—Eagle Scout. Every president of the United States automatically becomes an honorary Scout.

The term "boy scout" has come to be used half-derisively to describe a goody-goody type.

bra burner   Some activists for women's rights have regarded the bra (brassiere, in its original form) as a "demeaning symbol" of the way women dressed (or felt compelled to dress) to appeal to men. Spurred on by men who burned their draft cards at anti-Vietnam War demonstrations in the 1970s, some of the more zealous advocates burned their bras in public—a symbol of their liberation. Hence, any militant proponent of women's rights.

Brady Gang (Wild Bunch)   The most widely hunted gang of the 1930s. They terrorized the Midwest and, in the process of robbing banks and engaging in other criminal activities, killed two clerks and three police officers. They were imprisoned— but escaped. On October 12, 1937, they entered a Maine sporting goods store to place an order for two revolvers. The clerk recognized them and told the gang members that the guns would be ready in a few days. Meanwhile, he alerted the FBI. When the gang returned to pick up their purchase, they were ambushed by a team of FBI men. Al Brady and Clarence Shaffer died in the shoot-out. Dalhover was tried and executed. (See also BUTCH CASSIDY AND THE SUNDANCE KID.)

brain drain   Originally (1963) referred to the recruitment of highly trained professional talent from England to the United States with the promise of high salaries. One U.S. ad for help in a London newspaper read: "Brain Drain—or the Chance of a Lifetime." Later the term was applied to students from third world countries who came to the United States to learn and stayed to earn.

Now means any raid on talent, especially scientific, from one country to another, from one university to another, or from one industrial laboratory to another.

Use: "The most effective cure for a brain drain is to create opportunities for the gifted and well-educated at home." (*New York Times*, April 13, 1988, with headline "How Not to Stop China's Brain Drain.")

brain trust   Originally, intellectuals and university professors who were invited to Washington, D.C., to help fashion the New Deal programs of President Franklin Delano Roosevelt. They formed a kind of unofficial cabinet of advisors to the president. Among them were Harry Hopkins, Raymond Moley, Adolph A. Berle Jr. and Rexford Tugwell. President John F. Kennedy also surrounded himself with a "brain trust."

A body of eggheads or intellectuals whose combined knowledge and expertise are used to run a governmental, educational or business enterprise. Sometimes applied to brilliant students as well.

Brancusi, Constantin   Rumanian sculptor (1876–1957) who lived in Paris from 1904 and studied with Modigliani. His *Bird in Space* (1926) is quintessential Brancusi: a polished bronze abstract shape that suggests in the simplest possible form the soaring, upward-curving motion of a bird in flight.

Brando, Marlon   American stage and screen star (1924–). Brando's image was definitively set in his very first stage role, Stanley Kowalski, in Tennessee Williams' play *A Streetcar Named Desire*

(1947; screen version, 1951). He played the part of an uncouth, inarticulate, macho Polish worker, married to the sister of a faded, rather poetic Southern belle. Extremely physical, brutal, indifferent to the amenities of civilized behavior, alternately mumbling and shouting obscenities, he proved to be both repellent and attractive to the sensitive Blanche du Bois. Brando also starred in *The Men* (1950), *The Wild One* (1953), *On the Waterfront* (1954), *The Godfather* (1972), *Julius Caesar* (1953), *Last Tango in Paris* (1972), *Viva Zapata* (1951) and *Apocalypse Now* (1979). Brando speaks with his body, suggesting pent-up passion or violence.

Braque, Georges   French painter (1882–1963) who together with Pablo Picasso created one of the great innovative movements in 20th-century art—cubism. His early cubist paintings tend to be monochromatic and indistinguishable from those of Picasso. He painted mostly still lifes, e.g., *Black Fish* (1924), *Cafe Table* (1911), reducing objects to layered geometrical forms as they would seem if seen simultaneously from many points of view. Later, he introduced the techniques of collage, pasting pieces of newsprint and chips of wood to his canvases. In the 1950s, he did a series of paintings of birds with utter simplification of form. (See also CUBISM.)

Brechtian   Suggestive of the theories and plays of the German dramatist, Bertolt Brecht (1898–1956). Brecht is associated with "epic theater." He rejected suspension of disbelief as a working theory of drama and also rejected the Aristotelian aim of catharsis. His aims were didactic and his methods smacked of agit prop (agitation and propaganda). He saw the theater as spectacle and often used the music of composer Kurt Weill as in *The Threepenny Opera* (1928) and in *The Rise and Fall of the Town of Mahagonny* (1929). Brecht wished to create distance between the audience and the players and often used a narrator to address and instruct the viewers as to what they should be seeing. His plays proceeded in a succession of swiftly changing, brief scenes rather than in the traditional three-act format. Their mood was heavy as though outlined in black, like the paintings of the German expressionists. Their viewpoint was Marxist; their tone cynically and mordantly critical of modern society.

Other Brecht plays are *Mother Courage and Her Children* (1939), *The Good Woman of Sezuan* (1938), *The Caucasian Chalk Circle* (1944) and *The Life of Galileo* (1937).

Use: "...The opera [*The Crucible* by Robert Ward, based on Arthur Miller's play] unfurls like a Brechtian morality play." (*New York Times*, review by John Rockwell, December 9, 1988)

Bridge of San Luis Rey, The   Pulitzer prize-winning novel (1927) by Thornton Wilder (1897–1975) about five travelers who are killed on Friday noon, July 20, 1714, when a bridge over a canyon in Peru collapses. A witness to the disaster, Brother Juniper, a Franciscan friar, decides to investigate the events that brought the five together at that moment to share a common fate. Was it simply an accident or was it divine providence?

The bridge of San Luis Rey has become a symbol of shared disaster by persons otherwise discrete, as in a plane crash.

Bringing Up Father   The perennial battle of the sexes is the subject of this exuberant comic strip, begun in 1913 and drawn by George McManus.

Jiggs, formerly a mason, and his wife Maggie, a former wash woman, come into sudden wealth, having won the Irish Sweepstakes. The ugly, snobbish, egotistical Maggie wants to forget her origins. Jiggs, on the contrary, is always ducking out of the house to join his low-life pals at Dinty Moore's saloon for corned beef, cabbage and pinochle. Maggie, rolling pin in hand, awaits his return. As Jiggs tip-toes into the house, gingerly holding his shoes, Maggie tosses her rolling pin at him. It finds its target—unerringly. It epitomizes Maggie's "I'll show you who's boss here" attitude.

brinkmanship   The fine art of almost going to war, an art defined and practiced by John Foster Dulles, secretary of state under President Dwight D. Eisenhower from 1952 to 1959. Dulles was the chief architect of America's Cold War policy toward the Soviet bloc in Eastern Europe. He threatened to use nuclear power to stem U.S.S.R. aggression.

Used generally for stepping to the brink of hostilities, for using a variety of strategies short of all-out fight. A kind of flirtation without consummation in affairs other than belligerence, as in love or business or diplomacy. (See also COLD WAR; IRON CURTAIN.)

Broadway   A north-south-running street on the West Side of Manhattan in New York City, which gave its name to the theater district alongside of it. Broadway is a mecca for all ambitious theater people: actors and actresses, playwrights, directors, producers, technicians etc. Nicknamed the Great White Way, it is illuminated by marquees that have blazoned forth the names of all the glamorous theatrical greats of the century. To play on Broadway is to reach the zenith of professional theatrical recognition.

Bronx cheer   A sputtering noise made by extending the tongue between the lips and forcibly expelling air. Sometimes called the "razberry" (raspberry).

The Bronx cheer is generally confined to sports contests— especially baseball. Avid, highly partisan, excitable fans employ the Bronx cheer to express feelings of contempt or derision for individual teams or players—and, especially for umpires' decisions.

The Bronx cheer is also known as "the Bird," an expression of disapproval, contempt, etc. Often accompanied by hissing and booing.

Use: "In Poland, voters have just swept aside communist party candidates for the upper house. In the Soviet Union, new members of the legislature have given a *Bronx cheer* to their communist 'masters.'" (David Gergen, "Communism's Final Days," *U.S. News and World Report*, June 19, 1989)

Brooklyn Bridge   Suspension bridge over the East River connecting Manhattan and Brooklyn in New York City, built from 1867 to 1874. With its magnificent, vaulting Gothic arches, it has inspired many artists.

The term Brooklyn Bridge has become associated with gullibility: e.g., he is so convincing that he could sell you the Brooklyn Bridge; or, he is so naive he'd agree to buy the Brooklyn Bridge; or, he's so dishonest, he'd sell you the Brooklyn Bridge.

Use: Raymond Price, skeptical about the purpose of televised coverage of the Iran-Contra hearings, asks, "Is it really to find out what went wrong?...If anyone really believes that, I'll quote him a terrific price on the Brooklyn Bridge." (*New York Times*, July 12, 1987)

Brown V. Board of Education   See SEPARATE BUT EQUAL.

Buchenwald   Nazi concentration camp near Weimar, established in July 1937, where 50,000 people died from forced labor, starvation, beatings and the gas chambers. Many intellectuals from all over vanquished Europe were murdered here. Some were used as guinea pigs for infernal "medical" experiments. American forces that liberated the camp on April 12, 1945, found 20,000 living skeletons, and corpses stacked like firewood awaiting incineration. See also BEAST OF BUCHENWALD.

Buckley, William Frank, Jr.   Erudite, witty, articulate, ubiquitous spokesman for conservatism in America, he was born in New York City in 1925 and started his career in 1951 with the publication of *God and Man at Yale*, in which he castigated his alma mater for turning the sons of its wealthy supporters into "atheistic socialists." In the same vein, he once said: "I would rather be governed by the first 2,000 people in the telephone directory than by the Harvard University faculty."

In 1955 he founded and became the editor of the foremost conservative journal in the United States, *The National Review.* At its inception he said that he wanted to repeal much of the liberal social legislation of the preceding two decades. His magazine would "stand athwart history, yelling 'Stop'." He is the author of the column "On The Right." He has written many books, including *McCarthy and His Enemies* (1954), *Up From Liberalism* (1959), books on sailboat racing and, most recently, novels of mystery and intrigue. His instant recognition by the public, however, comes from his hosting of the Public Television debate show, "Firing Line." He does not suffer fools gladly, and on the air he takes every opportunity to demolish his opponents with formidable knowledge of the facts, daunting skill as a polemicist, polysyllabic abstruse words, withering wit, together with an icy charm and frequently raised eyebrows.

Buck Rogers   The first American science fiction comic strip, it appeared on January 7, 1929. Awakening from a five-century sleep, former U.S. Army Air Force Lieutenant Buck Rogers finds his beloved America in the hands of Mongol invaders. Aided by attractive young Wilma Deering, he liberates his country and prepares to take on a host of new enemies: "tiger men of Mars," "pirates from outer space," his arch-foe, "Killer Kane." With the help of a scientific prodigy, Dr.

Huer, Buck will eventually conquer all enemies and prevail over all the dangers that lie ahead.

Buck Rogers is the conqueror that all of us in our helpless state would like to be—strong and victorious against our known and unknown enemies. The young, especially, unable to cope with a world they never made and could not master, found that they could deal with a hostile and threatening universe—as Buck Rogers.

buck stops here   President Harry Truman, in his feisty way, was fond of using this slogan. It was his way of saying that ultimate responsibility lay with him, as when he fired General Douglas Mac-Arthur from his post as supreme commander of U.N. forces in Korea in 1951; or when he ordered the atomic bombing of Hiroshima in 1945.

Use: Admiral John Poindexter, during questioning at the congressional Iran-Contra hearings in 1987, protected President Ronald Reagan from implication in the sale of arms to Iran (for the purpose of funding the Nicaraguan Contras) by asserting that the buck stopped with him.

Burns and Allen   One of the most enjoyable husband-wife teams on radio, in the movies and finally on television. George Burns (Nathan Birnbaum, 1898–) and Gracie Allen (1906–1964) continued to delight their audiences until 1958 when Gracie retired. Subsequently, George tried to make it on his own. He wouldn't hear of looking for a substitute for Gracie. Finally, he took to doing a one-man show, cast as a geriatric roue.

The Burns and Allen formula looked deceptively simple. George was in show business, the center of problems created by "nutty friends, wacky neighbors, and a zany wife—Gracie." George played straight man to the harebrained (but lovable) Gracie, who "skewered common sense and...chatted about her bizarre relations."

Always fresh, always funny, always charmingly daffy, Burns and Allen were a unique American phenomenon, filled with innocent good humor and outrageous nonsequiturs.

bush league   Originally applied to small-town or minor league sports teams, it bears the stigma of the small-time, inferior, second-rate.

Use: "We all agreed that the new boss has no class. He is strictly bush-league." (See also MAKE THE BIG LEAGUE.)

Buster Brown   A comic strip character, Buster Brown appeared on May 4, 1902, and was instantly and enormously popular. Buster Brown was the well-dressed, 10-year old heir with an almost insatiable appetite for tricking and annoying his family and friends with explosives, paint, wrecked boats. Buster's constant companion was a "toothily grinning" dog called Tige.

Buster Brown is the archetypal mischief maker, juvenile outrageousness incarnate.

Butch Cassidy and the Sundance Kid   U.S. Western (1969) with Paul Newman and Robert Redford (playing outlaws pursued by a relentless posse); directed by George Ray Hill. In the film the two characters must jump off a cliff into a mountain river to escape a posse. Sundance says he can't swim. Butch answers, "You crazy fool, the fall will probably kill you."

Use: Headline in *New York Post*, June 1, 1988: "Reagan rides into glory with Butch and Sundance in university speech." (President Reagan had referred to the movie, in his address to the students at Moscow State University to illustrate the message that "sometimes it takes faith." (See also CASSIDY, BUTCH.)

But I have promises to keep And miles to go before I sleep   Penultimate lines of Robert Frost's poem "Stopping by Woods on a Snowy Evening." In the poem, a man on his way home from a New England village stops his horse and buggy on a road bordered by woods on one side and a lake on the other. He watches the snow falling. It is so quiet and so beautiful that he is tempted to stop there forever. His horse, however, gives the harness bells a shake. The sound wakes the man to his duty. He has promises to keep and miles to go before he can "sleep." Frost says that sometimes we long for the peace and stillness of death, but life's responsibilities and opportunities call to us.

Use: Headline from *New York Times* (August 27, 1988) about a black doctor who rose from the ghetto: "Doctor's Journey: Miles Still to Go, Promises to Keep."

Butler, Rhett   Hero of *Gone With the Wind* (1936), novel by Margaret Mitchell. (See also CLARK GABLE, SCARLETT O'HARA.)

C

Cadillac   Luxury car produced by General Motors and named for the city in Michigan where it is made. By extension, a Cadillac is something tops in its class.

Use: "Congress is grabbing for a Cadillac salary, but it already has a Rolls-Royce pension." (*Palm Beach Post*, February 4, 1989)

Caesar, Sid   See YOUR SHOW OF SHOWS.

Cagney, Jimmy   American actor James Cagney (1900–1986), born in New York City. Tough, cocky *Yankee Doodle Dandy* film star who could act, sing and dance. Started in gangster roles in *Penny Arcade* (1930) and later appeared in *The Roaring Twenties* (1939) with Humphrey Bogart. Known for his quick, jerky, chip-on-the-shoulder body movements and speech.

Calder, Alexander (1898–1976)   American artist famous for his mobiles, which are constructions of metal wire and painted aluminum so delicately balanced as to move with the slightest current of air. These mobiles are abstractions of organic forms like flowers, fish, animals, which fascinate by their constantly changing aspect in space.

"Candid Camera"   A very popular, long-running (1948–1967) TV program conducted by Allen Funt (1914–) and his crew of resourceful assistants. "Candid Camera" caught "unsuspecting folks in the act of being themselves" by trapping them in innocent-looking but

47

contrived settings. The results were by turns hilarious and embarrassing, but both audiences and victims hugely enjoyed themselves.

Capone (Scarface Al), Alphonse   America's most famous gangster. The most powerful and ruthless crime figure of his time, Capone (1899–1947) has been aptly characterized as a "heartless, mindless murderer" and "the evil genius of all gangsterdom."

Early in his educational experience, Al Capone beat up one of his teachers and was expelled from school. He was clearly cut out for a violent, non-academic career. Raised in Brooklyn's notorious Five-Points, Capone quickly rose in the rapidly burgeoning racketeering hierarchy of the Prohibition era.

In 1925, Capone moved his ruthless expertise to Chicago. By 1930, with an army of 1,000 gunmen and gangsters, he controlled all 10,000 speakeasies in Chicago—and ruled the entire bootlegging business from Canada to Florida.

At his peak, Capone boasted, "I own the police," "I own Chicago." Indeed, he could not have functioned as he did without some official connivance, support, fear, and indifference.

On February 17, 1929, St. Valentine's Day, Capone made his great and final mistake. He ordered what became known as the St. Valentine's Day Massacre. A group of his killers surprised seven members of a rival gang, lined them up against a wall and machine-gunned them to death.

Of course, everyone knew that neither this atrocity nor the numerous other atrocities could have been perpetrated without Capone's direct or indirect intervention. The FBI was especially miffed and infuriated. For years, it had been trying in vain to get Capone for the murders it "knew" he was responsible for. But the FBI couldn't prove it. The St. Valentine's Day Massacre changed its tactics. Shortly thereafter Capone was convicted on a long list of income tax evasion. Result: 11 years in the federal penitentiary at Atlanta. In 1934, Capone was transferred to ALCATRAZ, the toughest prison in the United States. His health rapidly deteriorated and he was released in 1939, suffering from terminal syphilis.

In common parlance, Capone is almost universally regarded as the quintessential crime boss, synonymous with the worst in organized crime.

Use: "The *Al Capone* of pigeon poaching came home to roost yesterday and the *Eliot Ness* of the Parks Department got him.

Domiano Parasimo, 73, of Brooklyn is suspected of trapping thousands of pigeons and selling them to poultry markets." (*New York Daily News*, June 23, 1988)

Captain Bligh   One of the main characters in *Mutiny on the Bounty* (1932), one of a trilogy of novels by James N. Hall and Charles B. Nordhoff that were made into a successful movie in 1935. Captain William Bligh is the tyrannical commander of a British vessel sailing to the South Sea islands in 1787. On the way home, his crew mutiny and set him and 17 others adrift in an open boat on the high seas. An excellent mariner, he makes it to England in the sequel, *Men Against the Sea* (1934). When some of the mutineers return to England, Captain Bligh brings charges against them. They are tried, convicted and hanged.

Based on an historical character, Captain Bligh has become a prototype of the rigidly authoritarian and eccentric sea captain for whom discipline represents the highest good.

"Captain Kangaroo"   Popular children's television show (1955–1975) staring Bob Keeshan. For a time, the only daily *show* that treated the very young with kindness and concern. Captain Kangaroo, with his distinctive cap and uniform and heavy gray moustache, was a sweet, kindly, somewhat "avuncular" presence. He was a welcome departure from the usual loud, silly animated cartoons served up to the impressionable young.

Captain Marvel   In the 1940 comic book, Captain Marvel is the alter ego of Billy Batson, an orphan without a home. He sells papers and lives in subway stations.

One day, a stranger leads Billy through an underground passage to meet the old Egyptian wizard, Shazam. The wizard, about to retire, passes on his secrets and powers to Billy. When Billy utters the magic word—Shazam—he becomes Captain Marvel, wearing a colorful gold and orange hero suit. When, as Captain Marvel, Billy wishes to return to his other self, he utters Shazam—and, presto, he is back in the subways selling papers. The magic word Shazam makes Billy into the world's "mightiest mortal"; he can leap great distances, repel bullets and fly at supersonic speeds. The word Shazam gives Billy

Solomon's Wisdom
Hercules' Strength
Achilles' Courage
Zeus' Powers
Atlas' Stamina
Mercury's Speed

Every month, one million readers the world over followed Captain Marvel's breathtaking exploits. *Shazam* and Captain Marvel became part of the English language.

Carnegie, Dale   Teacher, lecturer, author (1888–1955). His book *How to Win Friends and Influence People* (1936) sold almost five million copies up to his death, becoming one of the best-selling non-fiction books of all time.

Encouraged by the phenomenal sales of his book, Carnegie and his associates founded the Carnegie Institute for Effective Speaking and Human Relations. By 1955, the self-improvement courses created and administered by the institute had been taken by more than 450,000 people in 750 U.S. cities and 15 foreign countries.

Today's highly successful Dale Carnegie courses and seminars continue to speak to basic human needs and desires. The book is still selling briskly, a title that has long since passed into the language as a statement of fundamental longings and aspirations.

Carson, Johnny   (Nebraska-born former magician (1925–), he has dominated "late-show" television programming for more than 25 years. With a gifted crew of assistants, Carson created an easy, casual atmosphere within which to express his special brand of wit, slick vulgarity, ridicule of prominent politicos and commentary on current trends in America.

Carson commanded an enormous salary. Tens of millions watched his late show every night from 11:30 to 12:30. The style and the content of Carson's show exerted a far-reaching effect on the content and format of television's other one-man shows.

Carson launched the careers of many television entertainers. It is widely acknowledged that one guest appearance on the Carson Show and "you have it made."

Casey At the Bat   See THERE IS NO JOY IN MUDVILLE.

Caspar Milquetoast   This inspired creation of H.T. Webster first appeared as a comic strip character, *The Timid Soul*, in May 1924. He looked and thought and acted the role Webster created for him: pince-nez perched above his droopy white moustache, his shoulders stooped, his gait shambling, looking lean and tired. Ever fearful, ever undecided, he quietly accepted "the slings and arrows of outrageous fortune." Life seemed too much of a burden for him—filled with frightful people and frightening decisions—an accepting, beleaguered soul in a world he never made and could not control.

Caspar's many faithful readers recognized something of themselves in his self-inflicted dilemmas, in his doubts, his compromises, his self-abasement. He also provided someone they could feel sorry for and superior to.

The quintessential Caspar is shown waiting in a pouring rain on a busy downtown street corner, his hat collapsed damply about his face, water puddling around his shoes. The caption reads: "Well, I'll wait one more hour for him, and if he doesn't come then, he can go and borrow that $100 from someone else."

Cassatt, Mary   American born painter (1845–1926) who lived in Paris most of her life. Cassatt was a student and companion of Edgar Degas and exhibited with the Impressionists. Her paintings often had a mother and her children as their subjects.

Cassidy, Butch   American gangster (1866–1937?), born Robert Leroy Parker and raised on a ranch in Utah by his Mormon father. While still an adolescent, Cassidy fell in with bad company, engaged in cattle rustling, small bank robberies etc. Released from prison in 1890, he adopted the alias of Butch Cassidy and formed the famous Wild Bunch—a gang of ruthless desperadoes devoting their energies to such pastimes as train and bank robberies, stock thefts and murder. To a man, they were fiercely loyal to Butch.

Cassidy was the "brains" of the Wild Bunch, planning and executing their major depredations with exquisite skill and care. He boasted that he had never killed anyone. His associates could not make this claim. They felt quite at ease with the murders they had committed.

The widespread criminal activities of Cassidy and the Wild Bunch put the famous Pinkerton and railroad detectives on their trial. In the hot pursuit and the confrontations that followed, several gang members were killed or arrested. Realizing that he, too, would be caught,

Cassidy and his friend the Sundance Kid took off for South America. From this point on, accounts vary as to where the duo settled, what they did and when and where they died.

The prototypical free-lancing criminal, Butch Cassidy is widely regarded as one of the outlaw West's most romantic characters. (See also BUTCH CASSIDY AND THE SUNDANCE KID.)

Castle, Vernon and Irene   Elegant pair (1887–1918 and 1893–1969) who around the time of World War I developed and demonstrated a new style of ballroom dancing in which couples held each other in embrace. Their most famous dances were the Maxixe, the Castle Walk, the Castle Polka, the Tango and the Hesitation Waltz. Idolized for their stylishness in exhibition dancing, the Castles helped popularize social dancing.

A movie about the couple, *The Story of Vernon and Irene Castle* starring Fred Astaire and Ginger Rogers, was released in 1939 by RKO Radio Pictures.

Catch-22   Wildly satirical novel (1961) by Joseph Heller (1923–). The protagonist Yossarian is a bombardier in an American squadron stationed on a Mediterranean island during World War II. His commander is a fanatic bent on sacrificing his men to his own ambitions. In desperate efforts to survive, Yossarian feigns madness. But, argues the military bureaucracy, referring to regulation 22, how can one be mad if one is trying to get out of the war? There's the catch—catch-22!

Catch-22 is widely used to mean a paradoxical bind out of which one cannot work one's way, an absurd dilemma.

Use: "Headline for a September 6, 1988, *New York Post* editorial on the Soviet's exploding empire: "Moscow's Catch 22." and underneath: "…a fundamental contradiction endures: If the U.S.S.R. does provide its citizens with basic human rights, it will no longer be a communist totalitarian state. And no communist/totalitarian state in all of history has dismantled itself, let alone voluntarily."

Caulfield, Holden   Seventeen-year-old hero of J.D. Salinger's novel, *The Catcher in the Rye* (1951). In his book-length monologue, Holden reveals his disaffection from almost everybody in the world except his innocent young sister, Phoebe. His classmates and teachers at prep school, his own parents, affected girls, casual acquaintances he runs into during his long weekend in New York City, are all phonies, not to be trusted. He has a vision of standing in a field of rye at the bottom of a cliff so that he may catch the little children who fall off. He wants to protect the innocent children from the disillusionment they inevitably face in a world of grown-ups. Holden Caulfield became a cult figure for millions of youths all over the world. Young people dressed like him with a long scarf trailing around their necks; they used his racy language; and they adopted his attitudes.

Cavell, Edith Louisa   British nurse (1865–1915) executed by the Germans on October 13, 1915, on charges of espionage during World War I. She had treated the wounded of both sides, and so her death was viewed on the Allied side as a martyrdom.

The Center Cannot Hold   Phrase from "The Second Coming," a poem by William Butler Yeats (1865–1939). He writes:

> Things fall apart; the centre cannot hold;
> Mere anarchy is loosed upon the world...

What Yeats means is that Western civilization, as we have known it, is disintegrating. We are no longer bound together by commonly shared values and rituals. We recognize no authority. "The falcon cannot hear the falconer." It's each man for himself.

Use: William Safire, writing about Secretary of State James Baker's ill-advised attempts to undercut centrist policies in Israel: "The stakes are too big for this kind of stuff. We should not wearily assume that the center cannot hold; in Israel it can. James Baker should stop undermining The Shamir-Robin-Arens team and start supporting it." (*New York Times* Op-Ed page 6, June 19, 1989) (See also SLOUCHING TOWARD BETHLEHEM.)

Chagall, Marc   Born Moyshe Shagal (1887–1985) in Russia, he became a world-renowned painter and stained-glass maker who worked variously in St. Petersburg, Paris, Berlin, Jerusalem and New York. Chagall painted dreamlike fantasies out of the nostalgic elements of his boyhood in a Russian shtetl: rural village life, Russian folk tales, Jewish proverbs. Chagall's stained glass windows may be seen in the Hadassah Chapel in Jerusalem, on the facade of the Metropolitan Opera House in New York City, in the cathedral at

Rheims, France, and in many other places. A Chagall is a bright-colored pictorial folk tale.

chain reaction   The term comes from chemistry and physics. It is what happens, for example, in fission, when a single neutron splits the nucleus of a uranium atom into smaller parts, releasing two or three neutrons, each of which then attacks and splits nearby nuclei. The net result in fission is released energy. It was with this hypothesis that Enrico Fermi first succeeded in producing the chain reaction that made possible the making of the atom bomb.

In everyday use, a chain reaction is any series of happenings linked in such a way that one is the cause of the next, and so on.

Challenger   The explosion of the U.S. space shuttle Challenger 74 seconds after launching on the morning of January 28, 1986, at Cape Canaveral, Florida, with all seven astronauts aboard was the worst disaster in the history of space exploration. The tragedy was witnessed on television by millions of stunned viewers. One of the seven who died was Christa McAuliffe, a high school teacher from Concord, New Hampshire, who was supposed to have been the first "ordinary citizen" in space. The others were: Francis R. Scobee, commander; Michael J. Smith, pilot; Gregory B. Jarvis; Ronald E. McNair; Ellison S. Onizuka; and Judith A. Resnik.

The cause of the blow-up was found by the National Aeronautics and Space Administration (NASA) to be a weakness in the seal of a solid-fuel rocket booster. This terrible accident on the 25th flight of the shuttle brought the American space program to a standstill for about three years.

The Challenger has become a grim reminder of the possibility of catastrophe in space.

Use: "When working on the razor's edge of catastrophe, success demands constant training and easy communications from bottom up as well as top down—and that, in turn, demands leaders who are prepared to listen to and learn from their subordinates...These are among the principles that can help us avoid future BHOPALS, CHERNO-BYLS, Challenger's—or mistaken attacks on Iranian aircraft." (John Pfeiffer, *Smithsonian*, July 1989)

Chamberlain, Neville   British prime minister (1937–1940) whose name has become synonymous with appeasement. In spite of Hitler's broken promises—his rearming of Germany, his reoccupation of the Rhineland, his annexation of Austria—Chamberlain still thought he could do business with Hitler. In Munich on September 29, 1938, at a four-power conference—not including Czechoslovakia—Chamberlain capitulated to Hitler's demand for the German-speaking Sudetenland in return for guaranteeing the rest of Czechoslovakia's independence. Chamberlain acted, he said, "for peace in our time." Six months later, on March 15, 1939, Hitler's troops marched into Prague.

Use: Headline for *New York Times* Op-Ed article by Philip M. Kaiser, former ambassador to Hungary and Austria, February 5, 1988: "Reagan Is No Chamberlain." Reagan had been called an appeaser because of the I.N.F. (Intermediate Range Nuclear Forces) treaty with the Soviet Union. (See also MUNICH.)

Champs-Élysées   Very wide boulevard of upscale stores and restaurants in Paris, leading from the Place de la Concorde to the Etoile.

Chan, Charlie   Aphorism-spouting Chinese detective character created by the writer Earl Derr Biggers in 1925 and adapted for the screen in a long series of popular B movies from 1926 to 1949. His sayings were repeated by viewers as if they had emanated from Confucius; e.g., "When money talks, few are deaf" and "Man who flirt with dynamite sometimes fly with angels." Unlike hardboiled American private eyes, or the menacing Fu Manchu, Chan was courtly and soft-spoken. He was usually accompanied by his klutzy, bungling Number One (or Number Two) son, who supplied the comic relief. Oddly, Chan was never played by a Chinese actor. His two most authentic impersonators were Warner Oland, a Swede, and Sidney Toler, an American.

Chandleresque   Suggestive of the novels and movie scripts of Raymond Chandler (1888–1959), American mystery story writer. His books include *The Big Sleep* (1939), *Farewell, My Lovely* (1940), *The Long Goodbye* (1954) and *The Simple Art of Murder* (1950), a collection of 12 stories. Chandler used tough urban settings to depict racketeers, corrupt policeman and venal politicians.

Use: "Each of these individuals, of course, is another drifter cut loose from family ties and roots and in search of some elusive dream of home. Each has made the journey west to California, ending up in a tawdry, post-Chandleresque world of strip joints and cheap apartments." (*New York Times*, October 22, 1988)

Chanel, Gabrielle   Familiarly known as "Coco," Chanel (1886–1971) was a French designer of the haute couture whose understated, casual, slim and straight suits with collarless jackets became the standard of ultra-chic women's clothing, just as her Chanel #5 became a perennial favorite among perfumes. A Chanel is said never to go out of style. It is a classic.

Chaney, Lon   "The man of a thousand faces" used grotesque masks and horribly contorted physical postures to simulate fiendish characters in the silent movies. His most notable success was in the title role of *The Hunchback of Notre Dame* (1923). Chaney (1883–1930) was the undisputed star of horror films. Two actors who succeeded him in this genre were Bela Lugosi (*Dracula*, 1931) and Boris Karloff (*Frankenstein*, 1931).

Chaplinesque   Looking like or having the qualities of the "tramp," a character invented and played by Charles Chaplin (1889–1977), the greatest comic genius of the silent screen. The tramp was a homeless vagabond, a little guy with a derby hat, a cane, baggy pants and a duck-like waddle. He was a slapstick Mack Sennett type with a soul, wistful and trying to cope in an incomprehensible and intractable world. He first appeared in one-reelers and then in full-length movies like *City Lights* and *Modern Times*.

Chappaquiddick   Tiny island in Massachusetts where Senator Ted Kennedy drove off a bridge on the night of July 19, 1969. His 28-year-old companion in the car, Mary Jo Kopechne, was drowned. Kennedy received a two-month suspended sentence and one year's probation for leaving the scene of an accident. Although Kennedy, in a televised speech, said that he tried to save the girl, the unanswered questions of Chappaquiddick have continued to haunt his political career.

Chappaquiddick stands for political nemesis. It is a shady part of one's past that won't go away.

Use: Gary Hart's brief affair with Donna Rice proved to be his Chappaquiddick.

Charles, Nick and Nora   Sleek couple in the detective novel *The Thin Man* by Dashiell Hammett. They stand for debonair sophistication and wit.

Charlie   Originally, the Viet Cong or V.C. (uniformed members or guerrilla fighters of the National Liberation Front of South Vietnam). "Charlie" was the American military code word for the letter C, so Charlie became the enemy—eventually, the enemy of any kind in the Vietnam War.

Charlie Brown   Character in the comic strip *Peanuts*, created by Charles Schulz in 1950 and one of the most successful strips ever. Charlie Brown is the quintessence of meekness and failure.

Chauchat, Clavdia   See MAGIC MOUNTAIN, THE.

Checkers   Name of Richard Nixon's cocker spaniel puppy. Nixon invoked it in 1952 during a nationwide TV address in which he was trying to exculpate himself from charges that he had amassed a secret political fund for his vice presidential campaign on the Eisenhower ticket in 1952. Tearfully, he admitted that he had accepted the little dog as a gift, but that his children loved it and he was going to keep it no matter what. The American people, always responsive to dogs and babies, forgave him and accepted his explanation of the fund.

Now refers to any sentimental appeal that bypasses the real issues and tugs on the heartstrings instead.

Use: At the Republican Party convention in August 1988, Senator Quayle, the vice presidential nominee, was advised by some to make a Checkers-type speech—after it was discovered that he had avoided combat in Vietnam by using influence to get into the comparatively safe National Guard instead.

Chernobyl   Site of the Chernobyl Nuclear Power Plant in the Soviet Union. On April 26, 1986, due to "operator errors," explosions blew the roof off the #4 reactor and triggered a partial meltdown of the core's fuel. It was the worst nuclear power-plant accident ever. Thirty-one persons were killed and scores were subjected to radiation; 116,000 people within a 30-kilometer radius were evacuated. The Soviet Union did not make public this disaster until two days later, by which time serious radiation levels had been registered all over

Europe. Fear of contamination led to the call-out of civil defense teams and a prohibition on consumption of fresh produce and milk.

Chernobyl is widely used as a warning, a catchword by those opposed to the construction and operation of nuclear power plants near civilian populations. It spells disaster, meltdown.

Use: "Ethnic uprisings could be Gorby's political Chernobyl." (Headline in *New York Post*, March 4, 1988)

Chicken in every pot   Slogan of the Republican Party in the presidential campaign of 1928; a promise of continued prosperity under a new Republican administration. The entire slogan read: "A chicken in every pot, a car in every garage."

Connotes general prosperity for the masses. Sometimes used ironically to suggest the opposite.

Citizen Kane   Film about the controversial life of a publishing tycoon, modeled after William Randolph Hearst. Considered by many critics to be one of the greatest films ever made. Produced, directed, starred in and coauthored (with Herman J. Mankiewicz) in 1941 by Orson Welles (1916–1985), the onetime "boy wonder." (See also ROSEBUD.)

clear and present danger   See FALSELY SHOUTING FIRE IN A CROWDED THEATER.

cliffhanger   From silent movie serials, where every episode ended with a melodramatic, suspenseful situation designed to make the viewer come back for the outcome the following week. Literally, the hero might be left at the end of an episode clinging by one hand to the edge of a cliff. How would he escape? Wait till next week.

Any suspenseful situation not immediately resolved.

Clockwork Orange, A   Novel (1962) by English writer Anthony Burgess and film (1971) directed by Stanley Kubrick. The first half of the movie vividly depicts a teenage gang of the future rampaging through streets and homes. These young men are as hard-edged as the decor. Utterly lacking in human compassion or sensibility, they strike terror wherever they attack. They represent Burgess's terrible vision of a society tyrannized by children growing up without restraints of any kind.

Burgess's future seems to have arrived. Under the headline "A Clockwork Orange in Central Park" (*U.S. News & World Report*, May 8, 1989) the copy reads: "The attackers were children wielding rocks and a pipe, and the casual brutality of the crime shattered the springtime countenance of a city long accustomed to a daily drumbeat of murders, muggings and robberies."

clone   Term coined around 1903 from the Greek word *klon* meaning a slip or a twig. Biologists have discovered that, just as a plant can be reproduced from a small slip, an entire living system can be reproduced from a single cell, since each cell contains the DNA molecules of the whole organism. It is possible, therefore, to make a copy of a complex organic system (theoretically, even a human being) in a science laboratory. In other words, it is possible to produce a clone genetically identical to the ancestral unit from which it was derived.

Colloquially, a clone is a copy or a close imitation of someone or something else.

Use: "'One of the reasons I picked Lloyd Bentsen is because I know he will challenge me as Vice President,' the Massachusetts Governor said. And Senator Bentsen asserted, 'That's part of the strength and the character of this man: He wasn't looking for a clone of Michael Dukakis.'" (*New York Times*, July 14, 1988)

Clouseau, Inspector   Main character played by Peter Sellers in a series of films, including *The Pink Panther*, *The Return of the Pink Panther* and *The Revenge of the Pink Panther*. An inept, ineffectual, bumbling detective; a farcical parody of the tough private eye.

Use: During the Iran-Contra hearings in 1987 before a joint congressional committee, a member of the panel referred to Edwin Meese 3rd, the attorney general of the United States as a Clouseau because he allowed Lt. Col. Oliver North to shred potentially incriminating government documents in his presence as an investigator.

Coca, Imogene   See SHOW OF SHOWS.

Cohan, George M.   Actor, playwright, composer, producer (1878–1942) who dominated the Broadway musical theater for two decades.

Cohan spent 56 years on the stage. He wrote 40 plays, collaborated on 40 others, produced 150 other plays, wrote over 500 songs and made between 5,000 and 10,000 stage appearances.

Cohan's songs sold millions of copies of sheet music. Among his still popular songs: "Over There," "You're A Grand Old Flag," "Mary," "Give My Regards To Broadway," "I'm a Yankee Doodle Dandy." In 1940, Congress voted Cohan a special Medal of Honor. Cohan is the quintessential "song and dance man."

cold war   All-out hostility, short of a shooting war, between the Western democracies and the Soviet Union following the end of World War II. Ideological, military, economic and political rivalry between these two sides. The expression was coined in 1946 by Herbert Bayard Swope in a speech he wrote for elder statesman Bernard Baruch. Used today to indicate such a feeling between any two parties. The cold war came to an end with the tearing down of the BERLIN WALL in 1989.

Collyer brothers   Wealthy brothers Homer (1882–1947) and Langley (1886–1947), who lived like poverty-stricken recluses in a Harlem town house. When the police broke in, they found both brothers dead amidst mountainous piles of junk, garbage, old newspapers and magazines.

The Collyer brothers are synonymous with misers and irrational hoarders.

come up and see me sometime   See WEST, MAE.

comin' in on a wing and a prayer   From a World War II song about a pilot, written by Harold Adamson and Jimmy McHugh (lyrics) in 1943. Quoted now to mean just barely making it.

Como, Perry   In the 1950s, Como (1912–) was the "epitome of the super star" of television. His relaxed, easy, familiar, fresh, soft voice and his manner, his appealing personality, made him one of the most attractive performers of his time. His detractors' characterization of his "somnambulant style" had no effect on Como's vast and constant audience.

Comstock, Anthony   A lifetime crusader (1844–1915) against vice, obscenity and pornography. In 1873, Comstock established the New York Society for the Suppression of Vice, and remained as its secretary until he died 42 years later. Under his unrelenting pressure, the United States Congress passed the Comstock Act, which banned "obscene" materials, including prophylactics, from the mails.

The Post Office appointed him as special agent to enforce the law. Comstock pursued his mission as "smut-hunter" with unparalleled zeal. Among his "victories" was getting the Department of the Interior to fire Walt Whitman for his *Leaves of Grass* collection of poetry. At his insistence, New York City banned Margaret Sanger's books on birth control.

But Comstock didn't win all his battles. Sometimes his activities backfired. His attacks on George Bernard Shaw's *Mrs. Warren's Profession* contributed to the play's great success. Similarly, he focused international attention on the innocuous, mildly erotic painting SEPTEMBER MORN.

Eventually, Comstock became part of our language when George Bernard Shaw characterized his activities as "Comstockery," which the *Random House Dictionary* defines as: "Overzealous censorship of fine arts and literature often mistaking outspokenly honest works for salacious productions."

Use: Under the lash of local Comstocks, various individuals and organizations are at work censoring library and text books.

Coney Island   Seaside resort bordering the Atlantic Ocean at the southern tip of Brooklyn, New York City. At the turn of the century it was the most famous resort in the world. With its wide sandy beaches, its boathouses and hotels, its boardwalk, its fabled amusement parks and freak shows, it attracted hundreds of thousands of pleasure seekers. On a summer Sunday, the beach could be covered with a million bathers. At night all the electric lights went on, outlining the turrets of its buildings. Then it became the "City of Fire."

Coney Island, though in decline today, remains in the imagination as a symbol of carnival, with all the tawdriness and gaiety and magnificence intrinsic in that word.

Connor, Bull   Sheriff in Birmingham, Alabama, notorious for his use of dogs in trying to prevent black children from entering white schools. A brutish opponent of the civil rights movement in the 1960s.

Use: "The *Wall Street Journal* got its facts wrong when it described James O. Freedman, the liberal president of Dartmouth College, who accused the right wing *Dartmouth Review* of poisoning the intellectual environment of the campus, as the Bull Connor of Academia." (*New York Times*, May 11, 1988)

Conrad, Joseph   British novelist and short story writer of Polish birth (1857–1924) whose fiction is often based on his sea-faring experiences and adventures. His characters are often caught in strange, almost hallucinatory moral dilemmas, as in *Lord Jim* (1900) and *Heart of Darkness* (1902).

consciousness raising   A deliberate attempt on the part of women in the 1970s to convene in discussion groups for the purpose of making themselves alert to the various forms of their personal oppression. These groups were support groups. The women gained courage to recognize and free themselves of their dependency and feelings of inferiority.

The term (originally used by Mao to raise revolutionary consciousness in China) is now used not only for women's liberation but also for any person or group that needs to become more aware of its identity and integrity.

Cook's tour   An organized but superficial, inadequate, once-over-lightly tour of a country, city, any geographical area. So named after Thomas Cook, British travel agent.

Use: "We weren't at all happy about our last trip to China. Our tour guide gave us a real Cook's tour."

Cooper, Gary   Movie star (1901–1961) who started his career as an extra in silent Western movies and won an Oscar for his role as the sheriff in the great Western *High Noon* (1952). He is known for his monosyllabic Montana speech, his tall, lean frame, his craggy face, his quiet strength and his ability to ride horses. He won an Oscar for *Sergeant York* in 1941. One of his best known parts was Frederic Henry in *A Farewell to Arms* (1932).

Use: "Did he have long eyelashes and a boyish grin and gulp a lot, the way honest, upright Gary Cooper gulped in the old movies?"

(Russell Baker, satirizing Lt. Col. Oliver North, the "hero" of The Iran-Contra hearings, in his column on the *New York Times* Op-Ed page, August 5, 1987.)

Cory, Richard   Subject of a short, paradoxical portrait in the poem "Richard Cory" by American poet Edwin Arlington Robinson (1869–1935). Richard Cory is envied by everybody in his town. He seems to have it all: good looks, elegant manners, riches. But "Richard Cory, one summer night,/Went home and put a bullet through his head."

Richard Cory has become a tragic symbol of the despair that may lurk beneath the surface appearance of seemingly fortunate people. His life and death represent a little morality play about envy.

cosa nostra   "Our thing," an "alias" for the MAFIA. Allegedly coined by LUCKY LUCIANO and MEYER LANSKY, two of America's most powerful, most influential organized crime figures.

Coughlin, Charles Edward   A Depression-era radio chaplain (1891–1979) who lashed out at the communists and the "money changers" who, among others (he alleged), had brought America to the verge of chaos and hopelessness.

To the 30 million to 45 million of his radio listeners, Father Coughlin held out the hope that the nation would survive and "overcome." They wrote over 50,000 letters a week to his Shrine of the Little Flower in Royal Oak, Michigan.

By 1933, Father Coughlin had become a national hero—and a reckless one, as it turned out, hurling bitter invectives at President Franklin D. Roosevelt whom he called a "scab president" and "a great betrayer and liar."

Because Father Coughlin's weekly broadcasts were becoming increasingly inflammatory, CBS insisted that he submit his speeches in advance. He refused, so CBS did not renew his contract. Undaunted, and emboldened by a sense that he was destined to save America, Father Coughlin returned to the air, his air-time paid for by his faithful listeners.

In 1934, Father Coughlin founded the National Union for Social Justice. His rhetoric turned more raucous, his charges wild and outrageous, and his association with anti-Semites and pro-fascists ugly and threatening.

Appalled by his menacing excesses, the Catholic laity and clergy turned against him. In 1942, his Church silenced him. His hectic career had come to an end. Deserted by his former admirers and adherents, he vanished from the national scene.

Use: "America has had its peddlers of political hate, its Father Coughlin and its Joe McCarthy. "(*New York Times*, June 8, 1989)

countdown   Literally, counting backward from ten to one in the ultimate moments before a space launch or before a detonation. First used in the dramatic seconds before the atom bomb was tested. Now used to denote the seconds or minutes or hours or days before an important event or, jocularly, a not-so-important event.

counted out   In boxing, the referee gives the fallen boxer 10 seconds, counted out loud, to get up unassisted. If he cannot, he is considered "knocked out." The bout is over and he has lost.

In general use, to be counted out is to be beaten, finished, etc.

Use: There's plenty of fight in Allenby. So don't count him out.

Craig's Wife   Title of a Pulitzer prize-winning play (1925) by George Kelly (1887–1974). Harriet Craig, a selfish, narrow and domineering woman, is so obsessed with order and neatness that in the end her husband leaves her and she remains alone in her perfect house. She can't stand flowers because the petals fall; she can't stand guests because they mess up the house, etc.

To be characterized as a Craig's wife is to be stamped as a housewife neurotically addicted to compulsive straightening and cleaning so that nobody can relax in the house.

Crawford, Joan   American film actress (1904–1977). Born Lucille LeSueur in Texas. Starred in more than 80 films. Remembered mainly for sob sister, self-sacrificing roles like that of *Mildred Pierce.*

Crosby, Harry Lillis "Bing"   American popular singer (1904–1977). The career of "old groaner," as he was affectionately called, encompassed network radio, television, 50 movies, over 300 million records. In his uniquely unpretentious way, his quiet, intimate baritone made it all look so easy, so relaxed, so natural. Actually, his elegant paraphrasing, his "buoyant," faultless sense of rhythm, his fastidious diction and his special way with a song were anything but accidental. Crosby's art was the art that concealed art.

Bing Crosby was a legend in his time, a middle-American in taste, dress and inclination—a prototypical average guy.

Curie, Marie Polish-born French chemist and physicist (1867–1934) who, together with her husband Pierre Curie, studied radioactivity. She discovered the element radium and received a Nobel Prize for her find in 1911. She remains the prototype for women in science.

D

Dachau The first of the Nazi concentration camps, erected in Bavaria under the direction of Heinrich Himmler in March 1933, and manned by the SS. Dachau was the model for many other concentration camps. Over the camp gates was the motto ARBEIT MACHT FREI. Those who could work were spared for forced labor; those who were judged incapable of work (women, children, the old, the deranged) were killed. (See also AUSCHWITZ.)

Dagwood An unusually thick sandwich stuffed with a variety of meats, cheeses, dressings, vegetables, spices, condiments etc. This sandwich gets its name from the popular comic strip, BLONDIE, where Dagwood Bumstead makes these belly-busters for himself.

Dali, Salvador Surrealist Spanish painter (1904–1989) who went to great lengths to publicize his flamboyant persona as well as to promote his strange and disturbing art. His waxed mustache, turned upward like the horns of a bull, made him a caricature in the flesh; his surrealist images of melted watches— "The Persistence of Memory" (1931)—made an indelible impression on the public psyche.

Use: In the 115-degree Las Vegas morning, the ballpoint pen on the dashboard of the car had overnight melted like a Dali watch.

"Dallas" One of the most popular television shows of the 1980s. It has all the elements of the successful soap opera: larger than life characters; riveting conflicts about money and power; and lots of sex, intrigues, back stabbings etc.

The episode revealing which of "Dallas"'s 15 characters had shot J.R. (all of them had good reasons) was seen by more people than any program in the history of television up to that time.

"Dallas" takes place in Texas, a symbol of the opulence and power of the wealthy.

The centerpiece of "Dallas" is Larry Hagman as J.R. Ewing Jr., described by *Time* as "that human oil slick." He is the quintessential villain: power-hungry, cruel, vain, a ruthless womanizer, master of the shady deal. Through J.R.'s dealings and encounters, "Dallas" illuminates the false values and the ruthless pursuit of money and power he represented.

Acting his fat role with single-minded intensity, J.R. became "the man you love to hate."

Use: "Next year, I am going to France to teach young lycéens about American language and civilization. My students will ask me what this country is really like; they'll ask me if it's really like *Dallas* and *Dynasty*." (Caren Litherland, Letters to the Editor, *New York Times*, July 2, 1989)

Darrow, Clarence S.   In his day, Darrow (1857–1938) was widely regarded as one of America's most brilliant lawyers. He first gained prominence as a "political" lawyer for his successful defense of Big Bill Heywood, a radical leader charged with murder.

Later, Darrow achieved international fame defending Nathan Leopold and Richard Loeb, the "Thrill Killers" of little Bobby Franks. His plea, that both were "mentally and morally sick," saved them from the electric chair. They were sentenced to life imprisonment.

In his next sensational case, the famous Monkey Trial, Darrow defended Thomas Scopes, a schoolteacher charged with teaching the theory of evolution. The famous William Jennings Bryan was the attorney for the prosecution. Scopes was convicted and fined $100. In the court of world opinion, however, Darrow won the case.

To be called a Darrow is to take one's place in the pantheon of great lawyers who represent the underdog and the apparently sure losers. (See also LEOPOLD AND LOEB.)

Darth Vader   Villain of the epic space movie *Star Wars* (1977) and its sequels, *The Empire Strikes Back* (1980) and *The Return of the Jedi* (1983); all were produced and the first written and directed by George Lucas. As imperial master of the Death Star, Vader pursues the good guys (the rebels): Princess Leia, Luke Skywalker, Han Solo,

Obi-Wan Kenobi, the mystical Yoda, the robots R2D2 and C-3PO, and a host of others. He represents the dark side of the Force. Luke learns to master the good side of the Force. The Force "is an energy field. It is all around us...It gives us power. You can learn to make it work for you." At the end of the first movie, Luke blows up the Death Star.

Use: In an article about the strike of Eastern Airlines employees against management: "Mr. Lorenzo, who in some circles is viewed as the 'Darth Vader' of the industry, has shown nothing but contempt for Eastern employees, both union and non-contract." (*Palm Beach Post*, March 5, 1989)

Davis, Bette   American screen star (1908–1989) with huge rolling eyes, twitching spasmodic movements, raspy voice—easy to caricature. Associated with bitchy parts: the destructive waitress Mildred in *Of Human Bondage* (1934); Leslie Crosbie, the murderess in *The Letter* (1940); the title role of *Jezebel* (1938); the jealous, aging actress in *All About Eve* (1950). Bette Davis generated nervous intensity, a fierceness and independence bordering on intransigence.

day that will live in infamy   Words spoken by President Franklin Delano Roosevelt on December 8, 1941, after the previous day's attack by Japanese war planes on the American military bases at Pearl Harbor, Hawaii. The surprise strike had come in the midst of ongoing negotiations between the United States and Japan. Caught off guard, the Americans lost five battleships, 14 smaller ships, 200 aircraft as well as thousands of seamen, soldiers and civilians killed or wounded. The United States immediately declared war on Japan, and on December 11 the United States declared war on the other Axis powers, Italy and Germany.

The components of a day of infamy would seem to be outrageous activity, betrayal and shamefulness.

Use: When, in spite of worldwide protests, Pres. Ronald Reagan kept his word to German Chancellor Helmut Kohl to visit the military cemetery at Bitburg, Germany, where 49 of the 2,500 Germans buried there had been SS troops, many called that day (May 5, 1985) "a day of infamy."

D-day   June 6, 1944, the day of the Allied invasion of Europe on the Normandy beaches. Opening of the long-awaited Second Front in

World War II, under the command of General Dwight D. Eisenhower. D-day is generally used to mean *the* day of launching a new enterprise.

Dean, James   See REBEL WITHOUT A CAUSE

Dear Abby   Syndicated newspaper column (since 1956) written by Abigail van Buren, answering requests from readers for advice on handling personal moral dilemmas. Used mockingly in general parlance whenever advice in personal matters is sought, and where there are no easy, cliché answers.

Dear John letter   A letter to a soldier during World War II, from his girl friend or his wife, to announce the breakup of their relationship. The salutation "Dear John" and the cruel content of the letter became a bitter paradox.

A Dear John letter is still a letter of rejection, concealing a wallop behind the loving salutation.

Death in Venice   A novella (1913) by Thomas Mann. The hero, Gustav von Aschenbach, an austere classicist and writer in his 50s, is vacationing in Venice. There is a kind of decadence in the air, which exerts a strange fascination over him. He falls in love with a 14-year-old Polish boy, Tadzio, a boy of ideal beauty and grace. To overcome his infatuation he knows he must leave Venice, but he stays on. His unexpressed feelings become a passionate obsession. Venice is in the first stages of a cholera epidemic; Aschenbach becomes feverish and dies on the day Tadzio leaves.

"Death in Venice" has come to stand for the inner plague of self-indulgence and decadence. It exemplifies what may happen when Dionysian passion and license win out over Apollonian reason and restraint.

De Chirico, Giorgio   Artist (1888–1978) born in Greece of Sicilian parents, he studied in Athens, Munich, Italy and Paris. His early paintings, through the juxtaposition of incongruous elements caught in brooding shadows and cold light, suggest sinister events, as of a town just emptied of people. Some of his trademarks are classical buildings with arches and arcades stretching into infinity, a curtain flapping out of an open window in an empty house, a lone figure rolling a hoop down a deserted street. Typical is his painting *Mystery* *and Melancholy of A Street* (1914). His best paintings are hallucinatory, as in the 1920s series of wild horses galloping along shores strewn with broken Greek columns. His work is "metaphysical," eerie, dreamlike and disturbing. It touches the unconscious. In 1938 De Chirico wrote: "We who know the signs of the metaphysical alphabet know what joys and sorrows are present in a portico, on a street corner, within the walls of a room or inside a box."

A De Chirico is a dreamlike, almost surrealist evocation of scene.

Use: "Ian McEwan's fictional world is a dark and threatening place, combining the bleak, dream-like quality of De Chiricos citiscapes with the strange eroticism of canvases by Balthus." (Michiko Kakutani, reviewing in the *New York Times* [September 26, 1987] a novel called *The Child in Time,* by Ian McEwan.)

Decline of the West, The   Book written by the German philosopher and historian Oswald Spengler (1880–1936) and published in 1918. Its main thesis is that every culture passes through an organic life cycle similar to the human cycle. It predicts the decline of Western civilization and the growing ascendancy of Eastern cultures.

The great problems of Western democracies (crime, materialism, decadence, drugs, possibility of nuclear war) are taken to be proof of the decline of the West.

Deep Throat   Code name (derived from a pornographic movie of the same title) for the person who supplied information about the Watergate conspiracy and cover-up to Carl Bernstein and Bob Woodward, reporters for *The Washington Post,* who received the Pulitzer Prize for their investigative journalism on May 7, 1973. The identity of Deep Throat has so far not been disclosed.

Deep Throat is now used to refer to any secret source of information.

DeMille, Agnes   American dancer and choreographer (1909–) whose Rodeo ballet (1942) captured the exuberant spirit of the American West and influenced the choreography of many Broadway musicals, including *Oklahoma* (1943) and *Carousel* (1945). Her ballets are not merely decorative; they move the plot forward as in "Laurie Makes Up Her Mind" in *Oklahoma,* in which Laurie must decide between her rival suitors.

DeMille, Cecil B.   Pioneer director (1881–1959) of epic films, including *The Ten Commandments* (1923) and *The Greatest Show on Earth* (1952). DeMille's name is synonymous with colossal extravaganzas, lavish spectacles.

Dempsey, William Harrison (Jack)   Boxer who held the world heavyweight title from 1919 to 1925. Born in Manassa, Colorado, mining country, Dempsey (1895–1983) started life as a miner, found the work not to his liking, drifted into the tough, grimy existence of a boxer. A small man, Dempsey defeated many bigger men in the ring. Sportswriters called him "Jack, the Giant Killer," "The Manassa Mauler."

Dempsey has become a symbol of guts and fury in, at best, a not too gentle craft.

Dennis the Menace   Since it appeared on March 12, 1951, this comic strip has achieved vast popularity. In fact, *Dennis the Menace* has become a household word. Dennis, according to Maurice Horn, author of *The World Encyclopedia of Cartoons*, is a "...tousle-haired, enterprising tot whose counterfeit innocence, unflattering candor, and joyous vandalism are in delightful contrast to the docile conformity of the adult world..."

Dennis is the unpredictable, unstoppable disrupter of neighborhood and family peace. His helpless parents are often the target of his shenanigans. He is the contemporary counterpart of an earlier terror, PECK'S BAD BOY.

Use: "*Dennis the Menace Come In From the Cold.* Can Newt Gingrich save the GOP House Minority from irrelevance?"—Caption of a *U.S. News and World Report* article (March 27, 1989) on Newt Gingrich's possible ascension to leader of the Republican minority in the House of Representatives. The article refers to Representative Gingrich as an "exasperating Dennis The Menace."

Diaghilev, Serge Pavlovich   Russian-born impresario (1872–1929) famous mostly as the director of the Ballets Russes in Paris with Nijinsky as its star. Although he himself never choreographed a ballet, he exerted tremendous influence on the development of the ballet in the 20th century by gathering around him luminaries of dance, music and design who created the new ballet (and whom he helped to make into stars). Among these were the dancers NIJINSKY,

Karsavina, Danilova; the choreographers Fokine, Massine, BALANCHINE; the composers Stravinsky, Prokofiev, Ravel, Debussy; and the artists and designers Benois, Bakst, PICASSO, MATISSE, BRAQUE, Derain, Laurencin, DE CHIRICO. By force of personality, artistic integrity and brilliance, Diaghilev stamped his name on the world of art in the 20th century.

Diamond, Jack "Legs"   One of Prohibition's most feared, most hated racketeers (1896–1931). Many unsuccessful attempts were made on Diamond's life. For a time, he was thought to be "unkillable" and "unconvictable": "the bullet hasn't been made that can kill Legs Diamond."

Finally, his luck ran out. He was asleep in an Albany hotel room when two hired killers entered his room. One held him by the ears and the other shot him three times in the head.

Dick Tracy   One of the most famous and influential comic strip detectives. First appeared in 1931. Early on, Tracy watches, powerless, as his sweetheart Tess Trueheart is kidnapped and her father murdered. Tracy joins the police force to track down the criminals who were responsible for these two acts. In time, he becomes the symbol of avenging justice, relentlessly pursuing all evildoers at great peril to himself. He embodies the endless struggle between good and evil.

Dick Tracy is the first "realistic" comic strip. "Eagle-nosed," "square chinned," his violent, brutal encounters have exerted a great influence, not only on "the cops and robbers" strips but also on all action comics. Warren Beatty starred in the 1990 feature film, *Dick Tracy*.

Didi   See VLADIMIR.

didn't lay a glove on   In boxing, this describes a boxer who can't hit his opponent, or can't hit him hard or often enough to hurt or harm him. He is, in short, the inferior fighter, outmaneuvered by a more skillful opponent and, hence, likely to lose the match.

"Can't or didn't lay a glove on," in current use, means one is unable to do anything to injure a person's reputation, diminish his public standing, tarnish his image etc. A dramatic use of this expression occurred during the presidential primaries of 1988.

Use: Commenting on the heated exchange between himself and Dan Rather during an interview on CBS Evening News, Vice President George Bush said, "The worst time I've had in twenty years in public life. Two weeks before a primary. But it's going to help me because that bastard [Rather] didn't lay a glove on me." (*Newsweek Magazine*, February 8, 1988)

Dien Bien Phu   Where in May 1954 the French military forces lost a decisive battle against the Communist Viet Minh. In July 1954 the French signed an armistice at Geneva. They agreed to pull their troops out of Vietnam and they agreed to the division of Vietnam along the 17th parallel into two parts, North and South, to be reunited in the future by open elections.

The French had staked their national honor at Dien Bien Phu. They lost, as the Americans were to lose in Vietnam in 1973.

Dietrich, Marlene   Born Magdalena von Losch (1901–) in Germany. Blond, glamorous, wickedly sexy, sophisticated goddess of the screen—a femme fatale with perfect legs and a German-accented, husky singing voice. Her great role was as Lola in T*he Blue Angel* (1930), directed by Joseph von Sternberg, in which she dressed in a man's tuxedo and sang sexy songs in a cabaret.

Dillinger, John   The first American criminal (1903–1934) to be named Public Enemy Number 1 (1925) by U.S. Attorney General Homer Cummings. Until he reached the age of 22, Dillinger led a fairly prosaic existence. The last nine years of his life he devoted to an almost unparalleled succession of robberies, murders and prison escapes. His name spread terror throughout the Midwest. Released from prison in 1933, he shot 17 people, killing 10. His end came on July 22, 1934. Betrayed by female companion Anna Sage, known as "the woman in red," Dillinger was shot and killed by FBI men as he was leaving the Biograph Theater in Chicago.

Dillinger's name has become almost a metaphor for the brutal, merciless, senseless killer.

Use: The police bulletin read as follows: "Austin is wanted for three murders. He is armed and dangerous—another Dillinger."

Dilsey   Negro servant in *The Sound and the Fury* (1929), a novel by William Faulkner. She holds the Compson family together and cares especially for Benjy, the idiot son. She is compassionate and dependable. Sustained by her religious faith, she endures.

Dilsey is the black woman who has often compensated for the inadequacies of the southern white mother. She is a symbol of stability in the family.

DiMaggio, Joe   New York Yankees baseball player (1914–). One of the game's more sensational players, he never played to the stands. DiMaggio was modest, graceful, a man of "quiet elegance"—rare virtues anywhere. Even in his ill-starred marriage to MARILYN MONROE, he conducted himself with characteristic dignity and restraint.

DiMaggio's 13 years with the Yankees (1936–1951) brought him well-deserved honors: All Star team in 1936, Most Valuable Player for three years, Baseball Hall of Fame in 1955. Reaching for superlatives to describe DiMaggio's extraordinary achievements, the sportswriters settled for "Jolting Joe" and "The Yankee Clipper." Connie Mack, a true judge of baseball talent and achievement, said it all for DiMaggio: "The greatest team player of all time."

Disney, Walt   Hollywood producer (1901–1966) of cartoons and animated feature films combining cartoon and live characters. Creator of Disneyland. (See also MICKEY MOUSE, SEVEN DWARFS, DISNEYLAND.)

Disneyland   Amusement park covering 160 acres in Anaheim, California; completed in 1955 by WALT DISNEY. Here a child or a grown-up child can see Disney's cartoon characters come to life; here he can enter a world of fantasy or history, explore a medieval castle, ride on a stage coach or a Mississippi steamboat. Disneyland is synonymous with wonderland or fantasyland.

Dr. Kildare   The hero of a popular American television series: the archetypal, dedicated young physician, personable and appealing. Hence, any doctor embodying these characteristics.

Dr. Strangelove   British film directed in 1964 by Stanley Kubrick and based on *Red Alert*, a novel by Peter George. In the movie, Peter Sellers plays three rôles: the President of the United States, an RAF captain, and Dr. Strangelove, a mad German- American scientist. When a fanatical USAF general (George C. Scott) mistakenly launches an A-bomb attack on the Soviet Union, and fail-safe attempts do not work, and Soviet retaliation seems certain, the movie becomes a suspenseful black comedy about man's propensity for self-destruction in the atomic age. The full title of the film is *Dr. Strangelove Or: How I Learned to Stop Worrying and Love The Bomb*.

A Dr. Strangelove is a mad eccentric so in love with what he has created that he cannot think of the consequences of his deadly inventions.

Dodsworth, Samuel   The main character in *Dodsworth*, a 1929 novel by Sinclair Lewis. He is a retired manufacturer who longs to break through the limitations of small-town life by traveling abroad and being exposed to the culture of the Old World. In Europe, his wife has a series of disappointing love affairs. After many lonely months, Dodsworth himself falls in love with a cultivated American widow, Edith Cartright. At the end he plans to leave his rather immature wife and return to Edith who teaches him much about the possibilities of life even in his home town, Zenith.

Dodsworth is representative of the suppressed bourgeois who under the right circumstances learns to appreciate a more open way of life.

domino effect   Term derived from the game of dominoes. When dominoes are aligned and stood on end, pressure on one will be transmitted to the next and so on, until the entire series topples over one by one. Politically, the domino theory holds that the fall of one nation to communism inevitably leads to the fall of its neighbor and so on until the whole region is communist. The theory was applied in the 1960s to Asia and in the 1970s to Central America.

The cumulative, serial effect created by a single act or cause; e.g., convince the top man and all the rest of the organization will fall like dominoes.

Use: "We could muster all the legal arguments against curbing The First Amendment rights of cigarette advertisers, but we'll leave that to the lawyers. As we've said, we see the overriding issue as censorship by an elite— any elite—and the domino effect such censorship, once imposed, is guaranteed to generate." (Mobil ad in *New York Times*, September 10, 1987)

domino theory　See DOMINO EFFECT.

do not go gentle　From "Do Not Go Gentle Into That Good Night," a poem by the Welsh poet Dylan Thomas (1914–1953), addressed to his dying father. Recalling how death cuts off "wise men," "good men," "wild men," and "grave men" before they can achieve their purpose, the poet urges his father to "rage, rage against the dying of the light."

When quoted, the phrase applies in general use not only to those who are about to die but also to those who are exhorted to resist almost any force.

Use: "...Judge Robert Bork crossed them all up. Under no illusions about the vote count against him, he declined to go gently into that political good night." (William Safire, "Judge Bork's Victory," *New York Times* Op-Ed Page, October 11, 1987)

Doonesbury　A comic strip character created by Garry Trudeau. The strip of the same name began syndication in 1970. Doonesbury is "a C-minus college student and a minus in other enterprises, as well. He never quite succeeds in asserting himself or winning an argument with fellow students or scoring with campus co-eds."

The strip has a genuine satirical bite. Co-eds come off as shallow, empty, neurotic. Their male counterparts are just as pathetic. The police appear as sadistic monsters who find their greatest joy in cracking student's skulls. Political figures—high and low—get the rough treatment they deserve.

From the very first, Trudeau's *Doonesbury* was a sensation—deeply enjoyed by its readers—and resented and feared by the objects of its sharp, unsparing ridicule.

double dipper　An ice cream cone containing two portions (dips) of ice cream.

Now, applied to an individual who is collecting a pension from one department while he is being paid a salary for serving in another department of the same employer or organization.

Use: "General Larsen is a double dipper receiving a military retiree's pension while employed as a consultant in the Treasury Department."

doubleheader   Two consecutive baseball games played on the same day. A ticket for this day admits the holder to both games.

Use: We had a busy day. First, Jill's graduation, then a special luncheon at the Baldwin Hotel—a real doubleheader.

double play   See TINKER TO EVERS TO CHANCE.

doublethink   In George Orwell's novel *1984* (1949), the hypocritical and grotesquely flexible mode of thought imposed on society to reconcile its people to tyranny; e.g., War Is Peace; Freedom Is Slavery; Ignorance Is Strength. Doublethink refers to turning truth upside down to serve one's own interests. Sometimes written as "doublespeak."

Use: "By such doublethink, the colonel (Lt. Col. Oliver North of Iran-Contra gate) insisted to the committees that raising funds from foreign governments and private citizens in lieu of Congressional appropriations was complying with the 'letter and spirit' of the Boland Amendment." (Tom Wicker, *New York Times* Op-Ed Page, July 11, 1987)

doves and hawks   Two terms representing people with opposite points of view, they first came into use in modern times during the Cuban Missile Crisis of 1962. Doves advocated a conciliatory attitude toward the U.S.S.R; hawks advocated a tough policy, a showdown. The same terms were then used during the Vietnam War in the 1960s, doves urging a negotiated peace and quick withdrawal, hawks urging a continuation of the war until the communists were thrown out of Southeast Asia.

In general, a dove is a peacenik; a hawk is an advocate of aggressive policy, not only in international relations but in business as well.

Use: William Safire writes in the *New York Times* Op-Ed Page, July 14, 1988): "Mr. Dukakis [Democratic Party candidate for president] is essentially a liberal and a dove but realizes these positions are not likely to command a majority and has turned to Mr. Bentsen [vice presidential choice] for protective centrist coloration..."

downer   Drugs like VALIUM or the barbiturates that produce depression, relieve stress etc.

Also, any depressing experience or situation.

Use: "Today's stock market news was a downer. Our company lost at least $1 million."

down for the count   In boxing, when the boxer is knocked down and cannot rise before the count of 10, he is said to be "down for the count" (knocked out).

Informally, "down for the count" has a variety of meanings: beaten, defeated, done for, "dead."

Use: "The competition was too much for Bullfinch. After a tough fight, having spent a fortune, he went down for the count."

Dracula   Motion picture adapted in 1931 from the 1897 novel by Bram Stoker and the 1920s play by Hamilton Deane and John Balderston. Together with *Frankenstein* it launched the vogue for horror films. Its main character, brilliantly played by Bela Lugosi, became a figure in popular mythology as a human vampire.

Count Dracula is a cultivated Rumanian nobleman, impeccably dressed in white tie, tails and a black cape. His hair is black, his skin alabaster. He welcomes his intended victims to his castle in Transylvania where he feasts upon their blood.

"Dragnet"   An allegedly "real life" cops and robbers television drama (1952–1970). Each episode began with the following introduction: "The story you are about to see is true. The names have been changed to protect the innocent." On this documentary note "Dragnet" made its television debut. Its tightly written script, skillfully created suspense and understated acting held its large television audience glued to the screen for 18 years.

Jack Webb, the creator and producer of "Dragnet" was also its main character, Detective Joe Friday. Joe Friday is the archetypal "honest cop," the implacable foe of evil—tenacious, resourceful, unromantic. His clipped, monosyllabic speech ("Just the facts, ma'am") conceals his true compassion for his troubled and frightened clientele.

Dresden   City in Germany bombed into the ground by Allied air strikes, February 3, 1945. More than 130,000 civilians were killed and cathedrals and museums destroyed by 650,000 bombs and intense fire storms. Symbol of total devastation of war.

drop one's guard   In boxing, to lower the hand that protects one's chin. Hence, to leave oneself unprotected.

In general use, to relax one's defenses.

Use: "Before they went into the courtroom, the defense attorney cautioned his client not to drop his guard under the merciless cross-examination the prosecuting attorney was sure to subject him to."

Du Bois, Blanche   Heroine of Tennessee Williams' play *A Streetcar Named Desire* (1947). A faded Southern belle, she comes to live with her sister Stella and Stella's Polish working-class husband, Stanley Kowalski. She is repelled by Kowalski's vulgarity but attracted to his animal physicality. After Kowalski relentlessly exposes her shady past, brutally ridicules her airs and pretenses, spoils her last chance for a stable marriage, and rapes her while Stella is in the hospital giving birth to his child, she suffers a nervous breakdown. At the end of the play, she is taken away to a mental institution. The male guard, understanding her nature, offers his arm. She takes it and goes quietly, uttering the famous words: "I have always depended on the kindness of strangers."

A sensitive woman unable to cope with the brutalities of life.

Dubuque   City in Iowa associated with the hinterland, far from cosmopolitan interests or activities—similar to Peoria, Illinois ("Will it play in Peoria?").

Use: Harold Ross, founder of the *New Yorker*, announced that the new magazine was going to be "for caviar sophisticates, not for the old lady from Dubuque."

Duesenberg   The fast, expensive, classic car of the Jazz Age. The Duesenberg vanished from the market after the crash of 1929.

Dumb Dora   A very popular comic strip (1925–1930) about Dora Bell, a college-age brunette, her boy-girl dating and other related college activities. For obvious reasons, she was soon rechristened Dumb Dora. She had many dumb boyfriends whom she baffled, subdued and, in then-current fashion, "enslaved." Actually, of course, Dora wasn't as dumb as the strip's caption would seem to indicate. The pay-off line, "She ain't so dumb," was closer to Dora's real intelligence. While many girls are, in a sexist society, automatically labelled "dumb," Dora gave the lie to this stereotype.

Duncan, Isadora   American dancer (1878–1927) born in San Francisco, who became a legendary figure on two continents, not only because of her revolutionary dance style but also because of her much publicized free life style. She was a precursor of modern dance. She rejected the precise discipline of ballet movement and the traditional costumes of the ballerina. She wanted to be free of restraints. Dressed in Greek tunics, she danced barefoot, responding expressively and emotionally to symphonic music. She won wildly appreciative audiences all through Europe. In 1921, at the invitation of the Soviet Union, she set up a school in Moscow. It lasted until 1928. She became notorious for her many turbulent love affairs (Gordon Craig, the theater set designer; Sergei Esenin, the Russian poet; Paris Singer, heir to the sewing machine fortune). Her life was triumphant and tragic. She lost her two small children, one by Craig and one by Singer, in a car accident. She herself died when a scarf wound around her neck caught in the rear wheel of an open car on the Cote d'Azur and strangled her. In 1927 her autobiography, *My Life*, was published.

She continues to fascinate people by her legendary beauty, daring, passion and originality.

Dunkirk   Seaport in northern France from which allied troops and a British expeditionary force of about 340,000 men in danger of annihilation were evacuated under German fire from May 29 to June 4, 1940. The channel crossing, although a great military achievement, still claimed the lives of about 30,000 Allied troops.

Dunkirk is a successful retreat by heroic means, from seemingly sure defeat by overwhelming forces.

After the Dunkirk rescue, Churchill declared: "We shall fight on the seas and oceans; we shall fight...in the air...we shall fight on the beaches, we shall fight on the landing grounds, we shall fight in the fields and in the streets, we shall fight in the hills; we shall never surrender."

Use: "Pro-choice abortion groups suffered a judicial Dunkirk in the Supreme Court's ruling this week in *Webster v. Reproductive Health Services*. The Court stopped short of overruling the landmark *Roe v. Wade* decree of 1973, which created a constitutional right to an abortion. Nevertheless, a Court majority cast aspersions on the legal reasoning that went into the Roe decision, and positioned itself for a second assault in October." (Bruce Fein, *New York Times*, July 5, 1989)

Durante, James (Jimmy, Schnozzola)   American entertainer (1893–1980). A veteran of vaudeville, movies and the night club circuit, Durante found a new and colorful career in television. The audiences loved his old songs, his comic mugging, his deliberately concocted malapropisms, his unabashed hamming—and last but not least, the endless puns and fun provoked by his sizable nose. No one really knows who first nicknamed him Schnozzola; but it stuck—and he played his Cyrano-esque role lovingly.

Each show closed with Durante, caught in a spotlight, reverently removing his crushed hat and taking a melancholy walk away from the camera, paying a ritual farewell: "Good-night, Mrs. Calabash, wherever you are."

"Dynasty"   Inspired by the television prime time soap opera "Dallas," "Dynasty" was its main competitor from 1981 to 1987. The plot was a heady mixture of murder, intrigue, the endless struggle for money and power, frustration, finagling and infidelity. Joan Collins (1933–) as Alexis Carrington Colby, a sort of female J.R. Ewing, was the major source of the venom that permeated all of "Dynasty." Lacking "Dallas'"s depth of characterization, it compensated for this deficiency by providing a liberal application of "style and glamour." Some "class" was supplied by the appearance of former President Gerald Ford and former Secretary of State Henry Kissinger at a glitzy Carnival Ball in December 1983.

Though it enjoyed considerable popularity, "Dynasty" never quite achieved the dramatic impact of "Dallas."

E

Eastwood, Clint   Hollywood movie actor (1930–). Plays a macho American male, a loner, a tough guy, fast with the fists and the gun, willing to bypass the law and the bureaucracy in dishing out retributive justice on his own. Fulfills the fantasy of being the individual who can go out and clean up a mess by himself. He became a superstar with *Dirty Harry* (1971) in which he plays a cop hampered by red tape who relentlessly pursues a sadistic murderer. (See also MAKE MY DAY.)

Use: "The bodyguard I became acquainted with was a cross between Charles Bronson and Clint Eastwood. He packed two weapons beneath his suit, a pistol in a holster and what appeared to be a sawed-off machine gun tucked into the back of his trousers." (*Vanity Fair*, January 1989, article on Baron Thyssen)

Edison, Thomas Alva   Known as the "Wizard of Menlo Park," the town in New Jersey where he lived, Edison (1847–1931) was granted more than a thousand patents for his inventions. The best known of them are the incandescent electric bulb, the phonograph and records, the storage battery, the dictating machine, and the fluoroscope. With practically no formal education, he became an American myth, the genius of the technological revolution.

Edsel   Car named after Edsel Ford (1893–1943), son of Henry Ford. Launched with a media blitz in 1957, it became the biggest flop in automobile history.

The Edsel stands for a dud, a flop, an anticlimax to a big build-up.

82

Use: The following was the headline for three movie reviews in *Newsweek* (March 20, 1989): "One spanking new Chevy and two Edsels."

Eichmann, Adolph   Head of the SS Jewish section, Eichmann (1906–1962) was responsible for the deaths of millions of Jews in Nazi concentration camps. Kidnapped in Argentina in 1960 by Israeli security agents and tried for crimes against the Jewish people before an Israeli court of law, he claimed as his defense the fact that he was merely obeying the orders of his superiors. Eichmann was hanged in 1962.

Use: "Almost any choice a survivor makes is comprehensible, except forgiveness. Elie Wiesel writes novels; Wiesenthal hunts Eichmanns." (John Leonard reviewing *Murderers Among Us* in *New York Magazine*, April 24, 1989)

Einstein, Albert   German-born physicist (1879–1955) who found refuge in the United States from Nazi anti-Jewish persecution. Perceived as the preeminent brain of the 20th century; so much so, that he was asked to donate his brain for posthumous scientific study. He developed the theory of relativity, transforming our understanding of the relationship between space and time. His famous equation for energy, $E = MC^2$, was the theoretical basis upon which the atom bomb was built.

Use: "…of me, my mother would say, with characteristic restraint, 'this bandit. He doesn't even have to open a book—"A" in everything. Albert Einstein the Second.'" (Portnoy, in Philip Roth's *Portnoy's Complaint*)

Often used sarcastically as in: "An Einstein he's not."

Ellington, Edward Kennedy "Duke"   Black composer and band leader (1899–1974), known as "Duke" from childhood. A largely self-taught pianist with little formal training in composition, Ellington nonetheless became a major spokesman for jazz music. In his compositions, he used daring devices, blending, in his own words, "lush melodies with unorthodox, dissonant harmonies…"

Ellington composed music for theater, movies, radio, the concert stage. In 1969, he received the Presidential Medal of Freedom and in 1971 was inducted into the Songwriters Hall of Fame. Ellington's famous songs include: "Sophisticated Lady," "In My Solitude," "Don't Get Around Much Anymore."

Ellis Island   Entry port in New York Harbor for some 17 million immigrants to the United States who were processed there from 1892 to 1954. These were the poorest of the poor, who had traveled in steerage to America to escape the famines, wars and pogroms of the Old World. Ellis Island is located next to the Statue of Liberty, with its engraved lines of poetry by Emma Lazarus:
Give me your tired, your poor,
Your huddled masses yearning to breathe free,
The wretched refuse of your teeming shore,
Send these, the homeless, tempest-tossed to me:
I lift my lamp beside the golden door.
Ellis Island stands for the gateway to freedom and opportunity in the New World.

end run   In football, a play in which the ball carrier outflanks the opposing team by running around one end of the defensive line.
In general use, an attempt to solve a problem without confronting it head on, a diversionary tactic designed to achieve an illegitimate or illegal result.
Use: "While Cavazos [U.S. secretary of education] will chair two panels and introduce the President, he has not been given other major responsibilities. That not so subtle signal is the result of a classic Washington end run. The administrators who do business with the Education Department don't think the secretary is up to the job." (*Newsweek*, October 2, 1989)

enemies list   List of opponents of President Richard Nixon's administration who were considered fair game for harassment. The list was revealed by John Dean, an aide to Nixon, during the WATERGATE hearing.
Use: In a *N.Y. Post* article March 27, 1989, headlined: "Who's Gunnin' for Gotti?" we read: "The bizarre phony-bomb incident got cops shuffling through their list of Gotti's enemies once again. Topping the roster, of course, would be Gotti's arch foe— Vincent Chin Giganti, the eccentric boss of the Genovese family; the runners up on an Enemies list the size of a small-town phone directory . . ."

enforcer   See MURDER, INC.

Enola Gay   The American B-29 bomber from which Col. Paul W. Tibbets dropped the first atomic bomb on Hiroshima, a military-industrial city in Japan on August 6, 1945.

Entebbe   International airport in Uganda, where on July 4, 1976, Israeli commandos staged a spectacularly daring and successful raid to free 105 mostly Jewish hostages held by pro-Palestinian hijackers of an Air France jet. In a dramatic shoot- out, the commandos killed the terrorists, who were being supported by President Idi Amin and his troops. They then hustled the hostages onto three waiting transport planes and flew them 2,000 miles to Israel.

Entebbe stands for epic heroism, exultant victory against international terrorism, and triumph against overwhelming odds.

Erté   Born Romain de Tirtoff (1892–1990) in St. Petersburg, Russia, Erté (the name is derived from the French pronunciation of his initials) moved to Paris, worked for the then reigning French fashion designer Paul Poiret, and became himself a great costume designer and illustrator. Like Poiret, his designs are exotic, imaginative, sophisticated and avant-garde. His illustrations are works of art.

An Erté is an exquisite fashion plate.

Estragon (Gogo)   One of the two tattered tramps in Samuel Beckett's tragicomic masterpiece *Waiting for Godot*. (See also (DIDI) VLADIMIR and GODOT.)

every man a king   Phrase used by Huey Long (1893–1935), governor of Louisiana and later senator from that state, in appealing to the less affluent segments of the nation. Often labeled a demagogue, Long promised these people, in the depths of the Great Depression, a guaranteed annual income of $5,000 per family, thus making "every man a king."

evil empire   An empire in space held in a grip of terror by DARTH VADER, the villain of *Star Wars*, a 1977 film written and directed by George Lucas. In the 1980s President Ronald Reagan referred to the Soviet Union as an evil empire.

Use: Mary McCrory, writing in the *New York Post* about the Democratic and Republican candidates for president in 1988: "...if I were George Bush, I would smile when I attacked Michael Dukakis' hometown. Trying to make an evil empire out of Brookline, Mass., is a loser, and here's why."

expressionist   Belonging to that 20th-century movement in art that conceives the true purpose of art to be not the representation of nature but the expression of fundamental emotions like love, hate, fear, anxiety. Van Gogh, an early expressionist, wrote in one of his letters that he exaggerated the forms and rhythms of nature in order "to express...man's terrible passions." Expressionists reject Greek and Renaissance conceptions of beauty and use distortion to convey the force of an emotion. Although expressionism started in France with Van Gogh, Gauguin, Rouault, it spread throughout Europe: in Norway, Edvard Munch; in Belgium, James Ensor; in Germany, Ernst Kirchner and Emile Nolde; in Austria, Oskar Kokoschka.

Expressionist is associated with dark emotions, with heavy outlines, with mask-like grotesques. It is the opposite of "impressionist," which sees reality all in terms of light and joy.

F

fail-safe   A signal created by the U.S. Air Force to prevent comple-
tion of a retaliatory response to an enemy's preemptive atom bomb
strike, in the case of a false alarm. A double-check point at which
bombers already on their way to enemy territory can be recalled, a
fail-safe is insurance against atomic war by mistake.

Now, any scheme that is foolproof, even in so trivial a matter as a
recipe for a souffle.

Fairbanks, Douglas   Hollywood star (1883–1939), associated with
swashbuckling roles in derring-do films of historical adventure like
The Mark of Zorro (1920); *The Black Pirate* (1926); *The Iron Mask*
(1929); and *The Thief of Bagdad* (1924). Married to Mary Pickford in
1920.

fair deal   Term used by President Harry S Truman in his State of
the Union Message to Congress in January 1949 to characterize his
proposals for the nation. He called for an increase in the minimum
wage, more low-income housing, adherence to civil rights laws, and
greater social security coverage—a program intended to benefit the
disadvantaged.

fallout   Radiation released into the air from nuclear testing of
H-bombs or atom bombs. Radioactive particles fall to earth or into
water, contaminating the environment. A disaster in a nuclear power
plant, as in CHERNOBYL, also results in a widespread fallout.

Now used colloquially to mean the damaging consequences of an action.

Use: "No one, it seems, is immune from the fallout of the news. The case of the jogger and the wolf pack evokes fear—as much about the social contract as about personal safety—which hangs over the city as tangible as the full moon on April 19." (*New York Magazine*, May 15, 1989; Edwin Diamond, "Anatomy of A Horror.")

falsely shouting fire in a crowded theater   Phrase taken from the U.S. Supreme Court's decision in *Schenck v. U.S.* (1919), setting limits on the freedom of speech guaranteed by the first amendment to the constitution. Justice Oliver Wendell Holmes Jr. wrote: "The most stringent protection of free speech would not protect a man falsely shouting fire in a theater and causing a panic." The test for abridgement of free speech would be "whether the words are used in such circumstances and are of such a nature as to create a clear and present danger." For example, certain words that would be protected by the First Amendment in peace time would not be tolerated in war time. Thus, John Schenck's petition to have his arrest for distributing anti-draft pamphlets voided was rejected by the Court.

The phrase is often quoted when someone claims license to say whatever outrageous thing he thinks of, even in family squabbles. "Isn't there free speech in this country?" might be answered with, "but you can't shout fire in a crowded theater."

Falwell, Jerry   "Born again" Christian evangelist (1933–) on the nationwide TV program "Old-Time Gospel Hour." He founded the Moral Majority, Inc., in 1979 to become a formidable political activist, endorsing and supporting conservative political candidates with views similar to his own. He is against abortion, the Equal Rights Amendment and homosexual rights, and for, he says, traditional moral values.

Use: "...The most vocal demonologists of AIDS are the Falwells and Pat Buchanans." (David Gates, reviewing Susan Sontag's *AIDS and Its Metaphors, Newsweek*, January 30, 1989)

Farewell to Arms, A   Title of Ernest Hemingway's 1929 novel about love against a background of war. Frederic Henry, an American lieutenant in the Italian Ambulance Corps during World War I, falls in love with Catherine Barkley, an English nurse. When he is wounded, she comes to nurse him. They spend a few idyllic months together while he recuperates. He returns to the front and participates in the disastrous retreat from Caporetto. Disillusioned with the war, he makes his separate peace and deserts. He finds Catherine, who is pregnant, and they flee to Switzerland. There she dies in childbirth and the baby with her. Henry is left desolate. The rain, which has been a melancholy symbol of death throughout the book, falls steadily.

A farewell to arms is generally used to describe a personal truce, a private retreat from any kind of hostility.

fasten your seatbelts   Refers originally to the command given to airplane passengers on take-off and landing and during turbulent air conditions, the most dangerous moments in any flight. The term has come into general use to indicate anticipation of danger or any rough going. For example, toward the end of the movie *All About Eve*, Bette Davis, having just discovered that Anne Baxter, the ingenue she has befriended, has secretly been maneuvering to replace her in a starring role, turns to a roomful of people and says, "Fasten your seat belts. It's going to be a long, bumpy ride." In other words, "Gird yourselves, the war is on. Watch out for the flak."

Faubourg-St. Honore   Street of fashionable shops and haute-couture in Paris. Synonymous with elegant fashion.

Faulknerian   Having to do with the world, the style, the characters, the setting and themes in the work of William Faulkner (1897–1962), Nobel prize-winning American novelist and short-story writer. Faulkner lived most of his life in Oxford, Mississippi. Using the people and the history of the place he knew best, he became the greatest of the "Southern" writers. He created mythical Yoknapatawpha County with its county seat in Jefferson, Mississippi, and peopled it with declining aristocratic families of the Old South (the Sartorises and the Compsons) soon to be replaced by the rapacious poor white trash of the New South (the Snopes clan). The values of honor, courage, noblesse oblige, patriotism of a stable society are replaced by the cynicism and greed of a people without a past.

Faulknerian themes are many: the meaning of the past and its continued hold on the people of the South; the curse of slavery and its baleful effect upon race relations; the violence attached to Southern religiosity, class differences and sexual puritanism.

The Faulknerian style is often baroque, rhapsodic, using long sentences that seem to come out of the subjective dreams and subconscious of the characters. It is full of large symbols and allegorical overtones, as in *Light in August* (1932). Often Faulkner presents the same story from several points of view, as in *The Sound and the Fury* (1929) where the first version is told from the consciousness of an idiot Benjy, and then by each of his brothers, Quentin and Jason. He uses the same technique in *As I Lay Dying* (1930), the harrowing story of a family's pilgrimage to bury their mother in the town where she was born. Faulknerian humor is large and wild, as in the chapter of the horses rampaging through a house in *The Hamlet* (1940), the first of a trilogy about the Snopes saga. The Faulknerian world is strange, dream-like, full of violence and despair, often hilarious, peopled by "crazies," having the tone of remembered events recapitulated with conjecture, speculation and new interpretations. And yet it all hangs together because it bears the stamp of Faulkner as surely as the paintings in the Sistine Chapel bear the stamp of Michelangelo.

Use: "...this intricate first novel is pieced together out of fragments, fragments that only slowly cohere into a single narrative...The fractured structure (combined with windy loops of Faulknerian prose) belies an old-fashioned plot..." (Michiko Kakutani, *New York Times*, October 22, 1988)

fauves   Literally, "wild beasts" in French. The term was applied by an art critic to the painters whose work went on exhibit in October 1905 at a Paris salon. So brilliant and violent were the colors of their paintings that this critic felt that he had been thrust into a cage of wild animals. The fauves wore their epithet proudly. It gave them a sense of liberation to experiment not only with color but also with distortion of form. Most prominent of the Fauves was Henri Matisse (1869–1954). The fauves liberated all the world from a conventional use of color combinations.

Fauve is used for the riotous use of color, not only in painting, but also in dress, home decoration, etc.

Use: In a review of "Jerome Robbins' Broadway" in the *New York Times* (February 2, 1989), Frank Rich writes: "The dominant designer is Oliver Smith, whose glorious palette can encompass New Yorks as antithetical as those of 'On the Town' and 'West Side Story,' and whose collaborations with the costume designers Irene Sharaff, Miles White and Alvin Colt have no present-day match in technicolor Fauvist verve."

federal case   A case that comes within the jurisdiction of a federal court is generally held to be more serious than a case in the local courts. To make a federal case out of something is, with reverse logic, to exaggerate the significance, the weightiness, of a trivial fault, lapse or misdemeanor. A boy might say to his mother, "O.K. I forgot to take the garbage out. Let's not make a federal case out of it."

Fellini, Federico   Italian film director (1920–) who succeeds in mythologizing the materials of his own life by projecting unforgetta-ble images of it upon the screen. For example, in 8½ (1963) he surrealistically shows a human child climbing up the walls and across the ceiling in an attempt to get away from an adult with a whip. In *Amarcord* (1974) the heavy metal shutters of a shop clank down. Caught within is a little boy who is promptly smothered in the enormous breasts of the shopkeeper. (See also "LA DOLCE VITA.")

Feminine Mystique, The   Title of a seminal 1963 book by Betty Friedan, which launched the modern women's liberation movement. Friedan defines the feminine mystique as a lie that for generations kept women from realizing themselves as full persons with interests and longings beyond the bedroom, the kitchen and the nursery. Women themselves had been brainwashed into believing that work and interests outside the home were unfeminine. Friedan exploded the myth that the little woman was ecstatic in her domesticity. Her book changed the lives of millions of women—and men—worldwide.

Fibber McGee and Molly   Characters in the hilarious radio and TV comedy, who lived at 79 Wistful Vista from 1925 to 1960. What remains in most of our memories of this long-running show are Fibber's tendency to exaggerate (some charitably called it "fibbing"); Fibber's constant trouble with his friends—saved from disaster by Molly's good, old-fashioned common sense; and last but not least, Fibber's famous overcrowded hall closet, which would unleash its contents when opened. And it was designedly opened with great frequency. So much so that, in time, the closet disgorging its motley contents became a symbol of Fibber, his crotchetiness, his helpless-ness, his all-too-human frailties.

Fields, W.C.   William Claude Dukenfield (1879–1946), comedian of the silent movies and then the talkies. Paunchy, bulbous-nosed, bibulous, raspy-voiced, caustic, hating children and courting un-lovely women, he played in *My Little Chickadee* (1940); *The Bank Dick* (1940); *Never Give a Sucker an Even Break* (1941) and many others.

Fields is remembered for outrageous lines like "Anybody who hates children can't be all bad." He never touched water, he said, because "fish copulate in it."

Fifth Avenue   Street of fashionable shops and department stores from 34th Street to 59th Street in Manhattan (at one time, Cartier, Tiffany, Gucci, Bergdorf Goodman, Bonwit Teller, Saks Fifth Avenue, Lord and Taylor, Altman etc.). It is the route of the Easter parade in which people show off their new spring outfits, as in the popular 1933 song by Irving Berlin. From 59th Street north, it borders on Central Park and becomes a street of fine residences and museums. Fifth Avenue is a symbol of elegance and affluence.

fifth column   Phrase coined during the Spanish Civil War by fas-cist supporter Lt. General Queipo De Llano, to the effect that Franco had four columns of insurgents marching against Madrid and a fifth column within the city ready to betray it. Generally, subversives in sympathy with the enemy of their country and ready to commit sabotage in support of that enemy.

Use: "The machine-gun toting guards and concentration camp-type fences that more than 40 years ago were thought necessary to keep 120,000 Japanese—both American citizens and aliens—from formulating a home grown fifth column are, thankfully, only a memory." (*New York Newsday* editorial, April 26, 1988)

final solution   It was Nazi Germany under HITLER that added the word and the concept of "final" to the various "solutions" to the so-called Jewish problem. The problem had been seen by the emerging nation-states of Europe as the tendency of the Jews in the diaspora to remain a separate entity within the state, with their own religion, customs, language. Pre-Nazi "solutions" to this problem had been forced conversion, expulsion, exclusion from certain rights, including the right to engage in trades and professions. The Nazis' "solution" was truly final: genocide, extermination of a whole people.

The term is sometimes trivialized and used colloquially and even mockingly to mean the end, the ultimate solution to any problem.

Use: "Religious fanaticism has discovered censorship's Final Solution for that enemy of darkness, the world. I write that with a shudder." (Nadine Gordimer on *New York Times* Op-Ed page, February 22, 1989, writing about Ayatollah Khomeini's sentence of death upon Salman Rushdie for having written *Satanic Verses*.)

Finnegans Wake   Novel (1939) by James Joyce. So dense in word-making, so original and complex in design and content as to be virtually unreadable as a novel, it almost needs to be translated as from another language. The entire book represents an unconscious dream in which elements of history, mythology, philosophy and art coalesce in individual words and events. Based on Vico's cyclical philosophy of history, it begins with the second half of a sentence, the first half of which is to be found on the last page. Here is a sample:

"Whatif she be in flags or flitters, reekie rags or sundye chosies, with a mint of mines or beggar a pinnyweight. Arrah, sure, we all love little Anny Ruiny, or we mean to say, lovelittle Anna Rayiny, when unda her brela, mid piddle med puddle, she ninny goes nanny goes nancing by."

One might say of a given work that it was so incomprehensible that it might just as well be *Finnegans Wake*.

"Fire and Ice"   Short poem by Robert Frost (1875–1963) who writes:

> Some say the world will end in fire,
> Some say in ice.

Frost substitutes "desire" for fire and "hate" for ice, either one of which, if intense enough, can kill.

Often quoted literally to refer to death of the planet Earth by atomic warfare or a new ice age.

fireside chats   Informal radio talks to the nation begun by President Franklin Delano Roosevelt on March 12, 1933. He invariably began "My friends..." and spoke in simple language as if to "a mason at work on a new building, a girl behind a counter, and a farmer in his field." He explained to the people his proposals to fight the Depression and appealed directly to them for their support. Used by succeeding presidents thereafter.

first string   In sports, the players who regularly start in games as against those who are held in reserve or are substitutes.

In general use, the best members of a staff, business or professional organization.

Use: "Send only your first string people to the next conference. They'll meet stiff competition."

Fitzgerald, F. Scott   American novelist and short story writer (1896–1940), a member of the lost generation, associated most with the Jazz Age, a term he coined. He described his age as "a new generation grown up to find all Gods dead, all wars fought, all faiths in man shaken." He depicted the aimlessness and cynicism of the post-World War I expatriates in *Tender Is the Night* (1934) and the corruption of the American Dream in *The Great Gatsby* (1925). He and his beautiful wife, Zelda, became legendary figures, so wild, reckless and glamorous that they seemed to have stepped out of the pages of his novels. Both ended tragically, Zelda in an institution for the mentally ill and Scott Fitzgerald, drunk, sick, depleted in Hollywood.

five foot shelf of books   Charles William Eliot was the president of Harvard University from 1869 to 1909. In 1910, the joint efforts of Dr. Eliot and the enterprising publisher P.F. Collier launched Dr. *Eliot's Famous Five Foot Shelf of Books.*

According to a contemporary ad, written by the gifted Bruce Barton, "One hundred thousand businessmen are using the helpful reading courses which Dr. Eliot has laid out.

"They are reading the great histories, seeing the great plays, hearing the great orations, meeting the great men of history with Dr. Eliot...In all the world, there are only a few books...that have really made history. To read these few great works systematically and intelligently is to be well read.

"What are these great works?...Dr. Eliot has picked the few really worthwhile books out of the thousands of useless ones...and he has arranged them as the *Famous Five-Foot Shelf of Books.*"

To which Dr. Eliot adds: "I believe the faithful and considerate reading of these books will give any man the essentials of a liberal education, even if he devotes to them only fifteen minutes a day."

At the time and over the years, the *Five Foot Book Shelf* (as it came to be known) received its share of spoofing. Nonetheless, it has remained a metaphor for the well-read man.

Flaherty, Robert   Father of the documentary film (1884–1951) (although the term documentary was itself coined by a Scottish educator, John Grierson). Flaherty's first film, *Nanook of the North* (1922), which he made while living among the Eskimos in Hudson Bay country for 12 years, followed the daily patterns of existence in the life of one Eskimo and his family. *Moana* (1926) did the same for the people of Samoa. These were followed by *Man of Aran*, commissioned by Grierson; *Elephant Boy;* and *Louisiana Story.* Flaherty's ambition was to film the life of the peoples of the Earth.

He stamped his poetic sensibility, his powers of observation, his genius with the camera, on the documentary genre.

flak   Originally, German acronym for anti-aircraft fire in World War II. Then used for a barrage of words or complaints. Now used to denote criticism in response to a controversial idea; for example, a book contending that there is no discrimination against women in science, no matter how cogently argued and statistically proved, is sure to get plenty of flak from the feminists.

Flanders fields   Cemetery in Belgium where white crosses mark the graves of Allied soldiers fallen in World War I. The place has been immortalized in a poem written by the Canadian poet John McCrae (1872–1918). The poem begins:

In Flanders fields the poppies blow
Between the crosses, row on row,
That mark our place.

floor   In boxing, to knock down an opponent. The floored fighter is given 10 seconds—counted out loud by the referee—to get up unassisted to continue the fight. If he cannot, then he is "down for the count, knocked out, K.O'd, Kayoed."

In general, to floor means to defeat, overwhelm, surprise, confound, puzzle.

flower children   Young hippies of the 1960s counterculture who would offer a flower to policemen or military personnel as a symbol of their nonviolent, pacifist beliefs. Their slogan was "make love, not war."

Use: "He's like a flower child who thinks that if you remain a child you'll wind up as William Blake." (Pauline Kael describing Kevin Costner in *Field of Dreams; The New Yorker*, May 1, 1989) (See also HAIGHT- ASHBURY,HIPPIES, WOODSTOCK.)

Flynn, Errol   Actor (1909–1959). Born in Tasmania, he experienced real-life adventures in the South Seas equal to his swashbuckling roles in such movies as *Captain Blood* (1935) and *The Sea Hawk* (1940). He is also thought of as a debonair, charming seducer of women.

force, the   See DARTH VADER.

form follows function   See BAUHAUS.

Forsyte, Soames   "The man of property" in John Galsworthy's novel of the same name, the first volume (1906) of *The Forsyte Saga*, a series eventually comprising three trilogies, which follows the fortunes and changing mores of several generations of an upper-middle class British family. The BBC adapted the first six novels in a popular TV series in the 1970s.

Soames Forsyte is a hidebound solicitor who manages the family's business interests. He is stable and honest but unimaginative. He has "bought" his beautiful wife Irene as he has bought the paintings in his collection. They are all assets. She leaves him when she falls in love with Philip Bosinney, an architect whom Soames has hired to build a magnificent house for Irene. When Soames learns about his wife's affair, he asserts his property rights and forces himself upon her. The novel ends tragically with the suicide of Bosinney.

A Soames Forsyte is a man of wealth who looks upon the world as a column of assets and liabilities. He cannot create beauty but he can buy it.

Fort Knox   Since 1936, U.S. depository of gold bullion, located in Kentucky.

Fort Knox has come to stand as a symbol for any treasure house.

Use: "This is a Fort Knox of sorts, and the diligent reader will learn why former CIA Director William Casey was not to be trusted, along with brilliant considerations of such diverse materials as Hesiod, Homer...and W. H. Auden." (From a review of *Essays Ancient and Modern* by Bernard Knox, cited in *The American Scholar*, Summer 1989.)

foul ball   In baseball, a batted ball that falls outside the white foul lines. It is counted as a strike against the batter. If caught by a defensive player, the batter is out.

By extension, a foul ball has come to mean an unpleasant, undesirable, incompetent person. It has a wide variety of pejorative meanings, liberally applied to an unpopular, unattractive person.

Use: You know Jim. He's a foul ball. He spoiled the party with his silly mannerisms and off-color jokes.

Foxy Grandpa   This comic strip appeared just at the right time, January 7, 1900, when the comic strips were devoting themselves exclusively to the *Katzenjammer Kids* theme. The full-time preoccupation of the Kids was making the lives of their parents, their teachers and other authority figures miserable with their annoying, sadistic pranks.

Foxy Grandpa changed all that. He gave the Kids a taste of their own medicine, turning the tables on them with ingenious tricks of his own. The public relished seeing the Kids finally get their comeuppance. But the strip enjoyed a relatively brief popularity. By the end of the decade, interest in Foxy Grandpa's shenanigans evaporated. Nonetheless, Foxy Grandpa played his part in altering the stereotype of older folks as hapless victims.

Frank, Anne   Writer of *The Diary of Anne Frank*, a journal kept while she and her family were hiding out in an attic in Amsterdam during the Nazi occupation of Holland. The diary expresses with keen observation and honesty all of the feelings, the fears, the hopes, the frustrations, the budding sexual awareness of a young girl in such a fearful situation. The family's hiding place was discovered by the Nazis. All were sent to concentration camps and Anne Frank herself died at Bergen-Belsen at the age of 14. Anne Frank has become a symbol of hope in the midst of horror and despair.

frankly, my dear, I don't give a damn   Rhett Butler's final words of rejection to Scarlett O'Hara's pleas of helplessness in Margaret Mitchell's best-selling novel of the Civil War, *Gone With the Wind* (1936). The two were played by Clark Gable and Vivien Leigh in a 1939 movie.

free at last   See I HAVE A DREAM.

Freudian   Pertaining to the psychoanalytic theories, practices and terminology formulated by the Viennese neuropathologist, Sigmund Freud (1856–1939). Freud added a new dimension to man's understanding of himself; namely, the subconscious, to which are relegated repressions of instinctual sexual desires. These repressed desires emerge in garbled form in dreams and in free association. Freud postulated within each person the ID (primitive instinct), the ego (the developing self) and the superego (demands of culture), with the ego trying to accommodate the pull of the other two. Central to Freud's theories was the Oedipus complex (the child's natural sexual desire for the parent of the opposite sex). The child's eventual sublimation of this desire was necessary for his healthy development. Neurosis was caused by fixation on an infantile oral or anal phase of sexual development or by unresolved repressions. The psychoanalyst guided the patient, lying on a couch and freely associating, to relive his early experiences and through transference to work out the blocks to his normal development.

Freudian terms have become part of the vernacular but with little understanding of their meaning. Mostly, "Freudian" conjures up sexual obsessions and perversities. Everybody bandies about phrases like "castration complex," "death wish," "Oedipus complex," "Freudian slip," "fixation," "the id."

Use: Hemingway's second novel, *The Torrents of Spring*, was a savage parody of Sherwood Anderson, a writer who had been his mentor and who had befriended him in many ways. Dwight MacDonald theorized that Hemingway "had to kill the Freudian father in order to make his own place in the world of letters." (George Plimpton, *New York Times* Book Review, April 16, 1989)

Friday, Joe   See DRAGNET.

Friedan, Betty   See FEMININE MYSTIQUE.

führer   German word for leader. Now associated with a dictator of a particularly heinous virulence.

Use: "It is clear that the La Rouche conspiracy theory is designed to appeal to anti-Semitic right-wingers as well as to Black Muslims and nuclear engineers. But in trying to see Mr. La Rouche as a would-be Führer, Mr. King may be trying to tie together the whole unruly package with too neat a ribbon." (George Johnson, reviewing *Lyndon La Rouche and the New American Fascism* by Dennis King, *New York Times*, June 18, 1989)

G

Gable, Clark American movie star (1900–1960) who became synonymous with Rhett Butler, a role he played in the movie version of *Gone With the Wind* (1939); Butler, handsome, dashing, devil-may-care, dared to stand up to and eventually abandon the tempestuous Southern belle Scarlett O'Hara (Vivien Leigh). Gable starred in many films, including *It Happened One Night* (1934), *Mutiny on the Bounty* (1935) and *The Misfits* (1961).

game plan In sports, a team's meticulously planned strategy for winning a game.

In general use, any well-conceived, carefully worked out plan or course of action designed to achieve a specific goal, as in business, government, one's personal affairs.

Use: "If you expect to succeed in today's risky market, you've got to have a well worked-out game plan."

Gandhi, Mohandas Karamchand Also known as Mahatma (great-souled) Gandhi (1869–1948). Political and spiritual leader of India in its struggle for independence from British rule. Although he had been born into a rich Indian family and had practiced law in England, India and South Africa, Gandhi ultimately broke with his upper-class traditions and lived the life of an ascetic, taking vows of poverty and celibacy. He inspired and led a mass movement for Indian independence through non-violent means, civil disobedience, passive resistance, non-cooperation, protest marches, boycotts and strikes. He was arrested and imprisoned by the British many times. Periodically, he undertook fasts, "fasts unto death," to achieve his goals. He favored a return to simple village life and promoted, even by personal example, participation in cottage industries. In 1947, having finally brought England to its knees, he helped negotiate Indian independence. In 1948, at the age of 78, he was assassinated by a Hindu fanatic.

Lean, emaciated, wearing only a loin cloth, Gandhi struck an odd figure in modern times, but he was universally recognized as a symbol of selfless, non-violent struggle for freedom and justice.

gangbusters   "Gangbusters" was a very popular radio program in the 1930s. It usually featured violent stories of "crime and punishment," opening with sirens, shots, screeching of brakes. The police officers specialized in breaking up organized crime by sensational, forceful, aggressive means.

Over the years, gangbusters has taken on other meanings: having an unusual impact, done with great speed, force, success, strikingly effective.

Use: The new chancellor of the school came on like gangbusters with his reform program.

Gant, Eugene   Hero of *Look Homeward, Angel* (1929), an autobiographical novel by Thomas Wolfe (1900–1938). One of a large, rambunctious family living in North Carolina, he is a youth eager to break away and get to the "big city," where art lives. He has the ineffable yearnings, large ambitions and poetic sensibilities of certain very bright adolescents convinced of their own specialness and even genius.

Gantry, Elmer   Main character in the satirical novel of the same name written in 1927 by Sinclair Lewis and adapted for the movies in 1960. He is a charlatan and hypocrite who becomes a successful evangelist.

Use: "Unfortunately, [Jimmy] Swaggart's troubles revive Elmer Gantry stereotypes that cloud the fact that some TV evangelists, including Swaggart himself, have done good for others while doing good for themselves." (*U.S. News & World Report*, March 7, 1988)

Garbo, Greta   Born Greta Gustafsson (1905–1990) in Sweden. Perhaps the most beautiful face in the history of cinema. Reserved, mysterious, aloof, private; summed up in her famous but spurious line, "I vant to be alone." Her low, husky, accented voice thrilled moviegoers from the time of her first talkie, *Anna Christie* (1930), advertised simply: "Garbo Talks." She starred in *Flesh and the Devil*, a 1927 silent movie with John Gilbert, in *Anna Karenina* (1935), *Ninotchka* (1939) and many others.

Garbo: Feminine mystery combined with exquisite beauty.

Gaslight   Movie thriller (1944), directed by George Cukor and starring Ingrid Bergman and Charles Boyer, about a sophisticated man who subtly and insinuatingly tries to make his wife question her own sanity.

Use: Don't give me the "Gaslight" routine.

Gatsby, Jay   Central character in *The Great Gatsby* (1925), a novel by F. SCOTT FITZGERALD. In Gatsby we see the corruption and vanity of that part of the American dream that exalts great wealth as the means to happiness and success. Gatsby was a midwestern boy who fell in love with the beautiful Daisy, several notches above him in wealth and social class. To get her, he amassed a fortune from bootlegging and gangsterism. He got himself a mansion on Long Island and gave big parties where he felt like a stranger, an outsider. But Daisy had married the enormously rich and brutal Tom Buchanan. Gatsby's life was empty except for his continuing devotion to the dream of Daisy. In the end, his illusions as to the true nature of the very rich betrayed him. Fitzgerald deals sympathetically with this falsely romantic and, some say, tragic character.

Use: "The grandsons of Jay Gatsby made paper fortunes on Wall Street—greed is O.K., one of them said before the law caught up—and the godsons of Elmer Gantry got rich saving souls." (*Newsweek*, November 21, 1988, in a summing up of the Reagan presidency.)

Gaudi, Antonio   Spanish architect (1852–1926) who worked mostly in Barcelona. His buildings are like pastry pastiches, as if stone had been made as malleable as clay or wax and shaped into extraordinarily decorative and decorated organic shapes encrusted with glass, ceramics, etc. Some of his best known structures are the Casa Mila (1905–1910); the Church of the Sagrada Familia, of cathedral proportions; and the Colonia Guell Church and Park (1914).

Genovese, Kitty   At 3 A.M., the morning of March 13, 1964, Kitty Genovese (1935–1964) was murdered on her way home to her Queens apartment. Her killer, Winston Moseley, attacked her three times. First, he stabbed her on Austin Street in Kew Gardens. As Kitty staggered to her home, Moseley returned and stabbed her for the second time. He drove off. Then he returned again to find Kitty in the hallway of her apartment. There, he stabbed her for the third time— and left her dying. Moseley was later apprehended, tried, and sentenced to life imprisonment.

Police investigation revealed that at least 37 people witnessed the murder of Kitty Genovese. Not one called the police!

Some of the people who saw and heard what was happening said:

"I didn't want to get involved."

"Frankly, we were afraid."

"I was tired. I went back to bed."

"I don't know."

The behavior of the onlookers and witnesses has been labelled the *Kitty Genovese* syndrome, a dramatic illustration of the extent to which fear of crime has saturated our society and created a frightening, deliberate non-involvement in the lives of our neighbors.

gentleman caller   From *The Glass Menagerie* (1944), a play by Tennessee Williams. Amanda Wingfield, the mother of Tom, the narrator, lives in a largely imaginary past when as a Southern belle she entertained many gentlemen callers. Now abandoned by her husband, living in genteel poverty in St. Louis, she urges Tom to bring home a gentleman caller for his very shy, crippled sister Laura. Tom brings home Jim, a kind young coworker in the warehouse. Accidentally, Jim breaks off the horn of the unicorn, Laura's favorite animal in her glass animal collection. Nevertheless, Laura and Jim hit it off. She comes out of her shyness for once. But in a tender moment Jim confesses that he is engaged to another girl. Laura withdraws again into the world of her glass menagerie. The gentleman caller scheme has backfired, with the fragile Laura broken as surely as the unicorn.

A gentleman caller is one who calls on a girl and becomes instantly a prospective suitor.

gestalt   From the German word meaning form or pattern, gestalt psychology suggests that people respond not to individual elements within a scene or situation but rather to the pattern that they discern these elements to make. The whole is different from the sum of its parts. Different people may see different configurations emerging from the same collection of elements.

Use: Perestroika and glasnost are but two elements in a whole gestalt of revolutionary change introduced by Gorbachev in the Soviet Union.

Gestapo   Geheime Staatspolizei, the German secret state police organized in 1933 by Hermann Göring as a Nazi instrument of terror, for the suppression of all opposition to Hitler. Gradually it became absorbed into the SS (Schutzstaffel) under Heinrich Himmler, and merged with the SS's Sicherheits Dienst (SD), under Reinhard Heydrich.

"Gestapo" tactics refer to brutal, illegal, secret torture.

get to first base   In baseball, to get to the first of the four bases, in counterclockwise order as seen from home.

In general, to succeed in the first phase of an undertaking, to begin well, take a successful first step. In a romantic relationship, getting to first base is commonly understood to be the first step or steps leading to more or greater intimacy, attaining a status short of actual intercourse.

Use: "The likable Cynthia Nixon has no period sense...and gives us a Juliet who at fourteen, has seen it all. She meets Romeo at the party with mild curiosity and soon lets him get to first base, suggesting that scoring will follow apace..." (John Simon review of Joseph Papp's *Romeo and Juliet, New York Magazine,* June 6, 1988) (See also SCORE.)

G.I.   A regularly enlisted soldier in the U.S. Armed Forces. Originally an abbreviation from the "galvanized iron" trash cans used in the army; then from all "government issue" items, like GI uniforms, GI blankets, GI mess pans, and even GI haircuts; then applied to the soldier himself. GI used as an adjective means regimented, standardized.

Giacometti, Alberto   Swiss sculptor (1901–1966) whose thin, elongated, emaciated, skeletal, open-cage figures suggest the pain and isolation of modern man.

Use: From *New York Post,* March 28, 1989, quoting Leo Bassi, an Italian stand-up comic playing at the Perry Street Theater in New

York: "When Nero burnt Rome he did it for entertainment. What I loved at age 5 was fire-heating and pulling on my plastic soldiers to change their shape. In this way I pulled a G.I. Joe until it became a kind of Giacometti sculpture."

Gibson girl   An image of ideal American femininity created by the New York artist and illustrator Charles Dana Gibson (1867–1944). In pen and ink Gibson drew a wholesome, full-bosomed, small-waisted girl with long hair piled like a halo around her head. She wore a high-necked blouse with puff sleeves and a long skirt slightly flared at the ankles. She is engaged in athletic as well as social and romantic activities. Although her time was the turn of the century, the Gibson girl remains a vision of clean, wholesome, lovely womanhood.

G.I. Joe   Comic strip created during World War II (June 17, 1942) by David Breger (1908–1970) for *Yank*, the United States Army's enlisted man's magazine. The American troops, here and overseas, and the American public embraced *G.I. Joe* with universal affection. Based on Breger's experiences as a rookie, it quickly entered the language as both the military and civilian name for the American foot soldier.

give 'em hell, Harry   In his campaign for the presidency, Harry Truman told Alben Barkley, "I'm going to fight hard. I'm going to give them hell." "Them" were the "vested interests" and the "do-nothing Congress." At every whistle stop during the campaign, the crowds would shout, "Give 'em hell, Harry." Against the odds and the polls, Truman defeated Thomas E. Dewey.

glasnost   The Russian term for speaking out. Initiated by the charismatic leader of the U.S.S.R., Mikhail Gorbachev, glasnost is a relaxation of censorship, a thaw in repression, a new sense of liberation from restraint. Socialism with a human face.

Use: "The Chinese have taken a major stride toward glasnost by exhibiting decades' worth of photographic forgeries by their party propagandists." (*U.S. News & World Report*, March 28, 1988)

Godard, Jean-Luc   French film director (1930–) who made his reputation with *Breathless* (1959), a tradition-shattering movie with Jean-Paul Belmondo as a small-time Parisian punk and Jean Seberg as his American girl. Belmondo, who has stolen a car and killed a cop, is being chased by the police. He has grown up in a movie era and associates himself with the gangster heroes of American movies. Godard is associated with the Nouvelle Vague (new wave) films from young French and Italian film makers, beginning in the late 1950s, which broke with traditional concepts.

godfather   Originally, one who sponsors a child at baptism, the older and still most common use. More recently, however, godfather has acquired another meaning: a powerful leader of a criminal enterprise, especially of the MAFIA. In 1972, Mario Puzo's best-selling novel *The Godfather* was turned into the Academy Award-winning film of the same name, directed by Francis Ford Coppola and starring Marlon Brando.

Use: "As the reputed "godfather" of the Guadalajara cartel, Miguel Angel Felix Gallardo was allegedly responsible for smuggling as much as four tons of cocaine a month into the United States." (*Newsweek*, April 24, 1989)

go the distance   In boxing, being able to last the scheduled number of rounds without being knocked out or judged a technical knockout.

In general use, to go all the way to one's goal or destination.

Use: Jack surprised us all when he graduated from college. We never thought he'd go the distance.

Godot   The mysterious character who never shows up in *Waiting for Godot*, a 1952 tragi-comedy by Samuel Beckett, an Irish playwright who writes in French. Two tramps, Estragon and Vladimir, wait for Godot, but they are not sure where and when he is supposed to arrive. Two other characters come along: Pozzo, the master, driving the exploited Lucky at the end of a rope. What these characters represent has been a subject for intense speculation. Nobody really knows.

"Waiting for Godot" has entered the language to mean waiting endlessly and helplessly for somebody or something that never materializes.

Use: Waiting for cable TV in the Bronx was like waiting for Godot.

god that failed, the   Title of a book of autobiographical essays by six disillusioned writers who came to realize that their faith in the

Russian Revolution, in communism as practiced in the Soviet Union under Stalin, was a misplaced faith. Communism was a false god, the god that failed, and they rejected it. The writers were Arthur Koestler, Ignazio Silone, Richard Wright, André Gide, Louis Fischer and Stephen Spender. The book was edited by Richard Crossman and published in 1949.

Goetz, Bernhard   New Yord City subway rider who in December 1984 shot and wounded four black youths who tried to mug him. The case aroused passionate controversy because of general revulsion against widespread violence in the cities and the perception that police agencies were unable to protect the public. Indicted originally on four counts of attempted murder, Goetz eventually was found guilty only of carrying an illegal weapon.

Goetz's name has become synonymous, for some, with vigilantism, for others, with self-defense in the absence of police protection.

Gogo   See ESTRAGON.

Goldberg, Rube   Comic strip artist Reuben (Rube) Goldberg (1883–1970), who drew imaginative drawings of odd, daffy, highly complex machinery or gimmicks designed to achieve the simplest of ends. Rube Goldberg made an original contribution to the comic strip and to the English language.

Use: "It took parliamentary contortions worthy of Rube Goldberg—but Texas legislators last week finally adopted a spending and revenue blueprint that staved off financial chaos." (*New York Times*, July 26, 1987)

Golden Pond   A serene little lake in the country in the play *On Golden Pond* (1979) by Ernest Thompson. To their cottage on this lake an aged couple have retired to spend their last years in peace and loving tranquility. The couple were played by Hume Cronyn and Jessica Tandy on stage and by Henry Fonda and Katharine Hepburn in the screen version.

"Golden Pond" has become synonymous with an unspoiled, idyllic retreat.

Use: "So if old age, creeping senility and a battle between a father and his son were not enough to furnish a family play, imagine a case of chemical contamination on Golden Pond and one begins to see the trouble in store in *A Murder of Crows.* (From a drama review by Mel Gussow, *New York Times*, September 18, 1988)

Goldwynism   Any unwitting humorous twist or idiom attributed originally, perhaps apocryphally, to Sam Goldwyn (1883–1974), pioneer film producer. It is a modern version of a malapropism. Some examples are: "Include me out." "Anyone who goes to a psychiatrist ought to have his head examined." "I'll say it in two words: im-possible." "We have all passed a lot of water since then."

good fences make good neighbors   From the poem "Mending Wall" (1914) by Robert Frost (1875–1963). The line is ironic since Frost questions the need for fences between his apple orchard and his neighbor's pines. Neither has cows that might trespass. Frost writes:

> Something there is that doesn't love a wall...
> Before I built a wall I'd ask to know
> What I was walling in or walling out

But it is his neighbor "like an old-stone savage armed" who "moves in darkness...not of woods only," who doggedly clings to the old saw: "Good fences make good neighbors."

Often quoted to show the futility of outworn barriers between classes or nations. And sometimes *mis*quoted to insist that barriers are necessary to maintain peaceful relations.

Good Housekeeping Seal of Approval   In 1910, *Good Housekeeping Magazine* set up its own laboratories to test the products and claims of its advertisers. It accepted advertisements only for those products that passed its own tests for reliability, safety etc. It also checked the claims its advertisers made for their products. Originally, the products that passed its battery of tests received the Good Housekeeping Seal of Approval—a much prized award. It was widely accepted as a sign that a product measured up to Good Housekeeping's high standards. The Good Housekeeping Seal of Approval has now been extended to mean any significant stamp of approval.

Use: "Corporate is nervous money; it needs the NEA [National Endowment for the Arts] for reassurance as a Good Housekeeping Seal of Approval." ("A Loony Paradox of Cultural Democracy," by Robert Hughes, *Time*, August 14, 1989)

Goodman, Benjamin David (Benny)   Musician, bandleader (1909–1986). After playing with various jazz bands, Benny Goodman put his own band together in 1934. With the help of the gifted arranger, Fletcher Henderson, Benny developed his own "big band" style: Tightly woven, driving ensemble work overlaid with the improvisations of fine soloists. In short, Benny ushered in a new kind of jazz, swing, and quite naturally was crowned "The King of Swing"—a title he wore with dignity and aplomb.

Graham, Billy   Born in North Carolina (1918–) to Protestant fundamentalist parents, he was ordained as a Southern Baptist minister and became a preacher for American Youth for Christ in 1944. Graham launched blockbuster evangelical campaigns that lasted for months. These he called crusades. He packed huge meeting places like Yankee Stadium and Madison Square Garden with 75,000 to 100,000 listeners. The object was to get as many as possible to "decide for Christ." He carried his crusades into England, Hungary, Korea and even the Soviet Union (1984).

Billy Graham is the model for clean-cut, middle-class, optimistic Christianity.

Graham, Martha   American dancer, teacher and choreographer (1894–) who created and codified a new dance vocabulary that was to become the foundation of modern dance in America. Her dance technique was based on contraction and release of the muscles of the diaphragm, back and pelvis. She danced barefoot but with voluminous draperies to mask or reveal emotion. Her dance subjects were often literary in origin and Freudian in their psychological probing. Some of her most acclaimed works are: *Primitive Mysteries* (1931); *Letters to the World*, about Emily Dickinson, (1940); *Appalachian Spring* (1944); *Cave of the Heart*, about Medea, (1946); *Night Journey*, about Jocasta (1947); and *Clytemnestra*, (1958). All in all she choreographed more than 150 dances using members of her own company.

Grand Central Station   Located in New York City; one of the busiest, most crowded railroad terminals in the world. Hence, any place that is very busy.

Use: At noon, his office is Grand Central Station.

Grandma Moses   Born Anna Mary Robertson (1860–1961). Self-taught modern primitive painter who had her first one-woman show at the age of 80. In bright, clear colors she painted the rustic scenes and activities of her childhood in upstate New York. Many of her works have been reproduced on Christmas cards and indeed they all have a fresh celebratory air. A Grandma Moses has the quality of an old-fashioned sampler or a rural Currier and Ives.

grandstand play   In baseball, an ostentatious play explicitly designed to attract the attention and win the spectators' applause—especially those seated in the grandstands. Hence, any action designed to elicit applause, make an impression. It raises questions about the individual's sincerity and intent.

Use: McCarthy's vitriolic speech against the President was recognized as just another one of his grandstand plays.

Grant, Cary   American movie actor (1906–1986). Born a cockney in Bristol, England, he became a star famed for his tall, suave good looks and charm. Grant had a flair for light comedy, appearing in *She Done Him Wrong* (1933), *Bringing Up Baby* (1938), *Topper* (1937) and *To Catch a Thief* (1954).

Great White Father   Nickname for United States president, appeared in popular western novels about 1916. Now used to describe any important, influential, beneficent figure in industry, government, etc.

Great White Hope   The term originated in the early 1900s when Jack Johnson, the first black heavyweight champion of the world held that title for seven years (1908–1915). His unsavory life outside the ring, his falling afoul of the law, and his arrogance fed the desires of a considerable body of boxing fans to see the almost invincible Johnson beaten by a white boxer. Hence, the Great White Hope. On April 15, 1915, their wishes were fulfilled. In Havana, Cuba, Jess Willard, the then-current Great White Hope, and now a member of the boxing hall of fame, knocked Johnson out in the 26th round of a fight for the world's heavyweight championship.

Great White Hope is now applied generally to anyone who is expected to accomplish much in a specific field. It no longer bears any of its early racist overtones.

Use: Bradley is the Great White Hope of the computer industry. He is expected to make this industry as formidable as it was before Japan's ascendancy.

"The Green Hornet"   Program that ran first on radio and then on television, between 1936 and 1967. A special arrangement of Rimsky-Korsakov's "Flight of the Bumble-Bee" signaled the beginning of another episode of "The Green Hornet"—determined, unvanquishable fighter against crime. Britt Reid, the crusading editor and publisher of *The Daily Herald* is, of course, none other than the Green Hornet, crime fighter extraordinaire, in disguise. Only Kato, his faithful servant, knows that Britt is the Green Hornet's alter ego.

In his unrelenting battle against the forces of evil, the Green Hornet has: a souped-up 1966 Chrysler Imperial with a built-in TV camera that "sees" four miles ahead; exhaust apparatus to spread ice on the road to foil his pursuers; a special non-lethal gun that immobilizes "elements"; and a sting gun that goes through steel.

"The Green Hornet" is another of television's dramatizations of the "good guys" vs. "the bad guys."

Greenwich Village   A section of lower Manhattan in New York City, which in the early years of the century became the hub of a circle of artists, writers, theater people, radicals and bohemians experimenting with new art forms and unconventional life styles. Among them were Eugene O'Neill and the Provincetown Players, Edna St. Vincent Millay, Edmund Wilson, e.e. cummings, Maxwell Bodenheim, John Sloan, Edward Hopper and many more.

Still a neighborhood of town houses, tree-lined streets, antique shops, boutiques, galleries, book shops, restaurants and little theaters, it continues to attract the young and the young in heart.

gremlins   Imaginary imps who were blamed for all mechanical defects or failures in World War II.

Grosz, George   German painter and caricaturist (1893–1959) who immigrated to New York in 1932 and taught at the Art Students League. Grosz is identified with a series of savagely satirical studies of beefy German bourgeois types, hypocritical and complacent, which show his disillusionment with militarism, capitalism, and conformism in Germany at the end of World War I. For example, in

Germany, a Winter's Tale we see as if in a collage the pernicious influence of a clergyman, a general and a school master on an average smug German, against a tangled background of buildings that look like a huge jail.

ground rules   In baseball, special procedures or regulations applying to a specific ballpark or playing field.

In general usage, ground rules refer to agreed upon rules or procedures.

Use: Before the conference starts we'll have to draw up some ground rules: length of each presentation, time for discussion, etc.

Grover's Corners   The setting of *Our Town* (1938), a play by Thornton Wilder about the everyday lives of people in a typical American town, this one being in New Hampshire. A "Stage Manager" narrator introduces the townspeople: the newsboy, the milkman, the druggist, the gossip, the artist, the undertaker. The central characters will be the families of Editor Webb and Dr. Gibb. Young Emily Webb marries George Gibb. She dies in childbirth. She returns after death to observe the people she has been so familiar with and realizes the eternal verities in their simple, everyday actions, duties and relationships.

Guernica   The bombing of the Basque capital of Guernica by German warplanes on April 27, 1937, during the Spanish Civil War, was memorialized by PABLO PICASSO in his masterpiece *Guernica*. The painting depicts the horrors of war in terrifying images of dismemberment, chaos and suffering.

gulag   Russian acronym for Main Directorate of Corrective Labor Camps, a chain of forced-labor camps in the Soviet Union. The Russian Nobel prize-winner in literature, Aleksandr I. Solzhenitsyn, drew upon his own experiences as a prisoner to reveal the horrors of the camps in such books as *One Day in the Life of Ivan Denisovich*, *The Cancer Ward*, *The First Circle* and *The Gulag Archipelago*.

Now any prison or detention camp, especially for political prisoners.

Gulf of Tonkin   Waters off the coast of North Vietnam where communist patrol boats made "unprovoked" attacks against the U.S. destroyer *Madox*. In August 1964 Congress passed a resolution granting President Lyndon B. Johnson support for whatever action he deemed necessary to defend U.S. forces in Southeast Asia. The Tonkin Resolution was later thought to have been engineered by Johnson and the military, and was held responsible for the expansion of U.S. involvement in the Vietnam War.

Mentioning the Gulf of Tonkin Resolution is generally held to be a cautionary reference to a too-easy yielding to presidential demands for waging undeclared wars.

Gumps, The   Sidney Smith, the creator of *The Gumps* (1917), the most widely read comic strip through the 1930s, was fascinated by money and riches. A great storyteller and lover of soap opera melodrama, he made Andy Gump and his dedicated wife, Min (Minerva), the central characters of *The Gumps*, exemplars of the lower-middle-class, materialistic values he admired. Together with his wife and his billionaire Uncle Bim, Andy embodied the aspirations of millions of readers.

Smith died in an automobile accident in 1935. After his death, *The Gumps* lost much of its verve. It folded in 1959.

gung-ho   From the Chinese, meaning "work together." Adopted by Marine Lieutenant Colonel Evans F. Carlson as the slogan for his battalion. Known as Carlson's Raiders, they won a stunning victory over the Japanese in a surprise attack against Makin Island during World War II. This assault became the subject of the 1944 movie *Gung-Ho!*. Generally used now to mean enthusiastic, eager, all-out.

Use: After the coach's pep talk, the players were all gung-ho for the game against their arch-rivals.

guns before butter   Slogan coined in 1936 by Nazi political and military leader, Hermann Goering. "Guns will make us powerful; butter will only make us fat." He was urging Germans to sacrifice domestic comforts to an all-out preparation for war.

Phrase is now used to mean the sacrifice of amenities to hard realities.

guru   A wise man, a spiritual guide and teacher with a devoted following. Originally used for leaders in the Hindu religion, but now applied to elder statesmen, industrial geniuses, anyone with disciples.

Use: "...among body builders, Mr. Duchaine is the steroid guru, who they believe knows more about these drugs than anyone in the field of sports medicine... A guru who spreads the gospel of steroids." (*New York Times*, November 19, 1988)

Gypsy Rose Lee   Born Rose Louise Hovick (1914–1970). Her generation hailed her as the "Queen of Burlesque," America's most famous striptease artist. For perfecting her art "beyond that practiced by all contemporary practitioners," H.L. Mencken invented a word for Gypsy Rose Lee—ecdysiast.

In the 1920s, Gypsy Rose Lee was taking strip-tease lessons from the knowledgeable Tessie, the Tassel Twirler. By 1931, she had honed her considerable skills in Minsky's and other burlesque palaces. In her many subsequent appearances, she succeeded in raising the lowly, somewhat disreputable strip-tease to a graceful, stylish art.

Beautiful and intelligent, Gypsy Rose Lee became the darling of the New York intellectual set, to whom she was introduced by the famous sportswriter, Damon Runyon. While on tour, she wrote her first, best-selling novel, *The G-String Murders* (actually ghost-written by popular mystery writer Craig Rice). She appeared in the movies, on the Broadway stage and on TV.

H

Haight-Ashbury   District in San Francisco associated in the 1960's with hippies and other segments of the counterculture.

Hammer, Mike   Fictional private detective created by Mickey Spillane (1918–). Tough, ruthless, violent in speech and action, he pursues the bad guy with no holds barred, by-passing legalities when he deems necessary. He feels no sentimental remorse when he visits retribution upon a killer. He is in his own way incorruptible and he will risk his life for what he feels is right. He has a voluptuous assistant-secretary named Velda. Some of the novels he appears in are *I, The Jury* (1947), *Vengeance is Mine* (1950), *My Gun Is Quick* (1950), *Kiss Me Deadly* (1952).

hang up the gloves   In boxing, to retire, to withdraw from active participation. In general use, this expression has a similar meaning.
   Use: After 10 years as head of the company, Bill Morris decided to hang up his gloves.

Happiness Boys   The radio comedy team of Billy Jones and Ernie Hare, their name derived from their sponsor, Happiness Candy (1923).

Happy Hooligan   Fred Opper's great contribution to the pantheon of comic strip characters, *Happy Hooligan* occupied the avid attention of millions of readers from 1900 to 1932.
   In a sense, *Happy Hooligan* is an American Candide. The classic Irish Tramp with a red nose and a tin can for a hat, he is "a simple

115

innocent whose impulsive undertakings nearly always landed him in the hands of the law..."

Despite the bad luck that dogs his efforts at making the world a better, sunnier place for himself and for everyone else, Happy remains the unconquerable optimist, always smiling and hopeful. His brother, Gloomy Gus, is as long-faced as Happy is cheerful.

happy warrior   Originally, from William Wordsworth's "Character of the Happy Warriors" (1807), which begins:

> Who is the happy Warrior? Who is he
> That every man in arms would wish to be?

The expression was used politically when Franklin Delano Roosevelt applied it to Governor Alfred E. Smith of New York in a nominating speech in 1924 and then again in 1928, when Smith became the Democratic candidate for president. A liberal and a Catholic, Smith lost the election to Herbert Hoover.

Later the same nickname was given to Senator Hubert Humphrey, who, though he tried valiantly and with much optimism, never made it to the presidency.

In general use: one who joyously fights the good fight.

hard hat   The steel or plastic helmet worn by various workers, especially construction workers.

In general use, a "hard hat" has come to mean a conservative, a reactionary, a "right-winger."

Use: McFarland expects he'll win the election by appealing to the hard hats in his district.

Hardy, Andy   Teenage protagonist played by Mickey Rooney in a series of 15 enormously popular films made by MGM between 1937 and 1947. These movies purportedly portrayed the everyday growing pains of a good, clean-living boy in a typical American family in a small midwestern town. Andy would get into trivial scrapes and his father, a judge played by Lewis Stone, would have man-to-man talks with him. The series was given a special Academy Award in 1942 for "furthering the American way of life."

Use: "I realized how much of themselves these men [the early pioneering movie moguls] invested in the movies. They really believed in that Andy Hardy world. For Goldwyn, America provided a place where everything could be clean." (A. Scott Berg, quoted in a review of his biography *Goldwyn*, in the *New York Times* Book Review, March 26, 1989)

Harlem   Black district in Manhattan with its main artery along 125th Street, site of the Apollo Theater. It is associated not only with the problems of a black urban population—poverty, overcrowding, poor housing—but also with black creativity in jazz, dance and theater. In the 1920s, white patrons flocked to the reviews at the Cotton Club and Connie's Inn, while blacks themselves danced at the Savoy.

Harlow, Jean   American actress (1911–1937), born Harlean Carpenter in Kansas City, Missouri, she became the "Platinum Blonde" sex goddess of the 1930s. Brassy and often comic, she appeared with CLARK GABLE in *Red Dust* (1932) and *Hold Your Man* (1933).

"Have Gun, Will Travel"   The most adult of the 1950s television westerns. The "hero" Paladin, a surly, "hired gun," dressed in black and played with subdued conviction by Richard Boone, offered his services to the helpless and oppressed. Despite each episode's expected ending (virtue triumphant over evil), the tight writing and convincing, understated acting of Boone, attracted and held a wide spectrum of viewers.

Originally, Paladin was one of the legendary knights pledged to defend noble causes and protect the weak in the name of King Charlemagne. The modern Paladin's business card expressed this ancient code in a universally understood, contemporary idiom: "Have Gun. Will Travel. Wire Paladin. San Francisco."

Hawkshaw, the Detective   A very popular comic strip character introduced by its creator, Gus Mager, February 23, 1913. In its time, it became an American version of Sir Arthur Conan Doyle's immortal Sherlock Holmes. Actually, an earlier version of Hawkshaw was called Sherlocko. When it became obvious that Conan Doyle's representatives were about to launch a lawsuit contending that *Sherlocko* was a flagrant plagiarism, the publishers dropped Sherlocko and put Hawkshaw in his place.

Though Sherlock Holmes has displaced Hawkshaw in the minds and hearts of detective story aficionados, Hawkshaw is not entirely forgotten.

Use: "...The Times Bureau decided it was a job for Jeff Gerth, a reportorial Hawkshaw." (William Safire, *New York Times* Op-Ed page, February 9, 1989; the paper was piqued by what might be contained in the missing pages from a document issued by the Office of Government Ethics.)

haymaker   In boxing, a crushing, devastating punch, which usually results in a "knock-out" or "knock-down."

In general use, it carries the same sense of overwhelming force.

Use: "Under Mikhail Gorbachev's *glasnost*, Soviet visitors to the U.S. already have quadrupled in a year—and U.S. agents are hard-pressed to keep up. And here comes the *haymaker.* The expected arrival this summer of teams of Soviet inspectors who will roam over 22 different U.S. sites where mid-range American nuclear missles are made and stored." (*U.S. News and World Report*, February 15, 1988)

Hayworth, Rita   Born Margarita Cansino (1918–1987), a red-headed, glamorous, voluptuous American movie star and pin-up girl. Hayworth was married twice, first to Orson Welles and then to Aly Khan. A Hollywood love goddess.

Use: "A voluptuous figure in scarlet—from her Rita Hayworth pile of hair to her full lips to her drop-dead high-heel shoes—this mother is clearly the kind of powerful woman whom people don't get over." (Frank Rich, review of the play *Spoils of War, New York Times*, November 11, 1988)

Heart of Darkness   Short novel (1902) by JOSEPH CONRAD about a journey through the jungles of the Congo to rescue a legendary ivory trader by the name of Mr. Kurtz who is said to be very ill. It is an allegorical journey of the soul at the end of which the narrator, Marlow, finds the hero to have traveled backward into savagery, where he stares into the heart of darkness, the abyss of death and of evil in men's souls.

Use: "Some people were drawn to the story not because of a Conradian 'fascination of the abomination' but out of an obligation to try to make sense of this modern-day heart of darkness. (Edwin Diamond, "Anatomy of a Horror," an article on the rape of the

Central Park jogger, *New York Magazine,* May 15, 1989) (See also:
THE HORROR, THE HORROR.)

"Hearts and Flowers"   An immensely popular, sentimental song
of the early 1900s. Its melancholy tune "tears at the heart strings."
    Any maudlin, tear-jerking appeal is often labeled a "hearts and
flowers" presentation.
    Use: The board of directors was not impressed with Dalton's hearts
and flowers speech.

heavy hitter   In baseball, a player whose batting average is high,
who can be counted on to get considerably more than the average
number of hits per game or per season.
    In general, a heavy hitter is an important, influential person.
    Use: "*Heavy hitters* like the chairman and ranking minority mem-
bers of powerful committees collect much more than their ceilings
[in honoraria] and can give the excess to charity." (*New York Times,*
April 4, 1989)

Hefner, Hugh   Publisher (1926–) of *Playboy Magazine* (1953).
Playboy appealed to the young, affluent, urban male. It advocated a
life-style marked by extreme sexual permissiveness. The magazine
stimulated these impulses with nude photos of very attractive young
women surrounded by high-pressure advertising.
    Hefner organized and ran a string of private "Playboy" clubs staffed
by girls dressed like "bunnies": an exercise in extravagant hedonism.
Hefner himself, through his publications and other enterprises, pursued the kind of life style extolled in the pages of *Playboy.*

Held, John, Jr.   American illustrator and cartoonist (1889–1958).
After working, unsatisfied, for several magazines, Held found his
style and voice in the pages of *The New Yorker.* Here, he began to
capture the mood, feel and look of his skinny, flat-chested flappers of
the 1920s.

Hemingway, Ernest   American novelist, short-story writer and
journalist (1899–1961).
    In his own life, Hemingway stands for machismo, for pursuit of
the manly sports such as big game hunting (*Green Hills of Africa,*
1935; "The Short Happy Life of Francis Macomber" and "The Snows

of Kilimanjaro," 1938), deep sea fishing (*The Old Man and the Sea*, 1952), boxing, bull-fighting (*Death in the Afternoon*, 1932; *The Sun Also Rises*, 1926). He became an ambulance driver on the Italian front in World War I (*A Farewell to Arms*, 1929), covered the Spanish Civil War as a war correspondent (*For Whom the Bell Tolls*, 1940) and fought in World War II. His personal stance was pugnacious and challenging. When he could no longer pursue his macho activities because of illness, he committed suicide at the age of 61.

Hemingway has become synonymous with the *Lost Generation*, a group of American expatriates living in Paris after World War I (*A Moveable Feast*, published posthumously in 1964). (See also HEMINGWAY STYLE, HEMINGWAY CODE.

Hemingway code   A standard of behavior stated and exemplified by certain characters in ERNEST HEMINGWAY's novels and short stories. It is the ideal toward which the Hemingway hero strives: knowing how to lose well, courage in crisis, "grace under pressure," stoicism, loyalty to comrades, reticence, skill in manly endeavors. Santiago, the old man of *The Old Man and the Sea*, is an excellent example of the code, one who initiates the boy Manolin into what it takes to become a man. Wilson, the hunting guide in "The Short Happy Life of Francis Macomber," is another exemplar of the code.

Hemingway style   A taut style of writing first forged by ERNEST HEMINGWAY in the interludes and short stories of *In Our Time* (1925). Characterized by monosyllabic vocabulary, short sentences, stark dialogue, understated emotion, and dependence upon verbs and nouns rather than adjectives and adverbs, the Hemingway style exerted a strong influence on 20th-century fiction. (See also HEMINGWAY, ERNEST and HEMINGWAY CODE.)

Hepburn, Katharine   U.S. film actress (1909–). Represents high-spirited, independent, outspoken, classy career woman. Often teamed with SPENCER TRACY in movies that involve the battle of the sexes; e.g., *Woman of the Year* (1941), *Adam's Rib* (1949). She initiated this image as the young Jo in *Little Women* (1933).

Heston, Charlton   American stage and film star (1923–). Associated with epic roles: Moses and the voice of God in *The Ten Com-*

mandments, (1956); the heroes of *Ben Hur* (1955) and of *El Cid* (1961). His sonorous voice and heroic stature are often parodied.

hicksville   From hick or country bumpkin, thus any rural place far from the sophistications of city life. Always used disparagingly.

High Noon   Adult western (1951) directed by Fred Zinnemann. It tells the story of a sheriff (GARY COOPER) who must stand up alone against four desperados who will return at high noon on a certain day to kill him and to retake the town they had terrorized for years. The townspeople, out of abject fear, have deserted him. His new, young wife (Grace Kelly) is a Quaker who disavows violence, even in self-defense. Caught in a moral dilemma, and a situation of great personal danger, the sheriff decides to face the outlaws alone. Eventually he faces the leader of the outlaws in a classic confrontation scene on the town square.

High noon has become a parable of citizen responsibility against lawlessness, as well as a metaphor for fatal confrontation.

Use: U.S. scientists have grown so sensitive about the controversy surrounding the "cold fusion" experiments at the University of Utah that the National Academy of Sciences last week canceled a scheduled discussion of the complex affair because it feared the session might have turned into "a high-noon showdown" between believers and skeptics. (*U.S. News & World Report*, May 8, 1989)

hippies   Young people of the 1960s counterculture who affected long hair, slovenly dress, poverty, residence in city "pads" or country communes, and psychedelic drugs—outward symbols of their rejection of conventional society. They adopted "love" and "peace" as their bywords. (See also: HAIGHT-ASHBURY, WOODSTOCK, FLOWER CHILDREN.)

Use: "The translator's heart sinks at the sight of words like kommunalka, which he knows he must render as 'communal apartment'...The English term conjures up an image of a Berkeley, Calif. kitchen where hippies with headbands are cooking brown rice..." (Richard Lourie, "Why You'll Never Have Fun in Russian," *New York Times Book Review*, June 18, 1989)

hired gun   Originally a person hired to kill someone. Now applied to anyone hired to do a particularly difficult job.

Use: Publicity men getting out materials for both Democratic and Republican parties, creating 30-second "political commercials," were characterized by commentator David Brinkley as "the best hired guns in American politics." (ABC News, August 21, 1988)

Hiroshima   Japanese city destroyed by the first atomic bomb ever dropped upon a civilian population, on August 6, 1945. Four days later a second atomic bomb was dropped on Nagasaki with equally devastating effect. Japan surrendered to the U.S., thus ending World War II in the Pacific. The bomb was delivered by the Superfortress, the ENOLA GAY, piloted by Col. Paul W. Tibbets Jr. Symbol of the destructive power of atomic warfare.

his master's voice   One of the most famous ads ever created shows a fox terrier with his ear cocked to the large horn of an early record player. The ad for *Victor Records* carried the legend: His Master's Voice. In time, the attentive canine became known as "the dog everybody knows."

The English painter Francis Barrand was inspired to paint this picture when he saw his dog Nipper listening intently to the voices and music coming from the horn. The American rights to the painting were acquired in 1901.

Hiss, Alger   Highly respected State Department official sentenced on January 25, 1950, to five years in prison for perjury in denying that in the 1930s he had given secret documents to Whittaker Chambers, an agent for a Soviet spy ring. The evidence hinged on a borrowed typewriter and papers hidden in a pumpkin.

Referred to generally as a victim of Red-scare hysteria.

Hitchcock, Alfred   British film director (1899–1980) famous as the "master of suspense." Almost every one of his many thrillers achieved the status of an instant classic. He made *The 39 Steps, The Lady Vanishes* and *Sabotage* in England. After 1939 he made his pictures for Hollywood: *Rebecca* (1940), *Foreign Correspondent* (1940), *Suspicion* (1941), *Spellbound* (1945), *Dial M for Murder* (1954), *Rear Window* (1954), *Psycho* (1960), *The Birds* (1963) as well as *Vertigo* (1958) and *North by Northwest* (1959).

Once asked whether he ever considered making any other kind of picture, say a comedy or a musical, he replied: "I'm a typed director.

If I made Cinderella, the audience would immediately be looking for a body in the coach."

His signature on every one of his films was his appearance in some capacity as a walk-on. But his features actually became familiar to millions of fans through his commentaries on the TV series "Alfred Hitchcock Presents," beginning in 1955. He was short, pudgy, double-chinned, bald-pated and had a jutting lower lip from which emanated wry humor delivered with poker-faced imperturbability.

Hitler, Adolf   Fanatical leader (1889–1945) of the National Socialist Party of Germany. Hitler, born in Austria, was appointed chancellor of Germany January 30, 1933, and become Nazi dictator after the suspicious Reichstag fire in 1933. Hitler, also known as Führer, was responsible for German expansionism, World War II and the Holocaust. Author of *Mein Kampf*, a book setting forth his ideas of a pure Aryan race and society. Not taken seriously to begin with, he made the world pay heavily for not taking heed. Physically, Hitler was a figure of derision, with a slicked-down lick of hair across his forehead, a short bushy mustache, ramrod spine, arm raised stiffly in the Nazi salute, knickerbocker-uniformed and booted. But he was a mesmerizing orator and a master of propaganda. Hitler committed suicide April 30, 1945, rather than surrender to the victorious Allies.

To be called a Hitler is to be called evil incarnate; a monster, beyond the limits of the human; a brutal and deranged dictator. A Hitler is also a derisive term for an apoplectic caricature with a short moustache.

hit list   Originally, in Mafia circles, an alleged or actual list of individuals targeted for murder. In non-criminal circles, a hit list contains the names of individuals to be punished, demoted, removed from office etc.

Use: Nobody had seen it—but everyone knew that the president of the company kept a hit list of employees who were making trouble among their coworkers.

hitting below the belt   In boxing, the belt is an imaginery line above the hips, where a man's belt usually rests. A boxer who punches his opponent below this line ("below the belt") is said to have delivered a "foul blow"—and is penalized a number of points. If he continues to hit his opponent below the belt, he may be disqualified and forfeit the match.

In general use, hitting below the belt refers to an indecent, illegal, unsportsmanlike, against-the rules act or remark.

Use: Referring to Carlson's physical problems in campaign speeches was considered hitting below the belt.

Hokinson Girls   Inhabitants of cartoons created by Helen Hokinson (1893–1949). They were a good-natured spoof of well-fed, middle-aged, deadly serious clubwomen on the lookout for culture. They are shown at book discussion clubs, at flower shows, in department store mélées, in traffic jams of their own creation, at home wheedling maids. In all these situations, culture is the loser. Hokinson's partner, James Reid Parker, wrote the humorous captions for her drawings. Her *New Yorker* cartoons were collected and published in several books during her lifetime and posthumously, e.g., *The Ladies, God Bless 'Em* (1950), *There Are Ladies Present* (1952) and *The Hokinson Feature* (1956).

"The Hollow Men"   Poem (1925) by T.S. Eliot about modern man's lack of faith or conviction. He inhabits "death's dream kingdom," that is to say, death-in-life without hope of redemption. Eliot writes:

> We are the hollow men
> We are the stuffed men
> Leaning together
> Headpiece filled with straw. Alas!

Usually used today to denote people who are shallow, lacking in idealism, or stupid.

Use: "By resolutely following his script calling for Judge Bork to be referred to as 'Mr. Bork' and by shrinking from mind to mind combat, Edward Kennedy revealed himself again to be one of T.S. Eliot's hollow men, gesture without motion." (William Safire, *New York Times*, September 20, 1987) (See also NOT WITH A BANG BUT A WHIMPER.)

Hollywood   Fabled movie mecca of the world. Located in Los Angeles, California, where the weather is always mild and dependable, it has been the home of the big-time film studios from the pioneering days of the industry until today. Here William and Cecil B. DeMille, Sam Goldwyn, Louis B. Mayer, William Fox and the Warner Brothers built their empires. Here, movie stars and goddesses lived and worked amid glamor and glitter. Like the American Dream, it had its shabby side, too. Its power to corrupt has been vividly related in novels like *The Deer Park* (1955) by Norman Mailer and *The Day of the Locust* (1939) by Nathanael West. But in setting and disseminating in vivid screen images the patterns and values of American life, Hollywood has had immeasurable influence on the popular culture of the entire world. Hollywood, in the popular imagination, remains a place of star dust and dreams.

Hollywood Ten   HOLLYWOOD writers and one director who in 1947 were blacklisted by the motion picture industry itself, after they'd been held in contempt of Congress for refusing to testify before the House Un-American Activities Committee (HUAC) hearings, chaired by J. Parnell Thomas. They are generally considered victims of anti-communist hysteria and witch-hunting.

The ten are: Alvah Bessie, Herbert Biberman, Lester Cole, Edward Dmytryk, Ring Lardner, Jr., John Howard Lawson, Albert Maltz, Sam Ornitz, Robert Adrian Scott and Dalton Trumbo.

Holmes, Sherlock   Master detective created by Sir Arthur Conan Doyle (1859–1930) in *A Study in Scarlet (1887)*. He solved a variety of strange, exotic crimes through uncanny observation, intuition and ratiocination. He shared rooms in Baker Street, London, with his constant companion, DR. WATSON. The phrase "Elementary, my dear Watson," spoken by Holmes to his friend, has become part of the English language.

Holocaust   Nazi Germany's deliberate annihilation of six million European Jews during World War II. Hitler's "final solution" to the "Jewish problem." The systematic and technical proficiency of the mass murders in the gas chambers of concentration camps irrevocably altered our consciousness of the potential for human brutality and depravity. Although the Nazis also destroyed members of other groups (gypsies, Slavs, homosexuals, political opponents), the Holocaust refers specifically to the destruction of the Jews and their culture.

Now used to indicate mass murder of any people.

Hoover, J. Edgar   Head of the Federal Bureau of Investigation (FBI) under eight presidents. Before Hoover (1895–1972) was chosen to head the agency in 1925, the FBI was poorly staffed, badly led and scandal-ridden. Hoover was given a mandate to "cleanse" the agency. He did. Since his death in 1972, the FBI is still widely recognized as one of the most efficient, most brilliant organizations anywhere in the world.

Hoover established high professional standards for recruits to the department. Among other requirements, new members of the FBI had to be either lawyers or accountants. Hoover's almost fanatical insistence on the use of scientific methods in crime detection led to the establishment of the FBI Laboratory, probably one of the best-equipped, most sophisticated of its kind in the world.

Though he was guilty of some excesses and flawed approaches and though some presidents and other officials wanted to remove him, Hoover died in office invulnerable, untouchable, feared by all. The FBI remains a monument to him.

Hooverville   A shantytown put together out of crates and cardboard by the poor and dispossessed during the Great Depression in the U.S., when Herbert Hoover was president (1929–1933).

Has come to stand for any haphazard, temporary shelters.

Hopalong Cassidy   One of television's early "heroes" (1949–1951), "Hoppy," as he was affectionately called, was the nemesis of the villains of the Old West. Astride his faithful horse Topper, the silver-haired movie star William Boyd (1895–1972), dressed in black, played Hoppy to the delight of old and young and to the consternation of evildoers.

The predictable, but nonetheless enjoyable plots of the television series were drawn from Clarence E. Mulford's novels and from earlier low-budget movies.

Hopper, Edward   American painter (1882–1967) whose canvases suggest with compassion and even poetry the loneliness and alienation of ordinary people in ordinary American settings: a woman sitting alone at a window in an all-night cafeteria, or on a bench outside a railroad station, or standing in the lobby of a movie theater.

Even his houses and trees and gasoline stations are imbued through the play of light and shadow with a brooding, introspective loneliness. His subjects seem frozen in time. Although often labeled a realist, Hopper is subjective in emotional tone.

Use: "And the clear, clean morning light and the Edward Hopper streets and storefronts create a world where the script, by Leonard Glasser and George Malko, plays itself out in all its linear precision." (Pauline Kael, reviewing the movie *Out Cold* in *The New Yorker*, March 6, 1989)

the horror! the horror!   The last words of the dying Mr. Kurtz, an ivory trader in the heart of the Congo, in HEART OF DARKNESS (1902), a short novel by JOSEPH CONRAD (1857–1924). The words represent the ultimate, despairing vision of a man who went into the jungle not only to find and export ivory but also to bring civilization to barbaric natives. Instead, he found himself using brutal means, including human sacrifice, to subjugate the natives for his own purposes. What he discovered, and what the narrator Charles Marlow discovers, too, is that beneath the facade of civilized behavior shown by any one of us lies a substratum of savagery waiting to erupt. The jungle is within all of us.

The words "the horror! the horror!" are quoted seriously and sometimes mockingly to connote evil, the dark evil of death and savagery and sin.

hot line   Originally referred to a direct telephone link between the heads of state in Moscow and Washington for the purpose of averting a terrible mistake in a presumed nuclear first strike. Now refers to immediate telephone communication in any crisis. TV stations, for example, cite hot lines for getting help in domestic crises, for child abuse, for suicide threats.

Houdini, Harry   Born Eric Weiss (1874–1926). A world-famous American magician renowned for his baffling escapes from straight-jacket, chains, handcuffs, locked containers. Houdini's stage performances also included the disappearance and reappearance of men, women, animals. He never revealed the secrets of his extraordinary exploits.

In popular parlance, anyone who escapes from an apparently escape-proof setting is called a "real Houdini." One who causes people to disappear is also referred to as a "real Houdini."

Use: "A vicious gang of toughs 'systematically terrorized' an entire West Side Manhattan neighborhood for 20 years by murdering and dismembering its victims, a federal prosecutor charged yesterday...The gang leader, James Coonan, 41, and his cohorts 'made the bodies disappear—they did their Houdini act...'" (*New York Post,* October 20, 1987)

House Un-American Activities Committee (HUAC)   See MCCARTHYISM.

Howard, Leslie   Born Leslie Stainer (1893–1943). British actor who played sensitive, soft-spoken, gentle roles, e.g., Ashley in GONE WITH THE WIND (1939).

Howard Beach   Blue-collar neighborhood in the Borough of Queens, New York, where in 1986, a gang of white youths attacked four blacks and chased one of them, Michael Griffith, onto a parkway where he was struck and killed by a car. The whites were tried by a special prosecutor and found guilty of manslaughter. The incident raised racial tension in the city, but most blacks felt that justice had been meted out to the white racists.

Howard Beach has become a symbol of racial confrontation as well as a test of racial justice.

Howdy-Doody   Puppet, or marionette, on the television show of the same name. From 1947 to 1960, this four-foot puppet with 72 freckles (by an official count) provided lively, nonsensical, highly appealing entertainment for children—ably assisted by Clarabell, a clown with "the voice of an autohorn."

The host and creator of the "Howdy-Doody" show was Buffalo Bob Smith (1917–), a gifted ventriloquist with a true affection for children and an intuitive understanding of what made them tick.

The audience demand for tickets to the show was overwhelming; the waiting list was so long that—the show's managers reported—expectant mothers requested tickets for their unborn children!

How to Win Friends and Influence People   See CARNEGIE, DALE.

Hughes, Howard A billionaire inventor, industrialist, movie maker, eccentric and recluse(1905–1976). Howard Hughes was born in Texas to a wealthy family. In the late twenties he became a movie producer with *Hell's Angels* and many other hits to his credit. He studied aeronautics, designed planes and became an aviator who made and broke speed records. In July 1938 he and his crew flew around the world in three days, 19 hours, and 17 minutes, cutting in half the previous world record set by Wiley Post in 1933. He invested in Las Vegas casinos and associated with strange people who made unsubstantiated claims upon his fortune. Eventually he disappeared from public view, becoming a mysterious legend in his own lifetime and after his death. His last years were so mysterious that he became the subject of one of the most infamous publishing frauds of modern times. A writer by the name of Clifford Irving wrote the *Autobiography of Howard Hughes*, based, he claimed, on taped interviews with Hughes. McGraw-Hill and Time Inc., bought it for $750,000 and spent over a million dollars in publicizing it. The whole publishing world was agog, because nobody knew whether Hughes was dead or alive or mentally fit. A telephone call from Hughes, himself, to the publisher to the effect that he didn't know Irving from Adam exposed the fraud. Irving was sentenced to two and a half years in prison.

hundred days, the Originally, this expression referred to the period of time (March 20 to June 28, 1815) between Napoleon's escape from Elba and his defeat at Waterloo. In our time, "the hundred days" refers to the first hundred days of Franklin Delano Roosevelt's presidency in 1933. Under his dynamic leadership, Congress passed far-reaching, revolutionary legislation to deal with the problems of the Great Depression. Since then the first hundred days of a president's incumbency have become a measure of the direction and style of his administration. (See also: NEW DEAL.)

"Huntley-Brinkley Report" The superstars of TV reporting: Chet Huntley (1911–1974) conservative, straightforward, somewhat on the serious side; David Brinkley (1920–), liberal, glib, inclined to the sardonic. Both handled the news superbly—with style and distinction. TV has not found their equal. At its peak, the "Huntley-Brinkley Report" (1956–1980) reached an audience of over 17,000,000.

The program was famous for its coverage of the news, and for its closing signature:

Good-night, David.
Good-night, Chet.

Hurstwood, George   Tragic character in Theodore Dreiser's (1871–1945) novel SISTER CARRIE (1900). Infatuated with Carrie, he abandons his wife and his two selfish children, steals $10,000 from the safe of the fashionable bar in Chicago of which he has been the manager, and tricks Carrie into going with him to New York. There the police catch up with him, recover the money, and Hurstwood, accepting more and more meaningless jobs, finally is reduced to a Bowery bum. When he comes unwillingly to depend upon Carrie's rising earning power on the stage, he commits suicide.

Hurstwood is a weak man who is destroyed by his passion for another woman and by hostile forces that undermine his will.

I

Iacocca Lee A. Chairman of the Chrysler Motor Corporation. The son of Italian immigrants, Iacocca (1924–) became a marketing genius and the president of Ford Motor Company. In 1978, forced out of Ford, he took over the failing Chrysler, and through astute management and an unprecedented $1.2 billion loan guarantee from Congress he turned the company around to make a $2.4 billion profit in 1984. His autobiography *Iacocca* (1984), written with William Novak, sold 2.5 million hard cover copies by 1986.

Use: "Hailed as an Iacocca, he now must meet added competition." (Jan Carlzon, president of Scandinavian Airline System; *New York Times*, February 9, 1988)

I coulda been a contender A rueful remark made by Marlon Brando to his brother Rod Steiger in the taxi scene of *On the Waterfront*, a 1954 movie about union corruption on the Hoboken docks. The phrase, today used ironically, suggests wasted potential, lost opportunities.

I Cover the Waterfront Best-selling novel (1932) by journalist Max Miller, exposing crime and corruption on the waterfront.

Now expanded to mean a complete account of anything, "the whole story."

Use: When you address the delegates at the convention, be brief. Don't try to cover the waterfront.

id   FREUDIAN term for the primitive side of the psyche, the subconscious, associated with repressed sexual and aggressive instincts. The ego and the superego attempt to keep it in check, but every once in a while the id blows its top and runs amok, in civilizations as in individuals.

Use: "Père Ubu is a giant id let loose, without any reins on his appetite or his ambitions." (*Columbia Spectator*, July 12, 1989)

I do not choose to run   Calvin Coolidge (1872–1933), a man of few words and the 30th president of the United States announced in his usual laconic manner, on August 2, 1927: "I do not choose to run for president in 1928." That was that.

The phrase has since been used flippantly by anybody who turns down an offer to run for any office, no matter how humble or trivial. It is a way of saying "Thank you, but, no thank you."

I have a dream   Inspirational words, intoned with Biblical refrain and cadence, in a speech by Rev. Dr. Martin Luther King Jr., on August 28, 1963. To a crowd of 200,000 mostly black, peaceful demonstrators gathered at the Washington Mall to demand passage of a civil rights law, he said: "I have a dream that one day this nation will rise up and live out the true meaning of its creed: 'We hold these truths to be self-evident, that all men are created equal.'" He ended his stirring speech with the dream that his people would be "free at last, free at last, God Almighty, free at last."

A person need but say, "I have a dream," no matter how trivial or jocular or profound the dream, to call up overtones of the passionate eloquence of Dr. King's dream.

"I Love Lucy"   When Lucille Ball (1912–1989) died on April 26, 1989, episodes of "I Love Lucy," the longest-running show in prime time and syndicated television history (1951–), were lighting up TV screens in 80 countries. Conceived by Lucy and her husband Desi Arnaz, a Cuban band leader, "I Love Lucy" was an instant success. It became the most familiar, the most loved, the most rerun of all SITCOMS. Though Desi played his part well, Lucy was obviously the central character; a flawless comedienne, her dreams, plans and defeats touched millions all over the world. Her death at 77 evoked expressions of universal sorrow and appreciation, as:

Milton Berle, "The greatest woman clown in the world"; and the *New York Post*, "The true Queen of Television's Golden Age"; and President George Bush, "She was Lucy. She was loved. Lucille Ball possessed the gift of laughter. But she embodied an even greater treasure—the gift of love."

I'm from Missouri   Phrase used by Willard D. Vandiner, representative to Congress from Columbia, Missouri, from 1897 to 1905. In 1902, at a dinner given for members of a House Naval Committee inspecting the Navy Yard in Philadelphia, Vandiner expressed skepticism about a statement made by a previous speaker. Jocularly he said, "I'm from Missouri, you've got to show me."

Used (and not only by Missourians) to express doubt, as in "doubting Thomas," to challenge statements, and to demand proof in the form of direct evidence.

I'm in charge   Premature statement made by General Alexander Haig, the Secretary of State, shortly after the assassination attempt on President Ronald Reagan on March 30, 1981.

Generally used satirically for a pushy, rather arrogant assumption of authority.

in the ball park   Falling within the area where the game of baseball is played. It has come to mean acceptable, within reasonable limits.

Use: Markson offered $28 a share for Bartel Company stock. The company officers considered it well within the ball park.

I Never Promised You a Rose Garden   Novel (1964) by the American writer Joanne Greenberg (Hannah Green) about a sixteen-year-old girl's psychotic retreat into an imaginary world and her sympathetic psychiatrist's successful efforts to bring her back to the real world, however flawed it may be.

"I never promised you a rose garden" is an admission that whatever has been proffered was not perfect, but perhaps acceptable.

"I Never Saw a Butterfly"   Title of a poem, written by a child in a Nazi concentration camp, and then of a book containing the discovered writings and art work of the children exterminated in the camps. Sad, rueful, touching sentiment, a metaphor for all the missed life, the missed experience of beauty, of the one million slaughtered Jewish children. There were no butterflies, no tender frail beauties behind barbed wire and concrete.

"Information, Please"   Radio show. "Wake up, America. Time to stump the experts" opened the most literate, most urbane, wittiest quiz show on radio, from the late 1930s to the early 1940s. Every week the listening audience submitted questions about art, music, literature, nature, sports etc., to a panel of "experts," which included: *Oscar Levant*, a concert pianist; *John Kieran*, a sports writer for the *New York Times*, nature-lover and classical scholar; *Clifton Fadiman*, a critic, teacher, and editor; and *F.P.A. (Franklin Pierce Adams)*, a newspaper columnist for the *World* and the *New York Post*. His *Conning Tower* and *Our Own Samuel Pepys Diary* were a rare literary delight.

Innisfree   An idyllic country place on an island near Sligo in Ireland to which William Butler Yeats, in his poem "The Lake Isle of Innisfree," dreams of retiring from the "pavements grey" of London.

> I will arise and go now, and go to Innisfree,
> And a small cabin build there, of clay and wattles made:
> Nine bean-rows will I have there, a hive for the honey-bee,
> And live alone in the bee-loud glade.

Invisible Man   Novel (1952) by Ralph Ellison. The unnamed hero is a talented, idealistic black boy who grows up to be totally disillusioned with society, black and white. "I am an invisible man," he says in the opening sentence of the prologue. He is hiding in the basement of an abandoned New York City apartment house, which he has illuminated with a thousand electric bulbs to make himself visible. He has literally gone underground—and figuratively—to find his identity.

"Invisible man" is a term applied not only to blacks but also to other segments of society whose needs nobody seems to notice or care about.

Use: "As the biography progresses, we get more and more of the program notes (names, dates) behind which the real Langston Hughes, whoever he might have been, went into hiding, perhaps turning himself into his very own invisible man." (Rita Dove, reviewing *The Life of Langston Hughes*, vol. II, by Arnold Rampersad, *New York Times* Book Review, October 9, 1988)

iron curtain   Phrase coined by Winston Churchill in a speech at Fulton, Missouri, in 1946, shortly after the end of World War II to describe the absolute division between the Western democracies and the communist bloc of Eastern European nations dominated by the U.S.S.R. Soviet policies of secrecy and censorship had created an impenetrable barrier to communication and understanding between these two great ideological adversaries.

Now used seriously and sometimes ironically to denote a solid wall of secrecy separating two stubborn individuals, groups or nations.

Use: "Once the sale was consummated, a thorough housecleaning took place in the advertising department, but since that department and the editorial department are separated by an almost impenetrable iron curtain, little was heard by us in the upper regions of the considerable ruckus (and surely the heartbreak) being endured some floors below."(*New York Times* Book Review, October 4, 1987)

It Can't Happen Here   A novel by Sinclair Lewis warning Americans that indeed "it" can happen "here," "it" meaning a fascist dictatorship and "here" meaning the United States. The action of the novel takes place in 1936, one year after its publication, when fascism in Italy was already established and Nazism was on the rise in Germany. In the book, the newly elected president of the United States, Buzz Windrup, takes control of the Congress and the Supreme Court, suppresses labor unions and minorities and uses storm troopers, the Minute Men, to crush all opposition. The hero, Doremus Jessup, is the editor of a small, liberal newspaper in Vermont. In the course of his fight against the dictatorship, he comes to realize that liberalism will not work and he joins the revolutionary forces of the New Underground.

The phrase "it can't happen here" is always used ironically to mean it *can* happen here—whatever "it" is.

Use: Headline in *New York Post*, August 30, 1988, over a story about Costa-Gavras's film *Betrayed*, a "thriller about far-right military groups" and racism: "It Can Happen Here."

It Girl   Clara Bow (1905–1965) became known as the "It Girl" after starring in the movie *It* (1927), based on Elinor Glyn's titillating, mildly daring novel *It* (1927). More than any other movie actress of her time, Clara Bow personified the flapper of the 1920s. She was vital, fun-loving, vivacious and very sexy. Her Hollywood producer, B.F. Schulberg, starred her in pictures precisely tailored for her special persona: *Rough House Rosie, Dancing Mothers, Red Hair, The Wild Party.* Although they promised sex and sin, they were, by today's standards, quite innocent, invariably ending with Clara's marrying the "nice guy."

Today, any vivacious, provocative girl whom men find interesting and irresistible.

I and Thou   Philosophical book (1923; English translation, 1937) by Martin Buber (1878–1965), Austrian-born Israeli theologian. The book postulates two ways of relating to people: (1) the I-It relationship, which "focuses on a functional and manipulative treatment of other persons and things," and (2) the I-Thou relationship, which "provides for greater interpersonal knowledge and responsibility." The I-It way looks at people as objects; the I-Thou way sees people as subjects, and is, therefore, a more profound and sympathetic way. *I and Thou* had an important influence on psychology, education, ethics and theology.

It's a Wonderful Life   Movie (1946) directed by Frank Capra and starring James Stewart. Partly a fantasy, it tells the story of a sincere, hard-working but depressed young man who is about to commit suicide when his guardian angel comes along, shows him what the world would be like had he never been born, and convinces him that life can be beautiful after all. The young man returns to his family and they spend a happy Christmas together.

The phrase and the movie are optimistic, if sentimental, summations of everyday family life.

Iwo Jima   On February 23, 1945, men of the 28th Regiment of the Fifth Division of U.S. Marines scaled heavily fortified Mount Suribachi on the island of Iwo Jima (750 miles south of Tokyo) and planted the American flag on its summit. The scene has been immortalized in a famous photograph, which is now a symbol of the "can-do" attitude of the Marines.

Izzy and Moe In the 1920s, two of the Federal Prohibition Bureau's most successful agents (Isadore Einstein and Moe Epstein). Dubbed the "clown princes of Prohibition," they employed a large variety of disguises and ruses to pile up an unrivaled record of arrests and seizures of contraband liquor. Their score: over 5,000,000 bottles of liquor seized, 4,392 arrests, and convictions in 95% of the cases.

J

"Jack Armstrong, the All-American Boy" Radio show of the 1930s that met all of the demands of the network's code for children's programs.

The code excluded "torture, horror, use of the supernatural or superstition likely to arouse fear." And it banned vulgarity (in speech or action), kidnapping, and "cliff hanging."

"Jack Armstrong" proved that the themes of law and order, clean living, good sportsmanship and decent behavior could attract and hold large, young audiences.

Jamesian Suggesting the subtle psychological nuances of the thought processes and moral dilemmas in characters created by Henry James (1843–1916), the American novelist and short story writer. These niceties and ambivalences of thought are reflected in the "Jamesian" style, with its long, complex sentences full of modifying clauses and phrases and balanced elements. James can spend 20 pages having his heroine consider whether or not to accept a dinner invitation.

James concerns himself with the upper classes, their refinements of taste, etiquette and morality. He writes especially of the interaction of two cultures: the American seeming more honest, more robust, more unpolished; the European seeming more devious, more aesthetic, more compromised.

The novels that best embody these Jamesian characteristics of substance and style are:

The Portrait of A Lady (1881). Isabel Archer, a young, free-spirited American girl who inherits a fortune, turns down her sturdy American suitor, Caspar Goodwood, as well as a British lord, Lord Warburton, only to be manipulated by the devious Mme. Merle into marrying a cultivated bounder, Gilbert Osmond, whose illegitimate child Mme. Merle has secretly borne.

The Ambassadors (1903). The upright American hero, Lambert Strethers, is sent to France to bring home a young American friend who has fallen for the charms of Mme. de Vionnet. Strethers, himself, comes to appreciate the pull of the sensual and the aesthetic in European culture. He concludes: "Live all you can; it's a mistake not to."

The Golden Bowl (1904). Maggie Verver, an American heiress, marries an Italian prince. She does not know that her best friend, the beautiful and brilliant Charlotte Stant, has had an affair with the prince. Maggie's devoted father falls in love with and marries Charlotte. These four characters then try to work out a palatable modus vivendi. Eventually, the solution is that the father and Charlotte return to live in America.

Jazz Age   The period of the 1920s in the United States. The Jazz Age took its name from the new syncopated black music, which was in great part improvisational and seemingly abandoned. F. Scott Fitzgerald labeled his time the Jazz Age. In his books this signified unconventionality, a get-rich-quick mentality, defiance of Prohibition in speakeasies, wild partying.

At the end of *The Great Gatsby* (1925) the narrator says of Tom and Daisy Buchanan, Jazz-Age types, "They were careless people, Tom and Daisy—they smashed up things and creatures and then retreated back into their money or their vast carelessness, or whatever it was that kept them together, and let other people clean up the mess they had made..." (See also JAY GATSBY.)

Jeeves   The impeccable, omniscient and ever resourceful valet to Bertie Wooster in the comic stories of P.G. Wodehouse (1881–1975): *My Man Jeeves* (1919), *The Inimitable Jeeves* (1923), *Carry On, Jeeves* (1925) etc.

A Jeeves is an imperturbable servant with more savvy and elegance than his master.

Jewel in the Crown, The   First novel (1966) of the *Raj Quartet* by Paul M. Scott (1920–1978), dealing with Anglo-Indian relationships in India before Independence, when India was considered the jewel in the crown of the British Empire. The *Quartet* was popularized in a fine BBC television series in 1984.

Jewel in the crown means the brightest, best, most valuable of an assortment, whether of colonies or cities or even of one's children.

Use: "For almost a generation I proudly participated in the cult of Jerusalem, the jewel in the crown of modern Israel. I looked down upon Jerusalem's antithesis: Tel Aviv, the humid, nondescript, hedonistic, unheroic, soft coastal city." (Meron Benvenisti, *New York Times Magazine*, October 16, 1988)

Jewish mother   Proverbial over-solicitous Jewish mother who suffocates her children, especially her sons, with too much tender loving care, too much chicken soup, too many sexual and moral restrictions, too many admonitions. Satirized in innumerable skits, plays, novels and movies, including Philip Roth's PORTNOY'S COMPLAINT (1969) and WOODY ALLEN's *New York Stories* (1989). The term has been extended to include any all-embracing, hovering, over-feeding, over-worrying mother of any ethnic background.

Joads   The "Okie" (Oklahoma) family of sharecroppers in John Steinbeck's epic novel *The Grapes of Wrath* (1939). Driven from their home in the "dust bowl" by bank takeovers and absentee landlords, by poverty and drought, the Joads (all 12 of them plus Jim Casy, an itinerant preacher) pile into a dilapidated truck with their meager possessions, and head for California, the land of milk and honey, where jobs supposedly await them. The journey turns into a desperate odyssey with Ma Joad bent on keeping the family together at all costs. In California, the conditions of migrant workers turn out to be a nightmare of cheap labor and brutal deputies. Tom Joad, the central character and Ma's son, becomes a man with a mission. He joins Jim Casy in organizing the workers for better wages, working conditions and liberties.

The Joads are the oppressed and the poor among farm workers in America. They struggle. They endure.

Joe Palooka   This comic strip champion boxer appeared in 1928 when boxing was in especially bad odor. Joe Palooka's simple, corny charm immediately caught on with the public. Joe is a lovable character—not too bright, but not corrupt or vicious. His somewhat gauche, not quite literate, commonplace utterances on home, motherhood, fair play etc., did not sit too well with sophisticated readers. But the vast "general public" found Joe irresistible.

In his speech and behavior, Joe Palooka embodied the great simplicities—still immensely attractive to most Americans.

Joe Six-pack   The ordinary blue-collar American male, given to consuming six-can cartons of beer.

Use: "Mr. Bush's aides claim it was their gut kicking, flag-waving, lefty-bashing campaign, which caused élitist tut-tutting but worked to win over Joe and Josie Six-Pack." (William Safire *The New York Times*, October 13, 1988)

John Bircher   Member of rightist, quasi-secret political organization founded in 1958 by Robert Welch, a Massachusetts businessman. The John Birch Society was named after a United States intelligence officer killed in 1945 by Chinese Communists.

Now, anybody with extremist, reactionary, rabid anti-communist views.

Jolson, Al   Born Asa Yoelson (1886–1950). American singer and actor, Jolson's life was the great American rags-to-riches story. Born in Srednicke, Russia, the son of a rabbi, he was brought to America as a child. At the age of eight, he was singing in the streets of Washington, D.C., where his father had settled. Extraordinarily talented and irresistibly drawn to the world of entertainment, Jolson by turns was boy soprano, whistler, singer in bars, burlesque, minstrel shows, vaudeville and, finally, the movies and the stellar role in the first talkie, *The Jazz Singer*.

Appearing in blackface in vaudeville and musical comedy, kneeling on one knee, his arms extended, Jolson made entertainment history with his singing of such hits as: "Rock-A-Bye My Baby With a Dixie Melody," "Swanee," "Mammy," "Sonny Boy," "April Showers," "You Made Me Love You."

Jonestown   Town in Guyana set up by the Rev. Jim Jones, leader of a cult called the Peoples Temple. There, in the jungle of South America in November 1978 over 900 American men, women and children were persuaded by their fanatical leader to take part in a mass suicide by drinking a potion of Kool-Aid and cyanide. This gruesome ending was triggered by an impending congressional investigation of the cult's totalitarian slant and bizarre sexual practices. Jones had murdered several people, including California Congressman Leo Ryan, who had come to investigate the goings-on in Jonestown.

Jonestown has become a symbol of the brainwashing practiced by perniciously fanatical religious cults.

Joycean   Linguistically adventurous and exuberant, life-affirming, as in the works of James Joyce (1882–1941), Irish novelist, short story writer and poet. Some of Joyce's identifying techniques were the stream of consciousness and the interior monologue (see MOLLY BLOOM), diversity of architectural form in the novel, especially in *Ulysses* (1922), and experimentation with language bordering on the incommunicable, as in FINNEGANS WAKE (1939). In substance Joyce was anticlerical, robust in his appreciation of the sensual and whatever else was life-enhancing. As Joyce wrote at the end of *A Portrait of the Artist as a Young Man* (1914): "Welcome, O life! I go to encounter for the millionth time the reality of experience and to forge in the smithy of my soul the uncreated conscience of my race."

joy ride   Originally referred to the sense of freedom conferred by the mobility of automobiles. Now, a joy ride may refer to any irresponsible fling, to an action that is fast and reckless without regard to consequences.

Jukes   In *A Study In Crime, Pauperism, Disease, and Heredity*, Richard L. Dugdale advanced the thesis that criminal tendencies are inherited. He traced the criminal careers of 540 blood relations to bolster his theory.

The best known of Dugdale's "cases" were the Jukes, dubbed "the most depraved family in America," a group of rapists, thieves, prostitutes, murderers. Widely accepted in its time, Dugdale's position does not have much support today. To be labeled a "Jukes," however, still carries the original stigma.

Jungian   Pertaining to the theories of Carl Gustav Jung (1875–1961), a Swiss psychiatrist who broke away from Freud in 1913. Jung exalted the power and importance of the unconscious over reason. A life based on reason alone was an impoverished life, he thought. He predicated, moreover, a collective unconscious of the race made up of archetypal patterns recurring throughout the history of man. These took the form of powerful myths common to all cultures.

Jung believed that personal psychic health could be achieved only by bringing the conscious and the unconscious selves into harmony. He divided personalities into two types: introvert (in touch with the inner self) and extrovert (diverted by the outside world at the expense of the inner self).

The term Jungian is usually applied to large, overriding, mythic symbols, as in William Butler Yeats' poem, "Leda and the Swan," or to the mystical sense of déja vu in large, recurrent historical patterns.

K

Kafkaesque   Having the nightmarish atmosphere of a short story or novel by Franz Kafka (1883–1924), a Jewish writer born in Prague and who wrote in German. Kafka's works, all published posthumously by his friend Max Brod, express the anxiety, the alienation, the terror, the irrationality inherent in major events of the 20th century. They may be seen as parables and allegories open to various interpretations: political, psychological and theological.

On the most obvious level, Kafka attacks the unwieldy bureaucracy of Eastern European countries. On the psychological level, Kafka works out his subconscious struggle against an overpowering father figure. On the theological level, Kafka questions the morality of the invisible God and His Law, and he is tortured by man's inability to achieve salvation.

The Trial (1925), surely one of the most seminal novels of the 20th century, tells the story of Joseph K, an ordinary, sober, rational bank manager who awakes one morning to be told by two strangers at his door that he is arrested. They cannot tell him his crime, nor do they haul him away to court or prison. Ostensibly, he can continue as usual with his normal routines. But he becomes obsessed with his "case" and he seeks help in identifying his crime and clearing himself of it. He finds himself in airless, crowded, dream-like chambers suffused with an erotic atmosphere. At the end of a year, to the day, still ignorant of his crime and unsuccessful in finding his judges, he is taken out of his flat by two executioners who slash his throat and leave him to die in the street "like a dog."

Kafka's material seems related to that of the German expressionist painters; his settings evoke the atmosphere of Raskolnikov's guilt-haunted attics; yet his prose is simple, direct and completely accessible. It is his meaning that eludes us. As Churchill once said of Russia, Kafka is "a riddle wrapped in a mystery inside an enigma." Anyone who has ever fallen victim to some computer error on the part of a department store clerk or a traffic violations bureau clerk and has tried in vain to disentangle himself from it will have found himself, on a very minor scale, in a Kafkaesque situation.

Victims in the Nazi death camps, cramped together in tiers of bunks, awaiting certain extermination yet not knowing exactly when they would be called, nor what their crime was, outside of being born Jewish, found themselves in a Kafkaesque nightmare from which they would never awake.

Use: Mike Feder (a monologist on WBAI radio) "often reflects on growing up in Laurelton, where his attic bedroom overlooked 'the largest Jewish cemetery in Queens.' Sometimes, he reminisces about his mother, a high-strung, paranoid woman who committed suicide. He talks about his father, a gruff man who left his family when Feder was four. Other times, he rambles—irritable one minute, unabashedly sentimental the next, but always darkly funny. The overall effect is a little like having Franz Kafka riding beside you and bending your ear on the Jamaica-bound F train." (*New York Magazine*, October 31, 1988)

Use: "Street mendicants in the Soviet Union rise up swift as the agonized beggars of Bombay to plead a far more Kafkaesque need than money." (Francis X. Clines, "Out in Moscow's Streets, Looking For Justice," *New York Times*, July 16, 1989)

kamikaze   Literally, "Divine Wind." Japanese pilot who performed the suicide mission of crashing his plane loaded with explosives into an enemy (American) warship during World War II. One who performs a reckless, seemingly suicidal act.

Use: Michael Dukakis "had been floating along on a remarkable run of luck; weeks after, his opponents performed Kamikaze missions against one another while he stood smugly above the fray..." (*New York Magazine*, March 1988)

karate   A Japanese method of self-defense without the use of weapons. The practice of karate involves striking the body's sensitive areas with hands, elbows, knees and feet. These strikes are called "karate chops." Administered by someone trained in karate, they can have a devastating effect on the attacker.

In general use, a karate chop can mean any well-aimed blow to an individual, an institution, a plan, etc.

Use: "Every so often, the old pols on Capitol Hill demonstrate anew the manipulative skills that got them into positions of power in the first place. The latest example, the Democratic maneuver on the Medicare surtax, was the political equivalent of a Karate chop on one of the year's hottest issues. The blow was delivered by Senator Lloyd Bentsen to President Bush." (*New York Times*, May 3, 1989)

Kaye, Danny   Actor (1913–1987). Born David Daniel Kaminsky in Brooklyn, New York. Starred in 17 movies, including *The Secret Life of Walter Mitty* (1947), *Hans Christian Andersen* (1952), and *White Christmas* (1954). Known for his lightning-speed, rhyming patter songs, written by his wife Sylvia Fine, and for his good-natured, zany clowning.

Keaton, Buster   Slapstick comedian (1896–1966) known for his stony-faced stoicism. He appeared in *Day Dreams* (1922), a kind of early version of Walter Mitty; *The Three Ages* (1923), in which he played a Christian martyr thrown to the lions; *The Navigator* (1924); and *The General* (1927).

Kent State   Kent State University, Kent, Ohio. On May 4, 1970, National Guardsmen opened fire on Kent State students peacefully demonstrating against the U.S. invasion of Cambodia during the Vietnam War. Four students were killed and nine injured. The nation was shocked and outraged. Kent State has become a symbol of the excessive use of force against peaceful demonstrations guaranteed by the U.S. Bill of Rights.

Use: "Played out daily on the television screens of the world is a political melodrama that pits rioting half-armed civilians against orderly uniformed military. The anti-authority reflex that lies at the core of modern liberalism is activated. It is Kent State writ large." (Jeane Kirkpatrick, in the *New York Post*, February 13, 1989, criticizing a State Department report on human rights practices for unfairly exaggerating violations in Israel.)

Keystone Kops   Characters in Mack Sennett's short movie come-dies. Crew of inept, idiotic policemen engaged in slapstick antics in silent films like *In the Clutch of a Gang.*
Generally, ineffectual and bumbling figures of authority.
Use: "In our haste to finish the treaty by December 8, we lost sight of our negotiating objective. The result was a diplomatic chase worthy of the Keystone Kops and a slapdash finale that left significant details so unclear that the Senate threatened to block ratification until the confusion cleared." (*U.S. News & World Report,* June 6, 1988)

KGB   *Komitet Gosudárstvennoi Bezopásnosti* (Committee for State Security). Intelligence agency of the Soviet Union organized in 1954, responsible for internal security and for clandestine operations abroad. Associated with secrecy, brutality and terror, it is the fist of BIG BROTHER.
KGB is sometimes applied to any official using high-handed meth-ods of investigation; an agent of oppression.

Killing Fields, The   American film (1984) based on the Pulitzer prize-winning articles by *New York Times* journalist Sidney Schanberg. The film depicts the experiences of Schanberg and Dith Pran, his native aide, in the shifting fortunes and horrors of war in Cambodia.
Use: "Killing Fields of Mozambique"—editorial headline in *New York Times*—"...100,000 people have been massacred in Mozam-bique—mainly by Renamo, a rebel group waging a bush war against Mozambique's left-wing regime. Civilians have been shot, knifed, axed, bayoneted, burnt, starved, beaten, drowned & throttled. Nearly a million have fled into exile."

Kilroy was here   Ubiquitous inscription left by victorious Ameri-can troops on walls and other surfaces all over the world during World War II. The mysterious and fictitious Kilroy has been adopted as a sign of one's passing through.
Use: "War is unfamiliar, unimaginable, insane, appalling...and men who have fought...have had a deep need to record what they saw and felt. Not for *us*, I think, but for themselves, to say like the ubiquitous Kilroy, I was there." (Samuel Hynes, *New York Times Book Review,* July 31, 1988)

kindness of strangers   "I have always depended on the kindness of strangers," says BLANCHE DU BOIS at the end of Tennessee Williams' play *A Streetcar Named Desire* (1947), as she takes the arm of a gentlemanly guard on her way to a mental institution. She is referring to the many men who gave her solace— sexual and financial—in the years before she arrived at her sister Stella's flat in New Orleans.

Use: Caption under a picture of Nicaraguan refugees in a Miami shelter: "The kindness of strangers...Refugees without family in the U.S. live by the kindness of strangers." (*Newsweek*, November 14, 1988)

King, Martin Luther, Jr.   Foremost leader (1929–1968) of the Civil Rights movement in the United States. Espousing the nonviolent means successfully employed in India by Mahatma Gandhi, King organized mass demonstrations, marches and boycotts to protest racial discrimination, to implement equal rights legislation and to foster harmony between blacks and whites. In 1963, he led a march on Washington, D.C., where he thrilled 250,000 demonstrators with his now-famous "I have a dream" speech. In 1964 he was awarded the Nobel peace prize.

Often misunderstood and vilified, beaten and jailed, King was at last assassinated by James Earl Ray in Memphis, Tennessee. In 1983, Congress declared January 15 a national holiday to commemorate his life and achievements. His name is synonymous with America's moral conscience in seeking to attain racial harmony and justice. (See also: I HAVE A DREAM; MONTGOMERY, ALABAMA; PARKS, ROSA.)

King Kong   RKO movie (1933) about a monster, conceived by Merian C. Cooper, with special effects by Willis O'Brien. The plot: A movie producer, Carl Denham, and his crew arrive on Skull Island in the Indian Ocean to film a legendary creature, a huge, monstrous ape. The natives seize the heroine, Fay Wray, and are about to sacrifice her to King Kong, when the ape himself appears, snatches the girl and flees with her. A thrilling chase follows in which Kong kills prehistoric animals. Denham finally subdues the giant ape with sleeping gas. He brings him back to New York to exhibit him. Enraged by flashbulbs, Kong breaks his chains and runs amok in the city, causing general panic. Fay Wray is "safe" in a hotel room when Kong smashes through a window, seizes the screaming actress and carries her to the top of the Empire State Building. The military is called out. Fighter planes pump bullets into his body. Kong sets Fay Wray down gently on a ledge and he falls to his death.

Kinsey Report   Or *Sexual Behavior in the Human Male*, a groundbreaking, scientific study based on 12,000 personal interviews and questionnaires. Conducted by Dr. Alfred Kinsey (1894–1956), a professor of zoology at the University of Indiana. Kinsey switched from observing the birds and the bees to studying the sexual habits of homo sapiens. He presented statistically sound evidence on the frequency in white males of masturbation, orgasm, oral sex, marital and extramarital intercourse etc. The *Kinsey Report* shocked and titillated the nation, but it exploded many false preconceptions about sexual activity in the human male and probably served unwittingly to spread sexual freedom or, as some contend, license.

Kiplingesque   Displaying the imperialistic attitudes contained in the phrase "the white man's burden," coined by Rudyard Kipling (1865–1936), British author born in India, the locale of most of his tales and poems.

Kirche, Küche, Kinder   German for church, kitchen and children. The Nazi slogan for the proper sphere of women, a sexist concept of women's interests. A stereotype of woman's place in the world.

Klee, Paul   Swiss painter (1879–1940). Influenced by cubism, primitive African art, and children's drawings, Klee developed a pictorial language uniquely his own. In his later years he studied ideographs of all kinds; indeed, some of his works seem to have incorporated ancient hieroglyphics as well as cabalistic signs. His paintings are playful, inventive, witty, imaginative and musical.

K Mart   Chain of department stores carrying inexpensive items at cut-rate prices. Symbol of bargain-basement products.
    Use: "Bobbie Ann Mason seldom steps inside a K Mart and she doesn't watch much MTV... These are somewhat surprising admissions considering that Ms. Mason's fiction is as well known for its pop culture flotsam as for its western Kentucky setting and hard-luck working class cast." (*New York Times* Book Review, March 12, 1989)

knockout (also kayo, K.O.)   To win a boxing match by literally knocking an opponent unconscious or rendering him unable to get up unassisted after the referee has counted 10 seconds over him.

In general use, an overpoweringly attractive woman, a highly successful action.

Use: Tarleton's sales campaign was a knockout. It put sales for the 1988 model ahead of all the competition.

"Kojak"   In this long-running television drama (began 1973) of crime, pursuit and punishment in a large city, Telly Savalas was Kojak, a tough, crafty, unglamorous detective lieutenant with a curious appetite for lollipops. Kojak's low-keyed manner conceals his fierce hatred for the criminals who constitute his daily fare. Stocky, entirely bald, Kojak is not the typical nemesis of wrongdoers. Underneath his rough exterior there is a reservoir of great tenderness and concern for the injured and the oppressed. Despite his unorthodox manner and appearance, Kojak is recognized and cherished all over the world as the embodiment of the "good cop."

Use: "Dukakis is Kojak with hair." (*U.S. News and World Report,* July 18, 1988)

Kowalski, Stanley   Character in *A Streetcar Named Desire* (1947), play by Tennessee Williams (1914–1983). Uncouth, animalistic, macho, beer-guzzling and poker-playing, he is a blue-collar worker of Polish immigrant stock. He is married to Stella, who comes of finer Southern sensibilities. In the course of the play he ruins Stella's visiting sister BLANCHE DU BOIS, whose pretensions to culture and refinement are as a red flag to a raging bull. He destroys Blanche's last chance for marriage, and when he sneeringly rapes her, he destroys her sanity. There is little doubt that the playwright meant Kowalski to be the villain, and yet it is Blanche who is sterile and Kowalski who fathers a child with Stella, a child who will probably turn out to be more robust than the faded southern gentility represented by Blanche. The role of Stanley was brilliantly played on stage and screen by Marlon Brando.

Use: "[Andy Capasso] was a well-meaning Stanley Kowalski type." (*New York Post,* September 21, 1987) (See also MARLON BRANDO.)

K.P.   Originally, an abbreviation for the enlisted men who were the U.S. Army's "kitchen police"; later applied to the kitchen chores themselves.

Krantz, Judith   American writer (1928–) of blockbuster novels with mass appeal, she writes modern fairy tales about heroines who fight their way from impoverished, if aristocratic, beginnings to great wealth and power in the glamorous worlds of fashion and advertising. Along the way, Krantz indulges her sexual fantasies. Her novels are: *Scruples* (1978), which was adapted for a TV mini series; *Princess Daisy* (1980), which netted Krantz over $5 million in prepublication sales; and *Mistral's Daughter* (1980), about a French painter and the three women in his life, also adapted for TV.

A Judith Krantz novel is an easy read about women on the make in a glamorous world. (See also JACQUELINE SUSANN.)

K-ration   Named for Ancel Keys, an American physiologist who devised a small packet of food containing all necessary nutrients for a soldier's emergency ration out in the field. K-ration now stands for minimalism in the taste or aesthetics of food preparation or service.

Kristallnacht   Literally, crystal night. The night of November 9, 1938, when booted Nazis in civilian clothes under orders from Josef Goebbels rampaged through Berlin, smashing thousands of store windows of Jewish merchants. The streets were littered with glass. They set fire to synagogues, beat people with truncheons and killed at least 90 Jews.

The ostensible justification for this outrage was the assassination of Ernst von Rath, the third secretary of the German Embassy in Paris, by a young Polish Jew, Herschel Grynspan.

Kristallnacht is the urban pogrom, sometimes used to describe mob violence—destruction of property, looting, personal assaults—especially when aimed at a particular segment of the population.

Use: The streets were littered with broken glass. It was Kristallnacht in Watts.

L

La Dolce Vita   Italian movie (1961) directed by FEDERICO FELLINI. Marcello Mastroianni stars as a gossip columnist disenchanted with the trivial, cynical, shallow lives of Rome society. He senses that he is no better than the paparazzi (photographers) who swarm around these social butterflies, but he is too spoiled, too indolent, too corrupted by "the sweet life" to change his ways, even after he glimpses a vision of innocence and purity in the form of a young girl at the end of the film. Literally, "la dolce vita" means the sweet life, the life of pleasure, idleness and self-gratification.

Use: "His looks, his town houses and chateaux and yachts, would have qualified him for a role in *La Dolce Vita.*" (Saul Bellow, *A Theft*)

Lady Chatterley   Heroine of *Lady Chatterley's Lover,* a novel by D.H. Lawrence (1885–1930), privately printed in Florence in 1928 and finally published in an unexpurgated edition in Britain and the United States in 1960. The wife of a wealthy but crippled land owner, Lady Constance Chatterley is sexually awakened and fulfilled by the gamekeeper on the estate, Oliver Mellors, the son of a miner. In committing adultery with a man of lower social class, she has doubly transgressed. She bears Mellors' child and asks for a divorce. D.H. Lawrence describes her sexual encounters with Mellors with such explicit detail and language that his publishers were prosecuted for, but eventually acquitted of, obscenity.

A Lady Chatterley is a woman awakened to ecstatic sexual passion.

152

lame duck   Duck whose wings have been clipped. A congressman or president of the United States who is known to be serving his last weeks or months in office because he was either defeated for reelection or, as in the case of the president, he has served the allowed two terms. Lame duck incumbents have lost their power; they have had their wings clipped.

The 20th Amendment to the Constitution (the "Lame Duck" Amendment, 1933) shortened the time between the November election day and the January inauguration day (now January 3 for Congress and January 20 for the president), thus curtailing the period of ineffectiveness.

Any person in an important position who has no clout because he is on his way out.

Use: "Reagan is politically crippled, personally faltering and lapsing toward irrelevance. 'It's happened,' says one of his senior advisors. 'He's a lame duck.'" (*Newsweek*, July 13, 1987)

Lansky, Meyer   One of the founders (1902–1983) of the national crime syndicate, he was widely regarded as "the most shadowy of the organized crime leaders." He was the "brains of the combination," respected, feared, and frequently consulted by all the Mafiosi. He handled their money and deposited their millions in secret Swiss bank accounts. Lansky's personal wealth was somewhere between $300 million and $400 million.

Lardner, Ring   Sports writer, newspaper columnist, humorist, sardonic pessimist and short story writer (1885–1933) who had a keen ear for the nuances of the vulgar American speech used by low-life, uneducated, quirky characters in the world of sports and entertainment. He wrote *You Know Me, Al* (1916), a collection of stories devoted to baseball's more moronic practitioners.

Last Hurrah, The   Title of a 1956 novel by Edwin O'Connor, in which a consummate politician of Irish extraction, Frank Skeffington, at the age of 73, announces his candidacy for reelection as mayor. "...he felt the same undimmed flush of joyous anticipation. Much as he loved to win, he loved the fight to win even more, and in his appraisal of his own strengths he put in first place that of the born campaigner." Skeffington is based on the career of Boston Mayor James Curley. A last hurrah is a final farewell.

Use: "*Reagan's Last Hurrah.* Although he maintains scrupulous neutrality in the G.O.P. presidential race, Ronald Reagan is planning a drive on behalf of the winner during the campaign's final week. Aides say that in his last political hurrah as President, Reagan will barnstorm through the South and the West, where he remains highly popular." (*U.S. News & World Report*, February 29, 1988)

Las Vegas   City of gambling casinos and night clubs in Nevada.

Laurel and Hardy   Stan Laurel (1891–1965) and Oliver Hardy (1892–1957), a slapstick comedy team who made their best silent movies from 1927 to 1929: *You're Darn Tootin, Battle of the Century, Big Business, Two Tars* etc. Laurel played the role of the trusting innocent; Hardy, the more worldly type whose pompous airs and inflated ego were constantly punctured. Together, they managed to create chaos with the response of "Who? Me?" Their violence might start with pushing and pie- throwing and end with a crescendo of destruction all around them. They stand for escalating mayhem in an absurd and petty vein.
Use: "We are deeply into the era of Laurel and Hardy politics...When did the fender-ripping . . . of the 1988 Presidential campaign all begin?" (William Safire, "Laurel and Hardy Politics," Op-Ed page *New York Times*, November 7, 1988)

lead with one's chin   In boxing, to leave one's weakest point unprotected, to expose one's most serious weakness, to invite a knockout.
In general use, to leave oneself vulnerable to attack or serious trouble.
Use: "The defendant was leading with his chin when he questioned the judge's honesty and competence."

Lebanon   Small Middle Eastern country on the shores of the Mediterranean, once a prosperous and civilized paradise, but virtually destroyed by contending religious factions. It has been reduced to rubble and anarchy after 14 years of civil war.
A symbol of the disintegration of a political or national entity.
Use: "Do El Salvador's leaders really want to see their country turn into a Central American Lebanon?" *New York Times* editorial, January 23, 1989, on how the brutal right-wing and brutal left-wing

elements must come to some accommodation if El Salvador is to survive.

lebensraum   German for "living space." HITLER's justification for his expansionist policies in Europe.
Now, the need for more space. For example: In violating the zoning law, the developer claimed he needed lebensraum to remain profitable.

Lee, Lorelei   The predatory, blond flapper heroine of *Gentlemen Prefer Blondes* (1925), an immensely popular novel by Anita Loos (1893–1981). It was adapted for Broadway in 1926, made into a movie in 1928 and staged as a musical comedy with Carol Channing in 1949. The hit song of the musical, "Diamonds Are a Girl's Best Friend," sums up the philosophy of the Lorelei Lees of this world.

Léger, Fernand   French painter (1881–1955) enraptured by and fixated on the machine age, so that even his human figures seem made up of tubular, mechanized parts and geometric shapes. He paints bicyclists, acrobats, workers, all happy in a machine- like utopia.

Lennie   Character in John Steinbeck's popular novel *Of Mice and Men* (1937), which was made into a play (1937) and a film (1939). Lennie Small and George Milton are a pair of itinerant farm workers in Salinas Valley, California, who dream of some day owning their own place. Lennie is strong but retarded. George is small-boned but cunning. George protects Lennie. Lennie "loves" soft furry things and has been known to hug animals to death. When Lennie accidentally kills the promiscuous wife of the boss' son Curly, George protects him from an angry mob by first calming him with stories of their dream-place and then shooting him in the head.
A Lennie is a brawny but dim-witted person who can unwittingly destroy fragile things because he doesn't know his own strength.

Leopold and Loeb   In 1924, when Nathan Leopold was 19 years old, and his friend Richard Loeb was 18 years old, they murdered their 14-year-old friend, Bobby Franks, son of a Chicago millionaire—just for the intellectual challenge of committing the perfect crime. Both

Leopold and Loeb were brilliant, gifted college students, sons of prominent, wealthy Chicago families.

The parents of the two murderers hired Clarence Darrow, the famous criminal lawyer, to defend their sons. In his brilliant defense, Darrow depicted Leopold as a paranoiac and Loeb as a dangerous schizophrenic, arguing eloquently against putting them to death. The jury returned a verdict of guilty by reason of insanity and sentenced them to life imprisonment for murder, plus 99 years for kidnapping.

A "Leopold-Loeb" crime is marked by calculated, cold-blooded sadism carried out for "kicks," for thrills.

less is more   Dictum coined by Mies van der Rohe of the Bauhaus School, which also gave birth to another slogan: "Form follows function." "Less is more" encapsulated the aim of clean, unadorned, economical forms in architecture, crafts and industrial design.

Use: "Takeshita's Scorecard After A Year: Less Is More" (Headline in *New York Times*, October 23, 1988)

Use: "This summer less is more. Shorts are shorter. Swimsuits are skimpier." (*New York Times*, July 27, 1989)

Levittown   Housing development consisting of practically identical one-family houses mass-produced by the builder, William Levitt, on Long Island, New York, and throughout the post-World War II United States. Actually these were attractive and moderately priced and have become a standard for low-to middle-income housing, in spite of their uniformity.

Lidice   Village in Czechoslovakia demolished by the Nazis in retaliation for the murder of a top-ranking German official, Reinhard Heydrich, the "Hangman of Europe." The Germans executed 1,300 of its civilian inhabitants.

Lidice is a reference to brutal and ruthless destruction for the sake of revenge.

Commemorated by Edna St. Vincent Millay in her verse play *Lidice.*

life of Riley   A luxurious lifestyle, living "in clover," free from care of any kind. Perhaps based on early 1900s songs about "Reilly," especially *The Best of the House Is None Too Good For Reilly.*

Use: If you win the lottery, you can lead the life of Riley for the rest of your days.

lightweight   A professional boxer weighing between 126 and 135 pounds. Officially, he boxes in the lightweight division against men of comparable weight.

In general use, lightweight has derogatory overtones: inconsequential, unimportant, small-time.

Use: Pay no attention to Hilary's opinions about current trends in international trade. He's an intellectual lightweight.

light year   Term taken from astronomy, it is the distance traveled by light in a single year. The speed of light multiplied by the number of seconds in a year equals 5.88 trillion miles. The distance between stars is so great that it is measured in light years. For example, the distance from our sun to the nearest star is over four light years.

Used colloquially for a great distance, as to express progress, or for a long time, e.g., man's full understanding of the interaction between body and mind is still "light years" away.

Use: In the play *Lend Me a Tenor* Philip Bosco, who plays an excitable impresario, hears that his Italian tenor "has inconsiderately died before performing. Bosco greets this news with the deadest of pans, blank-faced and unblinking, and he sustains this for what seems like light years." (Monty Arnold, "Bravo Bosco," in *Playbill*)

Li'l Abner   Al Capp's enduring contribution to the mythology of the comic strip. Since he appeared in 1934, Li'l Abner has remained one of the most popular comic strip characters. Actually, the 19-year-old Li'l Abner is six-foot-three. Throughout the strip's long life, he has played the endearing role of "noble savage"—a figure American readers have been especially fond of since the days of James Fenimore Cooper's Chingachgook in *The Last of the Mohicans*.

The strip's skillful mixture of surprise, suspense and humor proved irresistible. The comings and goings of such characters as Sir Cecil Cesspool and Lady Cesspool, the appearance of the Schmoo, the potent Kickapoo Joy Juice, and other inhabitants of Dogpatch provided a delicious, bizarre brew for its readers all over America.

lineup   A list of players taking part in a game, as in baseball, football.

By extension, lineup has come to mean a list of participants in any activity of event.

Use: The lineup for the Constitution Forum contains some well-known speakers and scholars.

litmus test   A chemical test in which a piece of litmus paper is moistened with a solution. If the paper turns red, the solution is acid; if the paper turns blue, the solution is alkaline. Used figuratively today to mean a test of attitude in which there is only one decisive factor.

Use: "My private litmus test for the liberalisation currently under way in the Soviet Union was to see whether they would publish Grossman's novel [*Life and Fate* by Vassili Grossman]. They are starting to serialize it in a leading Moscow magazine and I'm absolutely delighted." (Tariq Ali, *Sunday Times Magazine*, November 15, 1987)

Little Orphan Annie   This comic strip, which made its debut in 1925, consisted essentially of a series of morality plays. The heroine, Little Orphan Annie, with her only friends, her dog Sandy and her doll Emily Marie, stands alone against the world. Daddy Warbucks, originally a munitions manufacturer, acquires extraordinary powers that enable him to mete out justice "arbitrarily, ruthlessly, and quietly."

The strip embodied its creator's (Harold Gray) conservative political and social views, and made it to the movies, to radio, to the phenomenally popular Broadway play *Annie*, and into the world of popular song with Annie's rendition of "Tomorrow, Tomorrow."

Little Rock   City in Arkansas where a major struggle for school integration took place throughout September 1957. Not until after President Dwight Eisenhower sent in federal troops, in a showdown with Governor Orval Faubus and a mob of white segregationists, were nine black children permitted to enter Central High School.

Little Rock has become a landmark in the continuing expansion of civil rights for blacks. It represents a hard-won triumph over school segregation.

Lloyd, Harold   Silent film comedian (1893–1971). Lloyd, with the horn-rimmed glasses, played hayseed characters who earnestly set out to make good in the big city. Along the way he had to take some pratfalls, but eventually his eternally optimistic Horatio Alger-type character succeeded. Slapstick stunt episodes involving chases and dangling from tenement roofs were both chilling and hilarious. His films include *Never Weaken* (1921), *Safety Last* (1923), *Girl Shy* (1924), *The Freshman* (1925).

Lolita   A nymphet in Vladimir Nabokov's satirical novel *Lolita* (1958). The sexually precocious Lolita inflames a college professor. Together they run away, from motel to motel, in a series of comic adventures across the breadth of the United States, with every scene offering readers a devastating picture of American manners, mores, morals and glitz.

Loman, Willy   Main character in *Death of a Salesman* (1949), a play by Arthur Miller (1915–). Willy Loman is a pathetic (some say tragic), confused, traveling salesman who is a failure at everything. Unable to make a living as he grows older, he daydreams about past glories (mostly imagined) and about missed opportunities as an entrepreneur. Having foisted his shoddy values about success onto his two sons, he cannot understand why success eludes them. At the age of 60 he feels discarded. Only his wife understands his perplexity at the disparity between his dreams and his reality. At the end, he commits suicide so that his son Biff may make a new start with the insurance money.
   A Willy Loman is a person who thinks he can make it on a smile and a slap on the back. He is discarded when he can no longer bring in profits for his boss.

Lonely Crowd, The   Scholarly work in sociology, (1950) which became a best seller in spite of its subtitle: "A Study of the Changing American Character." Written by David Riesman (1909–), it showed the relationship between socioeconomic development and national character. Riesman coined the now popular terms "inner-directed" and "other-directed." His phrase "the lonely crowd" has become a catchword for alienated residents of cities.

"Lone Ranger, The"   One of the most popular Western series programs, first on radio (1933) and then on television (1949–1961).

The opening of each episode captured the essence of the Lone Ranger's character and mission:

"A fiery horse with the speed of light...a cloud of dust and a hearty Hi-Yo Silver, the Lone Ranger. With his faithful Indian companion Tonto, the daring and resourceful masked rider of the plains led the fight for law and order in the early West. Return with us now to the thrilling days of yesteryear...The Lone Ranger rides again. Hi-Yo Silver and a-w-a-y"—to the accompaniment of pounding hoofs and Rossini's pulsating *William Tell* overture.

So popular had the Lone Ranger and his horse Silver become, that the "Hi-Yo Silver" call was, according to historian Irving Settel, actually used as a password by American troops entering Algiers during World War II.

The Lone Ranger is the sturdy archetype of the one good man against the evils of the world.

Use: "To his credit, Mr. Persico does not make his story a mindless saga in which [Edward R.] Murrow is the Lone Ranger, capable of accomplishing all that he did without a team of talented collaborators." From a review of a biography of Edward R. Murrow, *New York Times*, January 15, 1989)

Lonigan, Studs   Main character in James T. Farrell's trilogy: *Young Lonigan: A Boyhood in Chicago Streets* (1932), *The Young Manhood of Studs Lonigan* (1934) and *Judgment Day* (1935). Studs travels a path of moral and spiritual degradation as he changes from an outwardly tough but inwardly sensitive 15-year-old growing up in the squalor of Chicago's South Side to an out-and-out hoodlum who dies of alcohol and venereal disease at the age of 29. He is seen as a victim of our time, a boy who receives no meaningful direction from church, family, school or community. Farrell paints his character's world with an immense accumulation of naturalistic detail, including crude language, lewd attitudes toward sex, brutality against minorities.

loose cannon   Military term applied in 1986–87 to Marine Lt. Col. Oliver North, aide to National Security Advisor Admiral John Poindexter. From his office in the White House, North managed the various deals in what came to be known as the Iran- Contra affair: selling arms to Iran for the release of American hostages in Lebanon and diverting the profits to the Contras in Nicaragua. When these secret deals, made outside legitimate government channels, came to light, North shredded incriminating documents. He was dismissed from his job. North took the Fifth (see TAKE THE FIFTH) until he was granted limited immunity in testifying before the Senate panel hearings on Iran-Contra. Although he testified that he had acted on orders from Poindexter, he seemed generally to have had a free hand in far-reaching military and political transactions —for somebody who had the rank of Lieutenant Colonel.

Use: "Mr. Wallach [Robert Wallach, the personal lawyer and friend of Edwin Meese, the attorney general under President Reagan] was a loose cannon, which is why Mr. Meese should have watched him closely." (Reference to Middle East oil pipeline contract, *New York Times* editorial, February 24, 1988)

Lord Jim   Tragic hero of the novel *Lord Jim* (1900) by JOSEPH CONRAD. Guilty of a youthful, cowardly act in a moment of great confusion and indecision when, together with the rest of a ship's crew, he abandons ship before its passengers can be rescued, he spends the rest of his life trying to redeem his honor by some noble deed. In the end, his death is his salvation.

A Lord Jim is a romantic who cannot come to grips with his own human frailty.

Lost Generation   A term coined by GERTRUDE STEIN. "You are all a lost generation," she said to ERNEST HEMINGWAY. She was referring to him and his co-expatriate writers and artists who remained in Paris after World War I, without roots, without commitment, without illusions. See *The Lost Generation* by Malcolm Cowley and *A Moveable Feast*, a posthumous autobiography by Hemingway.

Louis, Joe (Joseph Louis Barrow)   Boxer (1914–1981). His long string of ring victories, mostly by knockout, earned him the sobriquet the Brown Bomber, and the world's heavyweight championship. He retired undefeated, having defended his title 25 times (but later returned and lost two fights).

Joe Louis was universally regarded as "one of the most beloved sportsmanly figures in boxing." In 1954, he was inducted into the Boxing Hall of Fame.

low blow   A boxer who hits his opponent below the belt is said to have delivered a low blow. For this infraction of the rules, the boxer may lose points, or lose the round, or, in some instances, be disqualified and lose the match.

In general use: an unfair, unsportsmanlike, cowardly attack.

Use: During the presidential campaign the candidates traded low blows in their TV ads. (See also HITTING BELOW THE BELT.)

Lower East Side   Immigrant ghetto, principally Jewish, of New York City in the early decades of the 20th century. Within this overcrowded, squalid area, in tiny railroad flats in dingy tenements on filthy streets were housed about a million Jewish emigrants from Eastern Europe (especially Russia and Poland), who had sailed in steerage across the Atlantic to seek freedom from persecution as well as economic opportunity in the Golden Land. With them they brought the Yiddish language and the ghetto culture of the shtetl. However, they were ambitious to enter the mainstream of America through education and hard work. Upward mobility sent these immigrants "uptown" and into the outer boroughs of New York.

The Lower East Side is a nostalgic symbol of poverty-stricken immigrants of all nationalities who eventually made it as full-fledged Americans and in the process contributed significantly to the economic, educational and artistic growth of the United States. The term evokes the smells, the foods, the pushcarts, the Sabbath preparations, the Yiddish-English argot, the sweatshops, the noisy vendors, the crowds of a bygone era.

lunatic fringe   Phrase used by Theodore Roosevelt at the end of his public career to describe men of excessive zeal within reform movements, "The foolish fanatics always to be found in such a movement and always discrediting it—the men who form the lunatic fringe in all reform movements."

Now used mostly to describe violent advocates of fundamentalist doctrines.

Lunt and Fontanne   Alfred Lunt (1892–1977) and Lynn Fontanne (1887–1983). Although each was a Broadway star before they were married, they became, after their marriage in 1922, the most glamorous couple in the history of the American legitimate theater. They appeared together in 27 plays, most of them sophisticated comedies like *The Guardsman* (1924), *Design for Living* (1932) and *Idiot's Delight* (1936). However, they were capable of brilliant ensemble acting in such serious dramas as Friedrich Dürrenmatt's *The Visit* (1960). They were stylish and urbane.

Lunt and Fontanne are as inseparable in theater history as caviar and champagne.

Lusitania   British-owned luxury liner sunk by a German submarine off the coast of Ireland on May 8, 1915. Among the 1,198 passengers who drowned, 128 were Americans. This was one of the events that eventually propelled the United States into World War I. The sinking of the Lusitania was condemned by Theodore Roosevelt as "an act of piracy."

M

Macavity The mystery cat in T.S. Eliot's book of poems *Old Possum's Book of Practical Cats* (1939). He is humorously described as "a fiend in feline shape," "the Napoleon of crime" and the elusive "bafflement of Scotland Yard," for

> He always has an alibi, and one or two to spare:
> And whatever time the deed took place—
> MACAVITY WASN'T THERE!

Macavity is a lightly ironic allusion to the sort of "criminal" who would steal a cookie out of the cookie jar.

McCarthyism From Joseph R. McCarthy (1907–1957), Republican senator from Wisconsin. As chairman of the Senate Committee on Government Operations, he first achieved notoriety by charging that communists and communist sympathizers had infiltrated the State Department. From 1950 to 1954 his witch-hunt for communists in every agency of government and the media paralyzed dissent and threatened to subvert constitutional liberties. He wrecked the careers and even the lives of many innocent people by unsubstantiated accusations, innuendo and bullying.

Today McCarthyism refers to the impugnment, by unfair and even malicious investigations, of a person's political loyalty or integrity in order to squelch dissent.

Use: "Capitol Hill's good old days, with heavy drinking and skirt-chasing discreetly ignored by the press, began to be numbered in 1969, when Teddy Kennedy drove off a bridge at Chappaquiddick. Subse-

164

quent scandals, from Wilbur Mills in the Tidal Basin to Gary Hart and The Monkey Business, kept notching up the minimum standards of official morality. Ideological sins have lost their bite, but there's growing fear of moral McCarthyism." (*Newsweek*, March 13, 1989)

McPherson, Aimee Semple   Or Sister Aimee (1890–1944), Canadian-born American evangelist and faith healer. She founded the Four-Square Gospel movement in 1918, which grew to encompass 400 branch churches in the United States and Britain. "Are you four-square?" is the greeting used by her followers. In 1923, she opened the lavish, 5,000-seat, permanent home of the movement, the Angelus Temple in Los Angeles, California. A consummate showwoman, she used all kinds of theatrical effects (music, lighting, costumes, tableaux) to attract followers. She made a fortune. In 1926 she and her mother (her manager) were indicted for fraud, but the charges were dropped. With her various love affairs, escapades, even a false claim to having been kidnapped, she made sensational headlines. She died of an overdose of sleeping pills in 1944.

She was a prototype of all those "healers" who make money out of religion and sensation.

madeleine   An oval-shaped French cookie that plays a key part in stimulating the train of reminiscences within Marcel, the narrator of *À La Recherche du Temps Perdu (Remembrance of Things Past)* (1913–1927) by Marcel Proust (1871–1922). One day, Marcel's mother serves him some madeleines. He dips one into his tea to soften it, and suddenly his entire childhood at Combray comes flooding back to him. Thus begins *Swann's Way*, the first novel of the series.

A madeleine suggests any object or gesture, anything that opens the floodgates of memory.

Madison Avenue   Street in Manhattan now lined with elegant international boutiques but usually associated with the world of high-powered, slick advertising.

Use: "The selling of the Republican presidential candidate in the '88 election campaign had all the earmarks of a Madison Avenue media blitz."

Mafia   A secret organization engaged in such criminal activities as loan-sharking, gambling, dope smuggling, prostitution, racketeering, infiltrating legitimate businesses, controlling unions.

The exact origin of the Mafia is not entirely clear. But on this much there is some agreement: It was founded in Italy in the 1300s to fight French oppressors. By the 1880s, it had established itself in America. From then on, it has devoted its energies to exclusively criminal activities.

In its present form, the Mafia was organized by Lucky Luciano and Meyer Lansky in the 1930s. The Mafia structure is usually built around crime families (about 24) located in major American cities. Each family is headed by a boss. Serving as his "assistants" are under-bosses (consigliere), lieutenants (capos) and soldiers (rank and file).

When Mafia families are not feuding or killing each other, they work together under a network of agreements, which, under the leadership of master criminals Luciano and Lansky, unified gangs into a "vast national criminal syndicate" with a board of directors, assigned territories and areas of influence, plus an enforcement arm—MURDER, INCORPORATED (defunct since 1940s).

Mafia is often applied to a small, powerful, highly organized clique or a group of "insiders" within a larger organization.

Use: "In President John F. Kennedy's time, some of his confidants and assistants were referred to as the "Irish Mafia."

Mafia kiss (kiss of death)   In Mafia circles, a kiss on the lips, when administered by a fellow-Mafioso, is a warning of impending danger or death. It is said that Vito Genovese, a Mafia boss, gave Joe Valachi, an associate, such a kiss "for old times' sake." Fearing that his days were numbered, Valachi turned informer and provided the government with some of the most sensational revelations in underworld history.

magic bullet   Popular name for salvarsan, a chemical compound for the treatment of syphilis. Syphilis had been a deadly scourge for centuries until Paul Ehrlich, a German physician and bacteriologist (1834–1915), discovered a substance effective against it. It is also known as "606" because it was the 606th substance that Ehrlich was experimenting with. In 1908 Ehrlich shared the Nobel Prize in medicine with Elie Metchnikoff for their work in immunology. Ehrlich named his discovery Salvarsan, meaning salvation, but the "Magic Bullet" has taken over in the popular imagination. Today, by extension, a magic bullet may be the longed-for cure for any deadly disease, whether medical or economic or social. In other words, a panacea.

Use: "Every gain in the fight against AIDS raises hope that a magic bullet can be fashioned to cure the disease." ("Making Do Without a Magic Bullet," *U.S. News & World Report*, February 20, 1989)

Magic Mountain, The   In German, *Der Zauberberg* (1924), one of the great novels of the 20th century, by the German writer Thomas Mann (1875–1955). It is a study of disease—specifically, the tuberculosis that brings the characters, as patients or visitors, to the Berghof Sanatorium in Davos, Switzerland, but symbolically, the malaise that infects all of Europe before the outbreak of World War I.

Hans Castorp, the main character, a German engineer of no special talent or virtue, comes to visit his sick cousin Joachim. He falls under the spell of the mountain, develops a touch of tuberculosis himself and stays for seven hermetic years. He falls in love with a languorous Russian woman, Clavdia Chauchat, "the Asiatic principle," who carelessly lets doors slam behind her. He also becomes the intellectual bone of contention between Settembrini, an Italian liberal humanist, and Naphta, a rigid absolutist and neo-fascist. The atmosphere on the mountain is febrile, erotic, contentious and self-absorbed.

The Magic Mountain is a place where one can let go. It is a place where one needn't bother with the duties or the constraints of the real world. It is a place to which people have withdrawn to concentrate on their own disease, their own psyche, a place where time is of no importance, where endless talk substitutes for action, where X rays are exchanged instead of snapshots, where shadows replace reality, where vague romantic and mystical notions replace the pragmatism of the bourgeois way of life in the flatland below.

Maginot Line   Named after Andre Maginot, French minister of defense from 1929 to 1932, this supposedly impregnable 200-mile-long system of fortifications was built by France along the Franco-German border. Unfortunately, the guns were fixed to face east. In 1940, early in World War II, the invading German armies simply outflanked the line by advancing through Belgium, thus rendering it useless. Symbol of fixed, inflexible system of defense that can be outmaneuvered.

Magritte, Rene   Belgian surrealist painter (1898–1967) who used incongruous juxtaposition of ordinary objects (a man's hat, a cane, an apple) for haunting effect. His planes of color were clear, flat and precise. His canvases make the viewer do a double-take: Can he have seen what he thought he saw?

Use: Mark Lamas, an innovative director of Shakespeare's plays, proposes that *Pericles* be produced "as a Magritte landscape with a rocking chair floating in the sky." (*New York Times*, March 5, 1989)

Maigret, Inspector Jules   Detective in the novels of prolific Belgian writer Georges Simenon (1903–1989). Maigret is of bourgeois origin. He is married and has a shabby little apartment on the Boulevard Richard-Lenoir and he goes home to lunch with Mme. Maigret. His chief recreation is going for walks with his wife and going to the movies. He smokes pipes, wears an overcoat and a bowler hat and he's clean-shaven. He is an intuitive detective who gets the feel of a crime by acclimatizing himself to the environment in which it was committed. Unlike Sherlock Holmes he does not use the process of ratiocination in solving his cases. Maigret's patience and compassion often get the criminal to confess.

Main Street   Novel (1920) by Sinclair Lewis (1885–1951) in which the Main Street of Gopher Prairie, Minnesota comes to stand for the provincialism of the majority of small towns in the United States. The heroine, Carol Milford, who is married to the kindly but rather ordinary town doctor, Will Kennicott, struggles in vain to rouse its inhabitants from their apathy and to introduce them to culture.

major league   See MAKE THE BIG LEAGUE.

make the big league (or major leagues)   In baseball, to be chosen to play in either of the two major professional leagues: the National or the American.

Big League or Major League means to attain the highest professional recognition, the best, the highest, the most important, most respected.

Use: "When Carlton was invited to join the front office staff, he knew he had at last made the major leagues."

make my day   Provocative words used by Clint Eastwood in the movie *Dirty Harry* (1971) as he aimed his gun at a thug. Words associated with vigilantes fighting crime on their own, without benefit of police.

"Make my day" laws in several states (Colorado, Oklahoma) legitimize the killing of intruders who use force after breaking into one's home.

Use: "It's not enough for the President [Reagan] to reach for his six-shooter, snorting 'make my day.' In the end, even worthy goals falter without the means and public support to implement them." (*New York Times* editorial, "Fast and Hasty Draw in the Gulf," May 27, 1987) (See also CLINT EASTWOOD.)

Malcolm X   Born Malcolm Little (1925–1965), a powerful, charismatic black American activist. In the political ferment of the 1960s, Malcolm X split from the movement led by Elijah Muhammad (The Nation of Islam) and formed his own group, *The Organization of Afro-American Unity*. The growing hostility and bitterness that had grown up between these groups reached its peak with the assassination of Malcolm X in a Harlem mosque on February 21, 1965.

Malcolm X has become a symbol of radical, militant black activism and separatism. In his time, he was a rallying point for the energies and aspirations of militant, revolutionary American blacks.

Maltese Falcon, The   Film classic (1941) directed by John Huston, based on detective story by Dashiell Hammett. HUMPHREY BOGART plays Sam Spade, a private eye hired by Mary Astor to retrieve a valuable piece of sculpture, the Maltese Falcon, from various sinister characters (Peter Lorre, Sydney Greenstreet), all of whom are plotting against each other. In an anti-romantic reversal, Bogart at the end of the film turns Astor in to the police for murder.

Use: In a review of *Stevie: A Biography of Stevie Smith* in the *New Yorker* (September 28, 1987), Clive James writes: "Barbara and Mc-Brien (the authors) were right to go in search of her. It was worth the legwork and the long stakeout. Stevie Smith is a rare bird, a Maltese Falcon."

Mandrake the Magician   Comic strip character who first appeared in the strip bearing his name on June 11, 1934. Mandrake was the music hall magician par excellence—complete with slicked, parted hair-do, waxed moustache and magic wand. Originally, Mandrake possessed supernatural powers. Later in the script, he assumed a more credible persona, relying only on his mastery of hypnotism and illusion, his extraordinary intelligence, ingenuity and courage to subdue his formidable enemies.

"Wearing a top hat and white gloves, the princess' attendant looks as if he is applying for the position of Mandrake The Magician." (From a review of Shakespeare's *Love's Labour's Lost* in *The New York Times*, February 23, 1989)

Manhattan Project   Code name given to the massive, all-out, secret American effort to develop the atomic bomb before Germany could produce one during World War II. A group of internationally eminent physicists (Enrico Fermi, Nils Bohr, Harold Urey, Ernest O. Lawrence, Robert Oppenheimer, etc.) were brought together at various locations in the United States (Los Alamos, New Mexico, Oak Ridge, Tennessee, etc.) to harness atomic fission. On July 16, 1945, they exploded the first atomic bomb at Alamogordo, New Mexico, (See also ATOM BOMB.)

Man in the Gray Flannel Suit   Title of a novel (1955) by the American writer Sloan Wilson. A Madison Avenue type executive who commutes daily from his suburban home to the big city.

Manson, Charles   Cult leader (1934–) of a "family" of drifters and hippies. They lived, totally dominated by Manson, in a commune outside Los Angeles where they practiced free love, experimented with drugs and held pseudo-religious rites with Manson as the central, Christ-like figure.

On the night of August 9, 1969, Manson and three of his female followers, Patricia Krenwinkel, Susan Atkins and Leslie Van Houten, entered the Beverly Hills home of Roman Polanski, murdered his pregnant wife, Sharon Tate, and four others—all shot, stabbed, clubbed to death. They used the victims' blood to scrawl messages— "Pig," "War" etc.—on the walls.

Two nights later, the murderers committed the same atrocities at the home of Leo and Rosemary La Bianca.

All the killers were captured, tried and sentenced to death. But a Supreme Court ruling outlawed the death penalty and gave them life sentences instead.

Manson and his bizarre crew are typical of the "crazies" of the time—essentially deranged, living in a world of their own, totally surrendering their will to their "leader," guided by homegrown, off-the-wall, exotic principles and practices.

Use: "The 'reason' Hedda Nussbaum gives for her failure to leave her monstrous lover, or to prevent him from harming her daughter, or even to call for help to save the child, is that Joel Steinberg had 'Supernatural, god-like powers over her.' We should remember that Charles Manson was godlike, too." (*Newsweek*, November 16, 1989)

Man Who Came to Dinner, The   Play (1939) by Moss Hart and George S. Kaufman about a character based on Alexander Woollcott, a drama critic and founding member of the Algonquin Round Table, infamous for his vicious wit. In the play, Sheridan Whiteside, a dinner guest in the home of a midwestern family, breaks his leg. He remains for several weeks, virtually a dictator, commandeering the entire household and hurling gratuitous insults at everybody. When in the last scene he is finally getting ready to depart, to the infinite relief of his enslaved hosts, he breaks his leg again.

"The man who came to dinner" is a guest who has overstayed his welcome.

Man With the Golden Arm, The   Naturalistic novel (1949) by American writer Nelson Algren (1909–1981). The main character, Frankie Machine, is a Chicago gambling house dealer whose addiction to heroin ruins him and drives him to suicide on Skid Row.

Now generally refers to heroin shooters.

"The March of Time"   A phenomenally popular radio news broadcast (1931–1945), it presented highly colorful dramatizations of important news events (also a movie theater newsreel, begun in 1935 by Time Inc.). Each program ended in a riveting, crescendo "TIME...marches O-N-N-N." For years, the announcer's voice was kept secret. Probably the most distinctive voice of its time, it was eventually revealed as that of Westbrook Van Voorhis.

Use: "'Boys, this is the nerve center of the newspaper,' he said, his voice heavy and solemn, like the voice of Westbrook Van Voorhis, the March of Time man, when he said 'Time Marches On.'" (Russell Baker, *The Good Times*)

Mariel   Port on northwest coast of Cuba from which refugees sailed in open boats to the coast of Florida in 1980. Mariel has come to be associated with mass migration from Central America.

Use: "Some 300 Nicaraguans arrive in Miami each week. We have a Mariel in slow motion." (*Newsweek*, November 14, 1988)

Marlboro Man   The central, commanding figure in the ads for Marlboro Cigarettes since the late 1950s. Dressed in a shearling jacket, cowboy hat and boots, a faint smile playing over his deeply-tanned features, he gazes, supremely confident, over the vast terrain: the archetypal "strong, silent man." He is master of all he surveys: the cattle, all the known and unknown rigors and perils around him. He radiates a quiet fearlessness. He is the quintessential embodiment of the virile American male.

Use: "The Los Angeles police are the toughest in the country, they will pridefully tell you, Marlboro Men on motorcycles, who take no lip from anyone and play it by the book." (*New York Times*, September 27, 1989)

Marlowe, Philip   A fictional detective created by Raymond Chandler (1888–1959). He is the chief character in *The Big Sleep* (1939), *Farewell, My Lovely* (1940), *The Lady in the Lake* (1943), *The Long Goodbye* (1953). He epitomizes the private eye. Trouble is his business. He operates from a one-man agency in Los Angeles and is only marginally financially successful. He is honest and loyal, witty, more educated than most private eyes and is able to quote Browning and Eliot, play chess for relaxation and enjoy classical music and art.

Marshall Plan   Plan proposed by United States Secretary of State George C. Marshall on June 5, 1947, for the economic recovery of Europe after World War II.

Use: "We need a Marshall Plan, a Berlin airlift for the cities." (Stella Schindler, director of New York Mayor Ed Koch's Office for the Homeless; quoted in *Newsweek*, March 21, 1988)

Marx, Groucho   Comedian (1895–1977), one of the zany Marx Brothers, prominent on stage, television and in film. The team consisted of *Harpo*, a mute kleptomaniac, master harpist and pantomimist. *Chico*, a pianist, philosopher, confidence man, master of broken English. *Zeppo*, fairly normal in speech and behavior, who left the group in 1933, and *Groucho*.

Groucho wore a long frock coat, sported an oversize cigar and a large, painted-on moustache. The mere appearance of an attractive woman activated his lascivious leer as he coyly wagged his eyebrows at his "prey." Bent over, lurching (not walking), Groucho seemed propelled by some interior mechanism. A "crack-shot wit," quick on the repartee, a lover of atrocious puns and insults, he "made mincemeat of logic and personalities."

Groucho wrote many of his own lines. Others were turned out by such gifted writers as S.J. Perelman, George S. Kaufman, Ben Hecht. Typical of Groucho's style and substance are these lines from one of his films: "I could dance with you 'til the cows come home. On second thought, I'd rather dance with the cows 'til you come home."

Marx Brothers   See MARX, GROUCHO.

"M*A*S*H"   Popular television series based on a fictional medical unit operating close to the front during the Korean War. MASH is an acronym for Medical Army Surgical Hospital. In the show, dedicated doctors and nurses cope with bloody war casualties by adopting a veneer of cynicism akin to black comedy. The last episode, in December 1983, was seen by 12.5 million viewers in the United States.

Synonymous with the kind of mordant with that permits people in the midst of mayhem to distance themselves from their natural responses and feelings.

Use: "Hospital emergency rooms are the M*A*S*H units of the drug wars, places where rhetoric is irrelevant and 'cool' turns deadly." (*U.S. News & World Report*, March 21, 1988)

Mastroianni, Marcello   (1923–) Italian film star idolized by women for his romantic good looks and his world-weary persona. Achieved international fame as the rueful, yet wistful journalist enmeshed in the decadent society of modern Rome in FELLINI's LA DOLCE VITA (1960).

Mata Hari   Margaretha Geertruida Zelle, a Dutch femme fatale who spied for the German secret service. She betrayed military secrets confided to her by Allied officers and was executed by the

French on October 15, 1917, at the age of 41. A Mata Hari is a female spy who seduces men to obtain secrets.

Use: "A swallow is an agent that seeks sexual contact with targeted individuals in order to gain access to information. The term for these modern Mata Haris began to gain popularity in the West in the 1960s." (*New York Times Magazine*, July 27, 1987)

Matisse, Henri   French painter and sculptor (1869–1954) who was the leading figure among the fauvists. As such, he liberated the world's conventional conception of color and color combinations. His canvases were vibrant with flat planes of brilliant color used to delineate not only his women and the decorative textiles of their dress but their backgrounds as well. Walls, carpeting, table cloths, household objects dazzled with an almost Moorish lavishness of color. Even late in life, when Matisse turned to découpés, his paper cutouts were riotous with unorthodox juxtapositions of color, except for his Blue Nudes, which were simply blue on white. The stained glass windows that he designed for the Dominican Chapel of the Rosary in Venice glowed with color.

Matisse's aim, philosophy and practice in painting can be summed up in one word: joy. He wanted to give the viewer the pleasure he experienced in the art of painting. And he painted what was joyful. His *The Joy of Life* (1905) is a pagan bacchanal. *The Dance* is a huge painting of a circle of figures holding hands and stomping with Dionysian ecstasy. His odalisques are women luxuriating in sensuous repose.

Mau-Mau   Anti-white terrorist society of Kenya, an East African British colony formed in 1925. Consisting mostly of Kikuyu tribe members under the leadership of Chief Jomo "Burning Spear" Kenyatta, the Mau-Mau murdered and pillaged all through the 1950s in an attempt to drive the white settlers from the fertile highlands. Kenyatta was sentenced to seven years of hard labor, but eventually became the first president of Kenya. Today Mau-Mau is associated with brutal revolutionary tactics and is applied to extremists, especially among black militants.

mean streets   From the title of the 1967 autobiography *Down These Mean Streets* by Piri Thomas, in which the author recounts the hazards of growing up Puerto Rican on the streets of Harlem.

medium is the message, the   A phrase formulated by the Canadian social scientist, Marshall McLuhan (1911–1980). Just as the means influence the end (the other side of the notion that the end justifies the means), McLuhan perceived that the medium of communication in an electronic age would have more potential influence than the message it carried. In fact, the medium *is* the message. He recognized that radio, TV, films, computers would radically alter the ways in which we experience the world, since these mass electronic media would make a global village of the world. He saw that these new forms of communication would have far-reaching sociological, aesthetic and philosophical consequences.

A catchword for powerful methods of presentation, as in violent video where the meaning is not clear but the brutality imprints itself.

Use: "God is not only present in these narratives but sometimes has a 'speaking part'...The messages are neither surprising nor profound...No new commandments are issued, no explications of old Scriptures given, but rather 'The medium is the message.'" (Dan Wakefield, "And Now, a Word from Our Creator," *New York Times Book Review*, February 12, 1989)

"Meet the Press"   A weekly TV press conference (1947–) with newsmakers from around the world. Originally conducted by the knowledgeable, skillful newspaper man Lawrence Spivak (1900–).

Me Generation   The generation after the activist, revolutionary, anti-Vietnam War, anti-nuclear, pro-civil rights generation of the 1960s seemed to observers to be "complacent and self-serving" and came to be labeled the "Me Generation." They seemed to lack altruism and commitment to any ideal. They sought college degrees to get rich quick. They became the YUPPIES instead of the HIPPIES of the previous generation.

The term "Me Generation" is applied to any individual or group that seems to act from selfish, self-aggrandizing motives.

meltdown   An ultimate nuclear reactor accident in which the core of radioactive material gets very hot and melts down into the earth. In 1979 the Three Mile Island reactor suffered a partial meltdown with little external radiation. In 1986 the CHERNOBYL reactor suffered a complete meltdown, with radiation spreading from the site to many parts of the world.

The concept of meltdown was quickly adapted to fit many disparate and often desperate situations.

Use: "What will it take to wake up the White House? U.S. stocks are now worth about $800 billion less than in August. Must the market undergo another meltdown before the administration accepts the urgent need to raise taxes by an extra few billion dollars less on the military?" (*New York Times* editorial, November 5, 1987)

melting pot, the   The notion that the vast majority of American immigrants have been or will be blended into a simple entity—Americans. A memorable statement of this concept is expressed in Israel Zangwill's (1865–1926) *The Melting Pot* (1908).

Use: "A melting pot is boiling over with resentment toward the newest arrivals: Boston's Chinatown." (*Newsweek*, February 20, 1989)

Member of the Wedding, The   Novel (1946) by Carson McCullers about Frankie Adams, a 12-year-old motherless girl whose only companions are her six-year-old cousin John Henry and the Negro cook Berenice. When her brother is about to be married and asks her to be a member of the wedding, she mistakenly thinks that she is going to make a threesome with him and his bride. She suffers terrible anguish when she realizes her error. Frankie has a lot of growing up to do within the year of the novel.

To be a member of the wedding is to "belong" to a group, whether a family or a club; to be an insider.

Mengele, Dr. Josef   Infamous doctor guilty of horrendous "medical" experiments, especially on Jewish children, at the Auschwitz death camp. Known as the "Angel of Death," he aided in the torture of four million helpless victims of the Nazis. Became a fugitive from justice and probably died in South America in 1979. Synonymous with one who commits inhuman atrocities in the name of science. A 20th-century monster.

Use: Writing of Kurt Waldheim, the former secretary-general of the United Nations, who was accused of Nazi war crimes, Shirley Hazzard concedes: "This is not a Mengele or Eichmann." (*New York Times* Book Review, March 27, 1988)

Mercedes Benz   High-priced, excellently tooled, German-made luxury car. Like a Cadillac, it is tops in its class.

merchants of death   From the title of a book by H.C. Engelbrecht and F.C. Hanighan, who in the 1920s sought to prove that nations go to war to advance or protect financial interests. Originally the merchants of death were munitions makers who stood to profit from war. Now the term is applied to the manufacturers and sellers of any product that is potentially lethal; e.g., drugs, tobacco, guns.

Use: *Merchants of Death: The American Tobacco Industry* is a book written by Larry C. White.

Merriwell, Frank   The hero of one of America's most popular boys' books. From 1896 through the 1920s the Merriwell books sold over 125 million copies. Unabashedly espousing honesty, courage, hard work, devotion to duty however difficult, fair play in sports and in life—the books were an inspiration to two generations of young Americans.

To be a Frank Merriwell means simply to live the clean, wholesome, exciting life—to exemplify the virtues embodied in the life and work of Frank Merriwell, the exemplar. Also to be a "goody-two-shoes," even though Frank Merriwell was not, by any means, a "sissy."

Ironically, Burt L. Standish, the author of the Merriwell stories, died in poverty. He received no royalties on the 205 books he ghosted or wrote.

Mersault   Central character and narrator of *The Stranger* (1942), an existential novel by the French-Algerian writer, Albert Camus (1913–1960).

Mersault is a young Algerian who is a totally uncommitted man. He is bound to no person, although he has a mother living in a nursing home and a mistress whom he sees on weekends. When his mother dies, he attends the funeral but feels no grief. As a result of a series of incidents in which he has played only a passive or acquiescent rôle, he comes to shoot an Arab who had pulled a knife on him. Mersault is tried, convicted of murder and at the end of the book awaits execution. He has refused apathetically to defend himself, for what difference does it make? We are all condemned to die sooner or later. He has refused the consolation of God or a chaplain. God is dead. Life is absurd and meaningless. There is no causality. We live only in the moment. That's all there is—the moment.

Mersault is modern man who must learn to live in an absurd universe without the constraints or consolations of God or religion.

method acting   A naturalistic style of acting developed by Konstantin Stanislavski (1863–1938), the great Russian theater director, actor, producer and teacher who founded the Moscow Art Theater. The "method" calls upon the actor to remember and use experiences and emotions in his own life, which will help him to identify with his role. The actor's performance thus depends upon psychological truth rather than on tricks and mannerisms. The method was adapted by the Actors Studio in New York, which has trained such exemplars of method acting as MARLON BRANDO and Paul Newman.

The "method" has become associated with such realistic and almost inarticulate roles as that of STANLEY KOWALSKI, played by Brando in Tennessee Williams' *A Streetcar Named Desire*.

Mickey Finn   A potent, doctored drink named after a Chicago bartender who operated in Chicago's notorious Whiskey Row. Finn's "ingredients," secretly added to whiskey or water, caused the victim to fall into a deep sleep from which he could not be aroused until the effects of the drink wore off. Finn's employees slipped this potion to lone customers. When they lost consciousness, they were robbed of everything they owned, all their clothes were removed, they were dressed in old rags and dumped in a strange, distant place. Finn is alleged to have sold his recipe to other criminally-inclined saloon-keepers.

A Mickey Finn now refers to any drink deliberately prepared to "knock-out," immobilize, the victim—sometimes in fun or as a practical joke; at other times, with sinister, criminal intent.

Use: "Top Court Slips Unions a Mickey—Dealing a stinging blow to organized labor, the U.S. Supreme Court yesterday said airlines and railroads do not have to guarantee jobs for some workers who go on strike." (*New York Daily News*, March 1, 1989)

Mickey Mouse   Engaging animated cartoon character conceived by WALT DISNEY (1901–1966), named by Mrs. Disney and drawn by Disney's associate Ub (Ubbe) Iwerks in 1928. Mickey was soon joined by his female counterpart, Minnie Mouse. Mickey Mouse has come to mean somebody or something silly or inconsequential.

Use: "It's like Mickey and Minnie have been kicked out of Disney World." (Quoted from a waitress speaking of TV evangelists Jim and Tammy Bakker's expulsion from the PTL empire; *Newsweek*, July 6, 1987)

Mildred   Mildred Rogers, the vulgar little Cockney waitress with whom Philip Carey becomes slavishly infatuated in the novel *Of Human Bondage* (1915) by the British author W. Somerset Maugham (1874–1965). Mildred is common, selfish, restless, petty and vindictive. She feels superior to the sensitive Philip because he has a club foot, but she uses him and very nearly succeeds in wrecking his life, as she wrecks his apartment one day in a fit of rage.

Mildred's image has been stamped upon the consciousness of every moviegoer who has seen Bette Davis in the movie adaptation of the book.

Miller, Henry   Prolific American writer (1891–1980) whose explicit, lusty and often hilarious treatment of sex shocked the censors into banning his books in the United States. Miller spent nine years as an expatriate in Paris. *The Tropic of Cancer* (1934) and *The Tropic of Capricorn* (1938), when purchased in Paris, had to be sneaked into the United States by intrepid travelers. Miller had much to do with loosening the puritanical sexual and social mores of his native land. In spite of his public image as practically a pornographer, he remained as in his boyhood an innocent, if exuberant, New York City street kid who had seen it all, the degradation as well as the glory. Miller's essays on literary censorship, "Obscenity in Literature" and " Obscenity and the Law of Reflection," reveal his attitudes on freedom of expression.

Miranda Decision   A landmark Supreme Court decision (*Miranda v. Arizona*, 1966) requiring law enforcement officials to tell anyone taken into custody that:

1) He has the right to remain silent.

2) Anything he says can be used against him.

3) He has the right to have his lawyer present while being questioned.

4) If he cannot afford a lawyer, the Court will appoint one to represent him.

"Miranda" stands as a symbol of continuing concern for the rights of the accused.

Miro, Joan   Spanish surrealist painter (1893–1983) known for his brightly colored, amoeba-like forms floating in rhythmic fantasy.

Miss Lonelyhearts   A short novel (1933) by Nathanael West (1903–1940), about a man who writes a column of advice to the lovelorn in a New York newspaper. His correspondents address their problems to "Miss Lonelyhearts." He agonizes over their sufferings. He becomes unwittingly entangled in the sordid life of one of these women, Mrs. Doyle. The result is that this Christ-like figure, who has taken upon himself the woes of the world, is murdered by her crazed husband.

Miss Lonelyhearts has become a generic term for practitioners of advice to the lovelorn.

Miss Marple   An amateur detective in the rather amusing, contrary-to-usual form of an elderly, gossipy spinster; created by Agatha Christie, British mystery story writer (1890–1976). Miss Jane Marple assumes disguises in order to get information about a crime. She may pose as a maid, as a member of a repertory group or riding lodge. A shrewd judge of human nature, she invariably solves her case. Miss Marple first appeared in *Murder at the Vicarage* (1930). Other Miss Marple stories include *The Body in the Library*, *4:50 from Paddington*, *What Miss McGillicuddy Saw*, *After the Funeral* and *Mrs. McGinty's Dead*.

Miss Marple was played by Margaret Rutherford in a series of four British films: *Murder, She Said* (1961) *Murder at the Gallop* (1963), *Murder Ahoy* (1964) and *Murder Most Foul* (1964).

Mix, Tom   Popular cowboy star in the silent movies of the 1920s who rode a black horse named Tony. He exemplified all the virtues and none of the vices of the typical cowboy. Although he eschewed violence, his pictures were full of action and daredevil stunts. His films included the Zane Grey westerns *The Lone Star Ranger* and *The Rainbow Trail*.

Model T   Car introduced by Henry Ford in 1909. It originally sold for $850 "in any color you choose as long as it's black," but by 1926, Ford's mass production assembly line had reduced the price to $350. Over 15 million cars had been sold by 1927.

The Model T now refers to anything sturdy, strictly utilitarian, basic, with no frills added.

Modigliani, Amedeo   Sculptor and painter (1884–1920) who was born in Livorno and moved to Paris in 1906, where he lived in extreme poverty and died of tuberculosis. Influenced by Brancusi and African carvings, he developed his own individual style in the mannerist tradition. A Modigliani woman is instantly recognized by the elegant elongation of the head, the neck, the body and the hands.

Molotov cocktail   Simple grenade that can be made by amateurs. It consists of a bottle filled with flammable liquid, like gasoline, and a wick that is ignited just before throwing. It was first used against tanks during the Spanish Civil War. Named after Vyacheslav Molotov (1890–1986), minister of foreign affairs for the U.S.S.R. from 1939 to 1945.

Monday morning quarterback   Anyone who criticizes the individual football players or the football team after the game or the play has been completed. Monday morning quarterbacking requires no experience or expertise, just a smattering of gall and ignorance—chutzpah.

Now applied to anyone who second-guesses any individual or group for the outcome of a game or performance.

Mondrian, Piet   Dutch painter (1872–1944) who lived in Paris, London and New York City. A Mondrian is a geometric composition of intersecting horizontal and vertical lines forming rectangles of various sizes, painted in primary colors plus black and white. Typical examples are *Composition in Red, Blue, and Yellow* and *Broadway Boogie-Woogie*. One sees Mondrians in all kinds of commercial designs.

Use: From the air, the town, with its precisely laid out streets and patches of color, looked like a Mondrian.

Monet, Claude   Preeminent and prolific French impressionist (1840–1926) famous for his studies of light and color, as in his series on Rouen Cathedral seen at various times of the day under different conditions of light. Influenced by Turner's canvases, Monet began to paint the water lilies in his pond at Giverny until he seems to have become obsessed with them. He created a series of huge murals, his Nympheas paintings, for the Musee de l'Orangerie in Paris.

Monroe, Marilyn   Film actress who became a cult figure, not just as a sex symbol but also as a fascinating study in contradictions for many intellectuals, who continue to produce books about her. Born Norma Jean Martenson in 1925, she committed suicide in 1962. The ultimate pin-up girl, she was sultry, exquisitely proportioned, played dumb blonde roles, but in real life she read Dostoevsky and studied with Lee Strasberg. She was both brazen and vulnerable. Her second husband was JOE DIMAGGIO, the baseball hero; her third husband was Arthur Miller, the playwright. Into adult life she brought her childhood traumas from foster homes and orphanages. Her talent was for light comedy in such films as *The Seven Year Itch* (1954), *Bus Stop* (1956) and especially *Some Like It Hot* (1959).

Montgomery, Alabama   Scene of organized boycott of buses, a movement led by Dr. Martin Luther King Jr. to force, through the technique of passive resistance, an end to segregation of whites and blacks on city buses. Since Alabama law prohibited organized boycotting, thousands of blacks were arrested and jailed. But on April 23, 1956, the Supreme Court of the United States ruled that segregation in public transportation is unconstitutional.

Montgomery has become a symbol of the struggle for civil rights and of the successful use of civil disobedience in removing unjust laws.

Moore, Henry   English sculptor (1898–1986). Moore rejected classical Greek and Renaissance ideals of beauty. A work must have, he said, " a pent-up energy, an intense life of its own, independent of the object it may represent. When a work has this powerful vitality, we do not connect the word Beauty with it." His figures look like primeval boulders that time and weather have eroded into almost human shapes. Moore's massive sculptures, carved out of stone, are noted for their spaces or holes within the framework of the statue. It is these empty spaces that are his signature.

Mother Teresa   (1910–) Nobel Peace Prize winner (1979) for her work with the poor. Born Agnes Gonxha Bojaxhiu in Skopje (now in Yugoslavia), of Albanian parents. She took her first vows as a nun in 1928 after training with the Sisters of Loretto, a community of Irish nuns with a mission in Calcutta. She took her final vows in 1937. In 1950 she founded the Missionaries of Charity, a Catholic religious order dedicated to "whole-hearted free service to the poorest of the poor." Mother Teresa has said, "To be able to love the poor and know the poor we must be poor ourselves." Thus the vow of poverty is exceptionally strict among the Missionaries of Charity. They care for and live among orphaned and abandoned children, sick and dying poor adults, lepers, battered and raped women.

Mother Teresa is the symbol of saintliness in her active life of service among the very poor and desolate.

Mouse That Roared, The   British film satire (1959) with Peter Sellers, based on Leonard Wibberley's 1955 novel. The tiny, bankrupt duchy of Grand Fenwick declares war on the United States in order to be defeated (naturally) and so be eligible to receive Marshall Plan aid. Ah, but suppose the penny-sized duchy were in danger of winning the war? Therein lies the comedy and the topical fun.

Moxie   Once-popular American soft drink (also called "tonic," or "pop" in the New England area). *Moxie* has acquired a variety of related meanings: dash, vigor, verve, strength, aggressiveness, heartiness, pep, courage, skill.

Use: "If we are going to succeed, we need a sales staff with more moxie."

Mr. Chips   Main character in *Goodbye, Mr. Chips* (1935), novel by James Hilton, and movie version in 1939 in which Robert Donat starred. Mr. Chipping starts out as a young, inexperienced Latin teacher in Brookfield, a boys' prep school in England. Shy, aloof, somewhat rigid in his adherence to rules, he is both feared and ridiculed by his students. Marriage to a warm and understanding girl changes him. After the death of his wife Katherine during childbirth, he devotes himself entirely to the school. Even after retirement, he remains on the campus, a living legend. In his 80s, on his deathbed, he overhears one of the masters saying to the doctor, "Poor old chap. Must have had a lonely life. Pity he had no children." "You're wrong," Chips says, "I had thousands of them, thousands of them—and all boys."

Mr. Chips is the prototype of the idiosyncratic but totally dedicated schoolmaster.

Use: "The advance publicity for *King of the Children*, from China, proved unreliable. It's a prettily photographed, rural Chinese Mr. Chips." *New York Times*, May 18, 1988)

Mr. Clean   The trademark of a popular liquid household cleaner.

Frequently applied to an individual of a perfect, unblemished character, scrupulously observant of all his duties, untouched by scandal or corruption.

Use: "[Tony] Coelho [Democratic member of the U.S. House of Representatives] stunned the Capitol Friday by telling the *New York Times* he would resign from Congress to spare his party a repetition of the Wright investigation. That opened the way for Representative Dick Gephardt of Missouri, who was already being urged by many Democrats to run for majority leader as the Mr. Clean alternative." (*U.S. News & World Report*, June 5, 1989)

"Mr. Rogers' Neighborhood"   Public television's low-keyed children's show. From a set designed to look like his own home, Mister Rogers, a Presbyterian minister, examines with kids the values, feelings and fears that are the staples of their lives.

In an easy, gentle manner, he deals with matters that concern kids: nightfall, rejection, disappointment, going to the dentist etc.

Mr. Rogers' neighborhood is a nice place to be—and a nice place to grow up in.

Use: "But if Mr. Bush's handlers could take their boy from Mister Rogers to Tarzan in three weeks, surely a similar make-over could be arranged for the Duke [Michael Dukakis]." (*New York Magazine*, September 19, 1988)

Mr. Smith Goes to Washington   Movie produced and directed in 1939 by Frank Capra and starring Jimmy Stewart. Mr. Jefferson Smith, a simple, honest man, head of the Boy Rangers, is tapped by the political machine of a western state to fill an unexpired term in the

Senate. The party bosses think they can manipulate him for their own greedy ends. But, of course, they have another thing coming. Mr. Smith is educated quickly and outwits and outfights the bad guys.

A parable of how an everyday citizen, an everyman, can fight corruption in high places and win.

Use: "In the end, Reagan was Mr. Smith come to Washington—a Jimmy Stewart figure who projected a purity of purpose but who could be as tough as Gary Cooper at HIGH NOON when provoked. His gunslinger image gave him the maneuvering room to face down the enemy even when he didn't always deliver on his threats." (*Newsweek*, November 21, 1988)

Mt. Everest   Situated in the Himalayas, it is the highest mountain peak in the world (29,028 feet) and, therefore, a supreme challenge to climbers and, metaphorically, to anyone struggling to reach a summit.

Use: "The New York City school system is the Everest of public education, huge and implacable, serving nearly a million students in almost 1,000 schools..." (*Newsweek*, January 15, 1988)

Mudville   See THERE IS NO JOY IN MUDVILLE.

Munch, Edvard   Norwegian painter and graphic artist (1863–1944) whose morbid view of life has touched the nerve of our century. He sees and depicts the skeleton beneath the living flesh and makes us aware, as did the medieval preachers, that death and corruption are the inevitable end of every joy in life. Munch's painting *The Scream* has particularly epitomized the anguish, frustration and desperation of the time, and might today be called the primal scream that psychiatrists advise us to express.

A Munch is always a reminder of Death.

Munchkins   The little, elfin-like people in the land of Oz from THE WIZARD OF OZ (1900) by L. Frank Baum. Now, any person of dwarfish appearance or low-level stature or simply a child.

Use: Headline in *U.S. News & World Report*, February 29, 1988— "Munchkin Marathon"—referred to the not very impressive candidates of both parties running for nomination for president of the United States in the election of 1988.

Munich   Four-power conference in Munich, Germany, on September 29, 1938, to decide the future of Czechoslovakia. The participants were Prime Minister NEVILLE CHAMBERLAIN of England, French Premier Edward Daladier, Generalissimo Benito Mussolini of Italy and Chancellor ADOLF HITLER of Germany. No representative from Czechoslovakia was present. England and France consented to Germany's annexation of the Czech Sudetenland for the promise of no further aggression against Czechoslovakia. Hitler invaded and conquered the rest of Czechoslovakia on March 15, 1939.

Munich stands for appeasement.

Use: "At home and abroad there is a strong dissenting view that sees the I.N.F. treaty as a new Munich." (Eugene V. Rostow, former director of the Arms Control and Disarmament Agency, quoted on *New York Times* Op-Ed page, February 5, 1988)

"Muppets, The"   According to reliable industry estimates, in the 1970s, "The Muppets"—an American TV program produced in England—was seen in 100 countries by over 235 million people, certainly the most widely viewed program in the world.

The presiding genius of this whimsical mix of muppets and people was Jim Henson (1936–1990) a fantastic puppeteer, comedian, character actor, writer, master of many voices. Ably assisted by a group of versatile, ingenious puppeteers, Henson created an American mythology equal, in some measure, to the magical Kingdom of Disneyland.

Among the lovable, endearing, unforgettable muppets (a combination of marionettes and puppets) were:

The host of the show, *Kermit the Frog*, the vaguely genial and bewildered master of ceremonies, trying to contain and direct the motley cast of monsters, animals, guest stars. With the very best of intentions, it all ends up in shambles.

Miss Piggy, a coyly corpulent "actress" determined to become the star of the show. In vain.

Rowlf, the shaggy dog, playing the piano with a demoniacal passion.

Fozzy Bear, he of the peaked head and tiny hat.

Statler and Waldorf, two aging, tart-tongued friends observing the madness on stage, demolishing each segment with what can at best be called "awful jokes."

More than 400 characters, with their corny gags and odd skills, gave "The Muppets" universal appeal. Their wit, warmth, vulnerability, their desperately futile and hilarious attempts to make some sense and order out of a world they never made and could not control gave them an almost human dimension.

Murder, Inc.   The enforcement arm of the national crime syndicate. Organized in the 1930s, it consisted of a group of professional killers available only for the business of organized crime in America. With the concurrence of its top leadership, MEYER LANSKY, Lucky Luciano, Frank Costello etc., Murder, Inc., is alleged to have committed between 400 and 500 murders—most unsolved.

Murder, Inc. (so called by the media) never acted against political figures, prosecutors, reporters. In the words of Bugsy Siegel, a high official in organized crime's hierarchy, "We only kill each other."

In the 1940s, Murder, Inc., began to fall apart, its disintegration hastened by the trial and conviction of a number of central crime figures. There is, however, some evidence that a similar organization has taken its place.

Murder, Inc., has enriched our language with such terms as "hit," "contract," "rub-out."

Murrow, Edward Roscoe   American broadcast journalist (1908–1965). Murrow's *See It Now*—a sophisticated television news presentation produced by Fred Friendly—set new standards for American reporters and commentators and became a "document of its times." To the practitioners of this new "advocacy journalism," Murrow was a saint. Essentially, the program was the world as seen by Murrow—a very personal, passionate view.

In 1954, Murrow broadcast a brilliant exposé of the tactics of Senator Joseph R. McCarthy (see MCCARTHYISM). Murrow's broadcast contributed significantly to alerting his listeners to the dangers Senator McCarthy posed to individuals and institutions.

Murrow was one of the most influential radio and TV commentators of his time.

mushroom cloud   White radioactive smoke rising in the shape of a mushroom to about 20,000 feet above the earth—when a nuclear bomb is exploded.

Mutt and Jeff   Two famous characters (1907–1950) in a comic strip of the same name. They are remembered mostly for their physical disparities. Mutt is the tall one, with an unruly, scraggly moustache; an insatiable bettor on the horses, perennially hopeful that the horse he bets on will hit the jackpot. Jeff is Mutt's pint-sized partner who imagines himself to be James Jeffries, the famous prizefighter.

Very little of Mutt and Jeff's character, adventures and misadventures are remembered today. What remains in our collective memory is the disparity in their height. When we encounter two individuals, of markedly different heights, our almost automatic comment is likely to be, "There they go—Mutt and Jeff."

My Lai   Hamlet in South Vietnam where 22 old men, women and children were massacred by an American detail under Lt. William Calley Jr. on March 16, 1968. Calley was court-martialed and convicted in March 1971, but his conviction was later overturned by a Federal Court. My Lai has become symbolic of the savagery that generally ordinary men can be guilty of under the stress of hatred and suspicion in wartime.

N

Nader, Ralph Consumer ombudsman and muckraker (1934–). His book *Unsafe at Any Speed* (1965) was an exposé of the automobile industry that led to the passage of the National Traffic and Motor Vehicle Safety Act (1966). He set up consumer advocacy groups like the Public Interest Research Group; with dedicated volunteers called Nader's Raiders, he investigated coal mine hazards, radiation dangers, insecticide use, slaughterhouse conditions and many other abuses. Ralph Nader's name is synonymous with consumer advocacy.

Nagasaki City in Japan destroyed on August 9, 1945, by the second and last atom bomb used by the United States to end World War II. Japan surrendered five days later. Thirty-six-thousand people were killed by the one bomb, dropped by the B-29 Superfortress, *Great Artiste.*

Naphta See MAGIC MOUNTAIN, THE.

Nash, Ogden American writer of light verse (1902–1971) marked by outrageous rhymes and lines of comically uneven length.
For example, "Introspective Reflection":

> I would live all my life in nonchalance and insouciance
> Were it not for making a living, which is rather a nouciance.

or

> Candy is dandy
> But liquor is quicker.

189

Ogden Nash stands for wit in versification.

Ness, Eliot   See UNTOUCHABLES.

never in the field of human conflict was so much owed by so many to so few: Winston Churchill's tribute in August 1940 to the Royal Air Force for its defense of Britain against the German aerial blitz during World War II.

The phrase has come to be used in other contexts, as when one attributes the gains in civil rights for black Americans in the 1960s to such outstanding heroes and martyrs as Dr. Martin Luther King Jr., Rosa Parks, James Meredith, Medgar Evers, James Chaney, Michael Schwerner and Andrew Goodman.

Never-Never Land   The imaginary land of the Lost Boys in the play PETER PAN by James M. Barrie.

Use: "When confronted about the closings and their effect on the old and the poor, Bishop Patrick Cooney, who spearheaded the reorganization, said he was 'dumbfounded' by the hostile reaction. 'Everybody is going to be in a parish,' he said. 'Nobody is going to be in Never-Never Land.'" (*New York Times*, October 14, 1988)

never underestimate the power of a woman   Originally, this simple, powerful statement appeared as part of an advertisement for *Ladies Home Journal* in the early 1940s—just at the dawn of the modern feminist movement in America.

New Deal   Program of reforms promised by Franklin Delano Roosevelt in accepting the Democratic nomination for president in 1932. In his first 100 days in office he proposed and Congress approved many bills to ease the effects of the Depression and ensure economic stability in the future. From 1933 to 1938 he established so-called alphabet agencies to carry out his reforms: WPA (Works Progress Administration); SSA (Social Security Administration); FDIC (Federal Deposit Insurance Corporation); NLRB (National Labor Relations Board); FHA (Federal Housing Administration); TVA (Tennessee Valley Authority); SEC (Securities and Exchange Commission) and many more. A wave of optimism swept through the country; a capable leader was at the helm.

"New Deal" now is used not only in its original context, but also for any sweeping new program or agenda for reform, whether on a domestic level or a political level.

Newport Seaside town in Rhode Island known for its great mansions, "country houses" to the super-rich.

newspeak In George Orwell's novel *1984* (1949), the reduced and simplified language designed to impoverish thought and ultimately to cripple the mind so that the people can accept totalitarian rule. Newspeak = doubletalk.
  Use: "Something close to Orwellian newspeak is therefore achieved by the new Harvard Law School guidelines when they use the term 'dissenters' to characterize the campus enforcers of this liberal orthodoxy." (Norman Podhoretz, *New York Post*, October 25, 1988)

Nighttown Section of *Ulysses* (1922), the novel by James Joyce, in which Leopold Bloom, the protagonist, visits the brothels of Dublin in the course of his wanderings on June 16, 1904.
  Use: "Following the reception, [Oscar] Wilde was taken to a club. There some of the young men are supposed to have importuned him to sample earthly examples of that beauty which he had been diffusing on a more ethereal level. Wilde seems to have gone along to nighttown, and perhaps did what they proposed." (Richard Ellmann; *Oscar Wilde*) (See also BLOOMSDAY; JOYCEAN.)

Nijinsky, Vaslav Russian ballet dancer (1889–1950). Nijinsky dazzled audiences with his technical virtuosity and exotic sensuality. He had sensational elevation. Leaping into the wings off stage, he seemed to be soaring in flight. As a youth, he studied at the Imperial Ballet School in St. Petersburg and then joined the Maryinsky Theatre where he soon became a star. His chief association, however, was with the DIAGHILEV Ballet in Paris. There in 1912 he created the erotic role of the fawn in *L'Après midi d' un faune* to the music of Claude Debussy. He pioneered modern ballet with his innovative choreography in *Jeux* (1913) and in *Le Sacre du Printemps* (1913), to music by Igor Stravinsky. The latter caused a riot on opening night. When Nijinsky married a Hungarian dancer, Diaghilev, his outraged lover, threw him out of the company. Nijinsky declined from that time on and eventually showed signs of dementia praecox. He spent his last years in mental hospitals.

1984   A novel by George Orwell published in 1949. A utopia in reverse, *1984* depicts a totalitarian society of the future in which every aspect of life is debased, mechanized and regimented. Winston Smith, the hero, wages a brief but hopeless struggle for independent thought and personal love. Arrested, tortured and brainwashed by the Thought Police, he ends by submitting to the overwhelming power of the police state.

The year 1984 has come and gone, but *1984* still stands as a warning against totalitarian repression. The novel has added many phrases to the language: 1984, BIG BROTHER, NEWSPEAK, DOUBLETHINK, as well as such topsy-turvy slogans as War is Peace, Freedom is Slavery, Ignorance Is Strength.

ninety-day wonder   In World War II, a disparaging, scornful description of an enlisted man who is commissioned as an Army officer after a 90-day course in officer candidate school. Obviously callow and inexperienced—and arrogant, too.

Use: "The department is falling apart. So whom do they send to keep it from collapsing? This ninety-day wonder."

99 44/100% Pure   From the first line of the first ad for Ivory Soap:
"The 'ivory' is a laundry soap with all the fine qualities of a choice toilet soap, and is 99 44/100% pure."

This slogan, part of Ivory Soap advertisements for more than 100 years, is universally recognized as one of the most effective in the history of advertising: simple, direct, unforgettable.

Interestingly enough, 99 44/100% has slipped into the language and become synonymous with absolute, 100% purity.

Nisei   Americans of Japanese descent. During World War II, they were forcibly evacuated from Oregon, Washington and California and relocated in guarded internment camps. Although they were American citizens, their rights were violated in the anti-Japanese hysteria after Pearl Harbor. Their property was confiscated. This action became a source of national guilt and disgrace. In September 1987 the U.S. House of Representatives made reparations to each of the 66,000 survivors with an apology and a payment of $20,000.

The Nisei are a reminder to the United States that it *can* happen here, that citizens of the United States were punished without due process of law for suspicion of disloyalty simply because they belonged to a certain ethnic group.

"Nixon vs. Kennedy debate"   For the first time in American political history (1960), two candidates for the presidency, Richard Milhous Nixon (1913–) and John Fitzgerald Kennedy (1917–1963), faced each other in a televised debate. Nixon looked tired, ragged, ill-at-ease. His jowly five o'clock shadow made him appear somewhat ominous. Kennedy looked young, handsome, vigorous, bright, eager and confident.

Nixon lost the election. Commentators and voters alike agreed that, in some measure, the merciless TV camera had contributed to his defeat.

Nobel Prize   Prize presented annually since 1901 in accordance with the will of Alfred Nobel, Swedish inventor of dynamite and other explosives, to "those who during the preceding year, shall have conferred the greatest benefit on mankind" in the fields of medicine, physics, chemistry, literature and peace. These categories have been expanded to include economics and physiology. The prize money comes from a fund administered by the Nobel Foundation, but the Nobel laureates are chosen by an independent committee.

no-man's-land   The disputed land between the opposing lines of deeply dug trenches on the Western Front in World War I. Allied and German forces faced each other and fired at each other and tried to overrun each other across this hellish space of land mines, barbed wire, dead bodies and torn-up earth.

Use: "Unless covert actions can be carried on covertly, the United States will have one arm tied behind its back in a deadly serious struggle in that no-man's-land between peace and war." (Raymond Price, *New York Times* Op-Ed Page, July 12, 1987)

"Not Waving but Drowning"   Title poem (1957) of a book of verse by the English poet Stevie Smith (1902–1971), about whose life with her aunt the movie *Stevie* was made. It is an ironic poem, with a tinge of black humor, about a man who is drowning and calling for help, but passersby on the shore think he is just waving high spiritedly.

The phrase "not waving but drowning" is used as a cri de coeur for help when one is floundering.

not with a bang but a whimper   The final line of T.S. Eliot's poem "The Hollow Men" (1925) in which the poet laments the spiritual stagnation, the emptiness, the vacuity and the paralysis of will of modern man, including himself. He concludes that his world will end not in any kind of affirmation, "not with a bang but a whimper."

Quoted often to express anticlimax, a kind of petering out of big beginnings or big expectations. Sometimes the line is reversed to read "The world will end not with a whimper but a bang," especially in connection with the threat of the end of the world in an atomic war.

Nude Descending a Staircase   Cubist painting by French artist Marcel Duchamp (1887–1968), which caused a scandal at the 1913 Armory Show in New York City. It shows successive superimposed images of a fragmented and mechanized figure moving down a staircase. Although it represented a revolutionary departure for art in its time, it has been greeted with derision and disbelief by laymen.

Nuke   Short for nuclear bomb. Used as a verb, to "nuke" an enemy is to atomize him, to hit him with ultimate power.

Nuremberg Laws   Laws enacted in September 1935 by the Nazi regime in Germany; they deprived German Jews of their citizenship and forbade intermarriage or sexual relations between Jews and Germans. These laws were called "The Law Respecting Reich Citizenship" and "The Law for the Protection of German Blood and German Honor." Together with 13 supplementary decrees, they outlined the course of Hitler's war against the Jews. The Jews became pariahs with no civil, political or economic rights.

The Nuremberg Laws are often referred to in connection with the definition of a Jew.

Use: "The fundamentalist Orthodox Jews of Israel are trying to impose Nuremberg Laws on all of Jewry."

Nuremberg Trials   Post-World War II Allied trials (1945–46) of Nazis accused of war crimes. The international tribunal in Nuremberg, Germany, sentenced nine criminals to death by hanging and established the principle of personal responsibility for crimes against humanity. Following orders from an upper command could not be used as an excuse.

Nureyev, Rudolf Hamitovich   Soviet-born and trained ballet dancer (1938–), he asked for political asylum while on a tour with the Kirov Ballet in Paris in 1961. Since then he has achieved sensational success in many companies in the Western world. One of the greatest male dancers of the century, he is a natural heir in expressiveness and virtuosity to NIJINSKY. He was Margot Fonteyn's principal partner for many years at the Royal Academy of Dance in London. He appeared in the 1972 film *I Am A Dancer* as well as in many filmed versions of his ballet performances.

Odd Couple, The Broadway play (1965) by Neil Simon, made into a film in 1968 and later into a TV situation comedy; about two ill-assorted men—fastidiously tidy Felix and slovenly Oscar—who set up housekeeping with hilarious results. Now, any ill-matched pair.

Use: Headline in the *New York Times*, August 7, 1987: "Odd Couple: A Marxist Soviet and an Islamic Iran."

Odessa steps Unforgettable scene in *Potemkin*, a 1925 film masterpiece by the Russian director Sergei Eisenstein. The movie depicts the suppression by Czarist troops of an insurrection aboard the Russian warship *Potemkin* in 1905. The memorable scene is a montage of boots and fixed bayonets inexorably advancing down the steps, red flag waving over the ship in the harbor and a baby carriage, with a baby in it, bouncing out of control down the long flight of steps leading to the harbor.

The scene produces a horrifying but symbolic effect by the juxtaposition of images of brute force with images of utter defenselessness.

off base In baseball, this means not touching one of the four bases. The player whose hit or whose teammate's hit has put him on first, second or third base must remain on or near that base while the ball is in play. If he is caught not touching the base by the defensive team and is tagged with the ball, he is "off-base," out, and leaves the field.

In general use, off-base means wrong, in error, badly mistaken.

often a bridesmaid but never a bride   One of the most potent slogans of the 1920s, this advertisement for listerine mouthwash started out like this:

"Edna's case was really a pathetic one. Like every woman, her primary ambition was to marry. Most of the girls of her set were married—or about to be. Yet not one possessed more grace or charm or loveliness than she.

And as her birthdays crept gradually toward that tragic thirty mark, marriage seemed further from her life than ever.

She was often a bridesmaid; but never a bride.

That's the insidious thing about halitosis (unpleasant breath). You yourself rarely know when you have it. And even your closest friends won't tell you."

Prominently centered over this doleful copy is the picture of the deeply distressed girl—the unknowing carrier of halitosis.

This ad sold millions of bottles of Listerine mouthwash—and added to our language "always a bridesmaid," a metaphor for any kind of frustration and disappointment.

O'Hara, Scarlett   Flirtatious, fiery, indomitable heroine of *Gone With the Wind* (1936), novel about the Civil War by Margaret Mitchell. A Georgia belle, rejected by her true love Ashley Wilkes, she spitefully or opportunistically is twice married and twice widowed. She then marries the dashing Rhett Butler who is more than a match for her. After their child is killed in a horseback riding accident, Rhett Butler realizes that her heart has always yearned for Ashley. Disgusted, he abandons her. The novel ends with the suggestion that Scarlett will endure and will somehow reconstruct her ruined but beloved ante-bellum Southern mansion, Tara.

Scarlett O'Hara has become a legendary figure who stands for a fiery-spirited, enduring woman.

O. Henry   Pseudonym of William Sydney Porter (1862–1910), a prolific American writer of humorous, ironic and poignant short stories known for their surprise endings and their observation of everyday New York types. One of his best known stories is "The Gift of The Magi" in which at Christmas a husband sells his only valuable possession, a gold watch, to buy his wife combs for her magnificent long hair, only to discover that she had cut her hair and sold it in order to buy her husband a fob for his watch.

An O. Henry situation is one marked by coincidence, ironic twists and surprise.

O'Keeffe, Georgia   American painter (1887–1986) whose style is so uniquely her own that she never had to sign her canvases. She is known for her sensual treatment of flowers. The viewer is drawn into the secret downy heart of a single flower, which is magnified to occupy a large canvas. After she moved from New York City to New Mexico, she painted desert landscapes with animal skeletons, Southwestern architecture and Indian artifacts. Her forms are always organic and monumental.

Okie   An impoverished farm worker from Oklahoma who in the 1930s tried to escape the dust storms of the ravaged land by moving to greener territories. In John Steinbeck's *The Grapes of Wrath*, (1939) Okie "means you're scum." (See JOADS, THE.)

on the ball   In baseball, to be alert, effective, extremely able, smart, knowledgeable, at whatever position a player is playing.
   In informal use, being on, or having something on, the ball indicates exceptional intelligence or ability.
   Use: "Seth is always on the ball. He knows which way the market will go."

on the button   In boxing, the button is the point of the chin, considered to be a boxer's most vulnerable spot. A well-directed blow here is often enough to knock out the boxer.
   In general use, "on the button" means in the precise spot or at the precise moment.
   Use: "He showed up for the appointment at 7 o'clock on the button."

one man, one vote   In *Baker v. Carr* (1962), the United States Supreme Court ruled that unequal election districts violated the Fourteenth Amendment to the Constitution. The Court mandated fair reapportionment according to the democratic principle of one man, one vote. The effect was to shift power from the sparsely populated rural areas to the densely populated cities.
   One man, one vote has become a catchword in any kind of decision making, whether on the political level or on the domestic level.

one on one   In sports, one-on-one refers to a single player facing or covered by one member of the opposing team.

In general, any circumstance in which an individual reacts face to face with another individual.

Use: They are going to have to resolve their differences in a one-on-one meeting.

one third of a nation   "I see one-third of a nation ill-housed, ill-clad, ill-nourished." These words were spoken by Franklin Delano Roosevelt at his second inaugural on January 20, 1937. He said he spoke not out of despair but out of hope. He promised to go forward with New Deal reforms to alleviate the plight of the poor. Refers to the poor and the disadvantaged.

one-two   In boxing, a two-punch combination, usually a short left jab then a hard right to the jaw of the opponent.

In general use, a two-part action or program.

Use: Fairlee beat the competition with a one-two program of brilliant advertising and low prices.

on the ropes   Description of a boxer who has been battered into virtual helplessness, leaning against or holding on to the ropes. He is clearly at the mercy of his opponent and just seconds away from defeat.

In general use on the verge of defeat, ruin, failure.

Use: Neglect and bad judgment had landed the once prosperous Harlan Fiske on the ropes.

oomph girl   In the 1930s and 1940s, a girl generously endowed with a constellation of "virtues," such as sexual attractiveness or "compelling carnality." Frequently referred to as a "sex goddess" or "sex queen."

In 1939, some press agents bestowed the accolade of "oomph girl" on the movie actress Ann Sheridan.

Use: Betty was the oomph girl of the Sales department.

open city   An undefended city. During World War II, Rome and Paris became open cities when their defenders chose to abandon them rather than risk destruction of their art and architectural treasures.

Orchard Street   Narrow, crowded street of pushcart vendors selling every conceivable ware at bargain prices to inhabitants of New York's LOWER EAST SIDE. A vestige of Yiddish immigrant life in the first part of the 20th century, Orchard Street is a symbol of cheap goods and animated bargaining.

Orwellian   Pertaining to the subject matter and style of the British writer George Orwell, the penname of Eric Arthur Blair (1903–1950), especially in those works which are satires on totalitarianism: *Animal Farm* (1945) and *1984* (1949). Orwellian acts or situations refer to the suppression of liberty or the distortion of truth.

Use: "it is not the usual violent horror story, although what happens is a horror nevertheless. This Granada Television Production from England comes across more in an Orwellian manner than in a style that flows with blood. There is a beating and forceful arrest, but the brutality of the state, hacking away at hapless individuals like a bully picking the wings off flies, is overt, constant and terrible." (Richard F. Shepard, *New York Times*, August 11, 1988) (See also BIG BROTHER; DOUBLETHINK; 1984; NEWSPEAK.)

Our Gang   Variegated group of children whose antics in silent films of the 1920s entertained the children of the world. Original members of the "gang" were Mary Kornman, Mickey Daniels, Joe Cobb, Farina (Allen Hoskins) and Jackie Condon.

Now applied to any cute cluster of kids or zany adults, for that matter, who are acting up.

Use: In a *New York Times* book review (November 19, 1988) of a biography of Andy Warhol, the critic cites the strong aberrant behavior of Warhol's associates, and concludes: "And so it goes, this perverse 'Our Gang' comedy, with Warhol as charismatic—though always detached— ringleader."

Our Town   See GROVER'S CORNERS.

out of the closet   Phrase used by homosexuals for abandoning secrecy and openly declaring their sexual preference. This was a tenet of the Gay Liberation Movement. By extension, to come out into the open with any hitherto concealed or camouflaged difference, whether personal or political.

Use: Referring to a memo written by Art Goodin for the Republican National Committee, Anthony Lewis in the *New York Times* (June 8, 1989) castigates Lee Atwater, chairman of the RNC, for his vicious smearing techniques: "The memo was entitled 'Tom Foley: Out of the Liberal Closet.' It argued that his voting record was similar to that of Representative Barney Frank, Democrat of Massachusetts, who is a declared homosexual. The phrase 'out of the closet' was a slyly unmistakable suggestion that Mr. Foley, too, is homosexual."

out of left field   In baseball, left field, seen from home plate, is the left side of the outfield past third base. Because of the vastness of the outfield and its distance from home plate, "to come out of left field" is a metaphor for something remote or unexpected.

Use: Miller's odd comments on the way the company was being run seemed to come out of left field. They took everyone by surprise.

overkill   Expression coined between 1945 and 1950 for the enormous capacity of a nation (at that time, only the United States) to destroy an enemy many times over with a plethora of nuclear bombs. The arms race between the U.S. and the Soviet Union, especially in strategic nuclear weapons, was denounced by pacifists as a foolish build-up for overkill.

In general parlance, overkill may refer to any over-zealous sales pitch, market saturation, propaganda campaign.

Use: "Politicians, from the White House to the statehouses, wrapped themselves in the flag with knee-jerk calls of overkill, including a constitutional amendment."(Al Neuharth, *U.S.A. Today*, July 7, 1989; in reference to the public reaction to the Supreme Court decision that burning the flag is a form of free speech protected by the First Amendment.)

over the top   From World War I trench warfare, when the troops charged out of the trenches by literally scrambling over the top. The British expression was "to jump off." To go over the top now means the launching and conclusion of a successful campaign (selling, advertising etc.).

Oz   See WIZARD OF OZ, YELLOW BRICK ROAD.

"Ozzie and Harriet"   One of television's longest running family comedies (1952–1966)—a story of the real, day-to-day life of an active, interesting, involved, decent, loving and lovable American middle-class family. What made this show unique was that Ozzie and Harriet were played by the real Ozzie and Harriet Nelson. And David and Ricky, their two growing sons, played themselves, too.

"Ozzie and Harriet" was a "real" show about real people playing themselves in an especially sweet, comfortable, believable America.

Use: "Residents of Seaford, Delaware, population 5,500, describe it as 'a conservative, God-fearing community'—an Ozzie and Harriet kind of place." (*New York Times*, May 28, 1989)

P

pack the court   President Franklin Delano Roosevelt's proposal in February 1937 (shortly after his election to a second term) to add as many as six justices to the Supreme Court (who would support his New Deal legislation). The "nine old men" on the Court, some of whom were over 70 but still disinclined to retire, had struck down as unconstitutional the National Recovery Act (NRA) and the Agricultural Adjustment Act (AAA). A furor arose over this blatant attempt to pack the court and Roosevelt had to back down.

To influence a vote or an action by padding membership in a committee or club or political organization with people of the desired views.

Pal Joey   Main character, a "heel," in a series of 12 stories originally published in *The New Yorker* and gathered in *Pal Joey* (1940) by John O'Hara, the American short story writer and novelist. The book was made into a successful musical in 1940 by Richard Rodgers and Lorenz Hart.

Pal Joey is the epitome of opportunistic, cynical Broadway types.

Palmer Raids   The post-World War I period in the United States ushered in a series of strikes. At its height, many citizens, thought to be anti-labor, received bombs in their mail. One of these bombs, mailed to A. Mitchell Palmer, U.S. attorney general, exploded on his stoop. Palmer, something of a fanatic, vowed to stamp out the "Bolshevik Revolution," which he held responsible for the current unrest.

On January 1, 1920, using the wartime Sedition Act, he authorized hundreds of his agents to invade homes in 33 cities: Over 4,000 American citizens and aliens were swept up in these raids. Many were held for a week without being charged. Friends and relatives who came to visit were themselves arrested on the grounds that they were likely to be revolutionaries or "Bolshies."

The Palmer Raids, as they came to be known, enjoyed brief public support. But challenges from the legal profession and the Wilson Administration soon led to the release of almost all the victims for lack of evidence. The raids yielded no signs that individuals or organizations were giving aid to America's enemies. Not a single spy was discovered. Nonetheless, Palmer succeeded in deporting some 600 aliens and two "anarchists": Emma Goldman and Alexander Berkman.

The Palmer Raids have come to stand for governmental persecution of unpopular groups and individuals, the filing of baseless charges and the violation of civil rights. In a sense, they foreshadowed the hysteria of the McCarthy era. (See also MCCARTHYISM.)

palooka   An athlete, especially a boxer, unskilled, incompetent or having lost much of his ability. Usually, an older boxer who has seen his best days in the ring, his senses and reflexes now dulled and erratic.

In general use, a crude, stupid, physically unattractive person inclined to senseless violence, easily led.

Use: The two men who held Palmer up looked and acted like palookas.

panzer   Referring to German armored divisions, especially tank units, used in World War II for lightning assaults. Swift, effective and brutal, as in a phalanx attack for a specific goal.

paper chase   From the English game of hare and hounds in which the hares drop pieces of paper as they run toward a fixed destination. The hounds try to follow the paper trail and catch up with the hares before they reach the designated spot. In 1973 the movie *The Paper Chase*, adapted from John Jay Osborne Jr.'s novel, popularized the term, as did the long-running TV series that followed. The movie dramatized the scholastic pressures upon a group of freshmen at

Harvard Law School, especially in a class intellectually tyrannized by a professor of law played by John Houseman.

Paper chase has come to mean running after a diploma or degree, especially in law school. It implies also the writing of many papers in pursuit of such a degree. Later the term included the paperwork in applying for financial aid.

Use: "Loss of predictable Federal operating support condemns major institutions like the library to an endless paper chase for public and private funds. A thousand forms must be filled out to win grants..." (*New York Times* editorial (September 3, 1988) on Dr. Vartan Gregorian's resignation from his post as president of the New York Public Library.)

paper tiger   An expression of contempt first used by Chinese leader Mao Tse-Tung in 1946 ("All reactionaries are paper tigers. In appearance, the reactionaries are terrifying, but in reality they are not so powerful.") and later by other communist nations to characterize the ineffectiveness of United States intervention. In 1965, however, Raul Castro, armed forces minister of Cuba, warned: "United States imperialism is no paper tiger."

Now, any person or thing that appears strong and powerful but is actually weak or ineffectual.

Use: "Today, the Warsaw Pact is not even a paper tiger, and the notion of a protracted nuclear war has become a sick joke." (Paul C. Warnke, *New York Times* Op-Ed page, April 13, 1990)

Park Avenue   Wide center-islanded street in Manhattan with elegant residential apartment buildings for the rich.

Use: Her upward mobility was marked by a mink coat, a Cadillac and a Park Avenue address.

Parker, Dorothy   Witty, sardonic American writer (1893–1967) of poetry, short stories and criticism. She wrote drama reviews for *Vanity Fair* and later *The New Yorker*. She was a member of the Algonquin Round Table together with such other luminaries as F.P.A. (Franklin P. Adams). She is known for her "Parkerisms":

(1) Men seldom make passes
 At girls who wear glasses.
(2) You can lead a horse to water

> But you can't make him drink;
> You can lead a horticulture
> But you can't make her think.

(3) She ran the whole gamut of emotions from A to B.

Parks, Rosa   First black person to defy the Alabama law that relegated black passengers to the back of the bus. For refusing to budge from the whites-only section in January 1956, she was arrested and fined. When she refused to pay the fine and threatened to appeal the decision to a higher court, she was jailed. Her case sparked the widespread boycott of buses in MONTGOMERY, ALABAMA.

Patton   General George S. Patton (1885–1945) Nicknamed "Old Blood and Guts." Achieved major victories with his tank units in World War II. A war hero, he was twice reprimanded, once for slapping a common soldier suffering from mental fatigue. His arrogance and outspokenness and eccentricities were immortalized in a brilliant portrait of him by George C. Scott in the film *Patton* (1969).

Use: "Let me confess right off that I was an early Lee Iacocca fan. I cheered when the Patton in pinstripes stormed Capitol Hill and won a reprieve for his troops." (From Patricia O'Toole's review of *Talking Straight* by Lee Iacocca, with Sonny Kleinfield; *New York Times* Book Review, July 17, 1988)

Pavlova, Anna   Ballerina (1881–1931). Born in St. Petersburg, Russia, Pavlova became the greatest dancer of her age, famous especially for her solo, "The Dying Swan," created for her by Mikhail Fokine. She studied at the Imperial Ballet School, made her debut at the Maryinsky Theater and became a prima ballerina there in 1906. She toured Europe, danced with DIAGHILEV's Ballets Russes in Paris and London, and performed at the Metropolitan Opera in New York City in 1910. She excelled in such classics as *Giselle, Swan Lake* and *Les Sylphides.* In 1913, she resigned from the Imperial Ballet, moved to London and opened her own school of mostly English dancers. She and her company toured all over the world, even in South America and Australia.

Pavlova became a household word in her time, a word synonymous with airy lightness and grace of movement suggesting poetic spirituality.

Pavlovian Pertaining to the experiments and theories of the Russian physiologist, Ivan Petrovich Pavlov (1849–1936), who won a Nobel Prize in 1904 for his work on digestive glands. In his experiments with salivating dogs he coined the term "conditioned reflex" and then showed how the behavior of human beings could also be modified by conditioning. His theories became the basis of a school of psychology, behaviorism.

Pax Americana The theory that the United States, the only country in the world in 1945 to possess the atom bomb, could impose world peace on its own terms. Reminiscent of the "Pax Romana" at the height of the Roman Empire.

Now, an imposed peace by one who assumes the frustrating role of policeman.

Peace Corps Organization of volunteers established by President Kennedy in 1961 for the purpose of training American men and women for peacetime service in mostly third-world or underdeveloped countries. Volunteers work in such areas as agriculture, education, health, or child care.

Use: Allan Bloom, in *The Closing of the American Mind*, writes of college students' attitudes: "It is the Peace Corps mentality, which is not a spur to learning but to a secularized version of doing good works."

Peanuts Since its first appearance as a daily feature (Oct. 2, 1950), *Peanuts* has become "the most successful strip in the history of comics." In addition to its millions of faithful, thoroughly enchanted readers, *Peanuts* earns more than $50,000,000 a year through reprints of the comic strip, books, TV specials, movies, a musical comedy, sweatshirts and other artifacts.

Ironically, when Charles Monroe Schulz, the creator of *Peanuts*, was trying to find a publisher for his feature (then called *Li'l Folks*), he was turned down by six syndicates.

The almost irresistible charm of *Peanuts* lies in its characters, what they feel, what they say, what they do. First, there is Charlie Brown himself—the quintessence of meekness and failure. His chief detractor is the ill-tempered, sharp-tongued Lucy Van Pelt. The intellectually precocious Linus, Lucy's brother, cannot cope without his security blanket. Then there is Schroeder, possessed by a consuming desire to play Beethoven on his toy piano. And Snoopy, Charlie Brown's beagle and totally unlike Charlie. In his phantasies (similar to those of WALTER MITTY), Snoopy is a great lover, a great writer and the most famous World War I ace.

Pearl Harbor   See A DAY THAT WILL LIVE IN INFAMY.

Peck's Bad Boy   A little hellion who devotes most of his waking moments to wreaking havoc and dismay upon his parents and the adult world in general. He does not spare his peers—but they get what mischief and malice he has leftover. Peck's Bad Boy is the creation of the humorist George Wilbur Peck (1840–1916).

Now applied to anyone—child or adult—who is mischievous, troublesome, breaks the accepted rules, makes a "pest of himself," creates trouble, whose behavior embarrasses his friends or colleagues.

Use: "Reports began circulating recently in Washington that the First Lady [Barbara Bush] was displeased with Lee Atwater's second career as an impersonator of Elvis Presley—with his doing occasional shows at clubs...She complained he was not paying proper attention to his job as national party (Republican) chairman. More importantly, she felt that his Peck's Bad Boy behavior was trivializing the image of the party her husband heads." (*New York Times*, June 10, 1989)

peel me a grape, Beulah   Famous line spoken by the well-padded, indolent movie star Mae West in one of her films. It represents the essence of laziness and false refinement.

Use: "Peel Me A Grape" appeared as a headline in the *New York Times* over an article about the Federal Food and Drug Administration's ban on the use of sulfites as preservatives for fresh fruit and vegetables. Under pressure from California growers, the EPA rescinded its own ban so that now it would be necessary to peel the grapes if anyone wanted to avoid harmful chemicals.

Penrod   Twelve-year-old boy in Booth Tarkington's novel *Penrod* (1914) who lives in a small midwestern city and has the typical, amusing adventures of a growing boy in a middle-class family of that time; e.g., he blackmails his older sister's suitor into giving him a dollar, with which he buys enough sweets to make him violently sick.

Penrod is a genre youngster in the tradition of Peck's Bad Boy, Tom Sawyer, and Huck Finn.

Pentagon Papers   Top-secret inquiry (commissioned by Robert McNamara, Secretary of Defense) into the origins and history of the U.S. involvement in Vietnam. On June 13, 1971, the *New York Times* published a summary of its findings. The papers had been leaked by Daniel Ellsberg, former deputy secretary of defense, who had come to assess the Vietnam war as immoral and the administration's presentation of it to the American people as dishonest. Ellsberg was tried and acquitted.

The Pentagon Papers have become a symbol of whistle-blowing in the highest levels of government and a reminder of the people's right to know just what their government is doing.

Peoria   Peoria is a small town in Illinois supposedly typical of average America. The ultimate test of commercial success is: Will it play in Peoria?

Use: "By Wednesday evening the television industry was already interviewing people described as expert on how things and people play in Peoria, and the early expert report was that the colonel [Lt. Col. Oliver North] was playing like *Beverly Hills Cop II*. He wasn't just a runaway gas bag; he was the genuine article—a TV smasheroo." (Russell Baker, *New York Times*, July 11, 1987)

perestroika   Russian for restructuring of the Soviet economy; title of a book by Mikhail Gorbachev, secretary general of the Communist Party of the U.S.S.R. Popularized during Gorbachev's visit to the United States for a summit meeting with President Ronald Reagan in 1987. Gorbachev favored a mixed-market economy rather than rigid Stalinist collectivization.

Adapted quickly from Russian into the English vocabulary to mean an overhauling of unsatisfactory conditions.

Use: "Perestroika in New York Schools, Please." (Headline of Op-Ed article by Andrew Stein, president of New York City Council, *New York Times*, February 6, 1988)

Perils of Pauline, The   Silent movie serial (1914) with Pearl White as its star. Stock ingredients were a scheming villain, a trusting girl and a hero who rescues her. Every episode was hair-raising, as Pauline battled redskins, was kidnapped by gypsies, etc. The "perils" went on from week to week in seemingly never-ending succession.

"Perry Mason"   An hour-long television show based on Erle Stanley Gardner's phenomenally popular detective novels. Perry Mason, the "hero," is a very successful lawyer-detective—played by Raymond Burr. Mason has never lost a case. He usually discovers the real thief, killer, embezzler etc., in the last minutes of the drama.

Perry Mason embodies the virtues of his profession: tenacity, resourcefulness, intelligence. His quick insights and finely-honed logic invariably lead him to the guilty ones. Essentially, Perry Mason is a protagonist in that oldest of struggles—the battle between good and evil.

Use: "Does this mean the debate format only works with provocative, *Perry Mason* style questions?" (Jeff Greenfield, *New York Times*, October 13, 1988)

Peter Pan   The boy who wouldn't grow up, in James M. Barrie's 1904 play, *Peter Pan*. One night he flies in through the open nursery window and teaches the Darling children—Wendy, John and Michael—to fly. He takes them to Never-Never Land, a country inhabited by all the wonderful characters of children's tales: Indians, mermaids and villainous pirates, the latter led by Capt. Hook. After the one-armed Hook is killed, the children return home to their distraught parents and their St. Bernard dog Nana. But Peter chooses to live with the rest of the Lost Boys in Never-Never Land.

A Peter Pan is an adult who remains locked into childhood, who refuses to relinquish the ways and attitudes of a child; in fact, he crows over his youthfulness and arrested development.

Use: "He's the hit-and-run lover. This darling, involved, sensitive man of your dreams turns out to be not your future husband, but rather your garden-variety Peter Pan, cringing at the thought of real love." (Dalma Heyn in *Mademoiselle*, March 1989)

Peter Principle   One of several mythical "laws" concerning how individuals advance in business, civil-service, not-for-profit organization etc.; as set forth by Laurence J. Peter, author of the book, *The Peter Principle:* "People tend to be promoted up to the level of their incompetence."

Use: Carton's dismal performance in his new job is just an illustration of the Peter Principle at work.

"Peyton Place"   A television program (1964–1969) based on Grace Metalious' best-selling novel, it was the first soap opera to become a major hit on prime time.

The show was set in the small New England town of Peyton Place where, according to popular stereotypes, all is sweet, good, kind and simple. The Peyton Place of the novel and of television, turns out, instead, to be "something with extra-marital affairs, dark secrets, assorted skull-duggery..." Events run the gamut from infidelity to murder.

Peyton Place is a synonym for dark deeds in dark places. Underneath its soap opera–ish plot and characterization, it is an unlovely portrait of human meanness, cruelty and ruthlessness. It was something of a "first" for television to strike so unsparingly at America's fond illusions about small-town life and people.

Picasso, Pablo   Spanish-born painter, sculptor and ceramist (1881–1974) who worked in Paris from 1900. The most protean artist of the 20th century, he went from the poetic pathos of his Blue Period (e.g., *The Old Guitarist*, 1903) to the cerebral abstraction of cubism and collage cubism (e.g., *Les Demoiselles d'Avignon*, 1907, and *Ambroise Vollard*, 1910), to his Classic or Rose Period of monumental figures tenderly modeled (e.g., *Mother and Child*, 1922), to the "cut-paper style" of *Three Musicians*, (1921) and *Three Dancers* (1925). Picasso was quicksilver, constantly experimenting. His name in the popular mind, however, stands for a kind of perverse distortion of the figure and for fragmentation, as in his powerful *Guernica*. A Picasso seems deliberately misshapen and angular.

Piltdown Man   Fossil remains of early man, found in Sussex, England, in 1908; proved to be a hoax. They had been put together from a human skull and the jaw of an ape.

Use: John Talent, an Australian scientist, launched a "full-dress investigation into what he now believes may be one of the biggest cases of scientific fraud since Piltdown man." (Wm. F. Allman, *U.S. News & World Report*, May 18, 1989)

pinch hit   In baseball, this involves sending in a player to take another player's turn at bat—to pinch-hit for him. The pinch-hitter is used in various situations, including: (1) to bat for a poor hitter at a critical point in a game; or (2) to face a particular pitcher from whom he may get a hit.

The term "pinch hitter" was coined by sportswriter Charlie Dryden in 1892, to indicate that the player sent into the game was expected to get his team out of a "pinch" or difficult or tight spot. Now used in any similar situation.

Use: Bernard was asked to pinch hit in the boys' wear department until a new manager was hired.

pinch hitter   See PINCH HIT.

Pinteresque   Like the style and subject matter of the British playwright Harold Pinter (1930–) in such provocative and difficult plays as *The Caretaker* (1960), *The Homecoming* (1965) and *Betrayal* (1978). Elements of his style include seemingly ordinary colloquial speech with hidden or ambivalent meaning, long pauses and silences almost musical in effect, an atmosphere of menace or eroticism or derangement. The totality of effect is unsettling, almost surreal.

pin-up girl   Popular term for free publicity pictures of movie actresses distributed to men in the U.S. Armed Forces during World War II. The girls in these pictures were all provocatively clad and immensely appealing. Their pictures were pasted, glued and pinned in barracks, crew's quarters, airplane cockpits, footlockers and bars all over the world. Wherever soldiers, sailors, pilots or Marines were stationed, the pictures followed them.

The most popular pin-up girl was Betty Grable.

Pin-up girl is now used for any sexually attractive girl.

plastic   A synthetic polymer made from long chains of molecules strung together in chemistry laboratories. Plastic was a truly original invention since it was not made out of any raw materials in nature. The miracle plastics have been cellophane (1912), acetate (1927), vinyl (1928), plexiglass (1930), acrylics (1936), melmac (1937), styrene (1938), formica (1938), polyester (1940), nylon (1940), polyethylene (1942) and others. Plastic has revolutionized everyday, useful objects, and decorative ones as well. It can be used as a coating for the preservation of paper, as in plastic credit cards. In fact, credit cards are often referred to as plastic money. The whole concept of plastic is one of ersatz materials, and by extension one hears of plastic emotions, plastic tears, plastic smiles.

play hardball   Literally, to play baseball because the ball used in baseball is smaller and harder than the ball used in the game of softball. The smaller, "hard"-ball is more difficult to hit and field than the larger and softer "soft"- ball. Hence, baseball is considered the more difficult and more dangerous game.

In general use, the person who is said to play hardball "means business." He is not concerned about the niceties or the amenities or even the rules—if he can bend or disregard them. He is determined to win at all costs.

Use: "Mr. Gorbachev plays diplomatic hardball." (William Safire, *New York Times* Op-Ed page, September 19, 1988)

plumbers　From a sign tacked up by Nixon aides on the door of Room 16 in the Old Executive Office Building across the street from the White House. One of the aides' assignments was to investigate and plug up leaks of information to the press, such as the leak to the *New York Times* of the Pentagon Papers, on the Vietnam War, by Daniel Ellsberg. Their obsessive hunt led to the hiring of ex-CIA men for illegal break-ins (as into the office of Ellsberg's psychiatrist and into the headquarters of the Democratic National Committee in the Watergate complex). G. Gordon Liddy and E. Howard Hunt were eventually convicted of conspiracy to break-in, together with many others involved in what has come to be known as the Watergate scandal.

A plumber is one who tries to stop leaks of information.

Podunk　The mythical small town, with all that it implies in limited access to cultural activities, narrow points of view, constricted aspirations and experiences.

Pogo　Comic strip created in 1948 by Walt Kelly, a "graduate" of the Walt Disney Studios.

All the inhabitants of *Pogo* live in the great swamp of Okefenokee. They represent various "herbivores" and "carnivores" a fascinating melange of social types and classes.

Dominating this teeming scene are: Pogo, opossum: wise, warmhearted, kind, outgoing and self-effacing; and Albert, the Alligator, Pogo's friend, a self-centered anarchist.

One of the memorable *Pogo* lines has found a secure place in our language. "We have met the enemy and they are us."

Pollock, Jackson An abstract expressionist American painter (1912–1956) who conceived the unique method of laying huge canvases flat on the ground and dribbling paint all over them. Although he started with color, by 1951 he was using only black and white. The Philistine public at first hooted at his marbleized effects, but gradually he was perceived, at least by the critics, on his own terms: an innovator to whom the act of painting was more important than the painting itself. His seemingly formless works were imbued with the rhythms of his own controlled frenzy. His works include: *One* (1950); *White Light* (1954); *Blue Poles* (1953).

Use: "Martin Scorsese's sketch of the rugged, tormented painter Lionel Dobie in the trilogy *New York Stories* is the most sophisticated cinematic under-the-skin account of an artist I've seen. Even so, in the background, you discover the shade of *Jackson Pollock*, slinging paint and brooding in bars. Some stereotypes never die." (Kay Larson, *New York Magazine*, April 24, 1989)

Pollyanna Title character in a 1913 novel by Eleanor H. Porter. An eleven-year-old girl who comes to live with a rather dour maiden aunt in Vermont after her father dies, she evinces a totally sunny disposition in the face of every negative circumstance. She makes a game, in fact, of finding "something to be glad about." A Pollyanna is generally a derogatory name for one who sees good in everything, who is excessively and saccharinely optimistic. "Don't be such a Pollyanna!" is a put-down for one who constantly looks at the bright side of things.

Ponzi, Charles Ex-dishwasher, ex-forger, ex-smuggler of aliens into America, high-living Charles Ponzi (1877–1949) became the arch-swindler of his time. His get-rich-quick scheme promised a gullible public a 50% profit on their investment in three months. The money came pouring in.

Ponzi's scam was simplicity itself. As the new money rolled in, he used part of it to pay interest to the investors. Part went to defray the expenses of running the elaborate enterprise. The rest Ponzi squirreled away for himself. Ponzi banked on an endless flow of new money, but that didn't happen. Eventually the money stopped coming. The scheme collapsed. Ponzi went to prison for his elegant swindling.

In the long and colorful history of larceny, "Ponzi" has become a synonym for cheating on a grand scale.

Use: Carlson bilked his clients of millions. But despite his ingenious and apparently irresistible get-rich-quick plans, he ended up another Ponzi—penniless and in prison.

pop art   Art that uses the images of popular culture. Examples include the flags of Jasper Johns, the comic strips of Roy Lichtenstein, and the Campbell soup cans, Coke bottles and Marilyn Monroes of Andy Warhol. These images, popularized by the mass media, are shown up as the icons of modern American taste and values. Thus American painters and sculptors of the mid-1960s attempted to transmute "camp" into high art.

Popeye   Character in the comic strip *Thimble Theater*. The strip first appeared on December 19, 1919, and as a full-color Sunday page, April 18, 1925. Other characters were Olive Oyl, her cantankerous brother, Castor Oyl, and the hero Ham Gravy.

Popeye, the Sailor Man, appeared January 1929 making *Thimble Theater* one of the most successful strips of the 1930s. The readers had never met anyone like Popeye—a tough-talking, wise-guy, all-powerful sailor. The source of Popeye's omnipotence was uniquely, disarmingly simple—a can of spinach he always carried with him. Faced with some seemingly impossible challenge, Popeye would whip out his old reliable can of spinach and slurp down its contents. Thus fortified, he was up to any Herculean task—equal to, if not surpassing, *Superman.*

Popeye appeared in a movie and in movie and TV animated cartoons produced for Paramount Studios by Max Fleischer.

Portnoy   Alexander Portnoy, main character in *Portnoy's Complaint* (1969), an exuberant Rabelaisian tale of hilarious woe by American novelist and short story writer, Philip Roth. In a book-length monologue addressed to his psychiatrist, Portnoy presents himself as the victim of an over-solicitous Jewish mother and an ineffectual Jewish father. His mother is an expert in all the tricks of inducing guilt in her rebellious son. Outwardly a good little Jewish boy, secretly Portnoy seeks refuge in masturbation and other sexual perversities which only aggravate his guilt and shame.

Post, Emily   Author (1873–1960) of *Etiquette: The Blue Book of Social Usage* (1922), a book on manners for a democratic, upwardly mobile American population desiring standards for polite behavior. It made the top of the best-seller non-fiction list, and by 1945 had sold 666,000 copies. "What would Emily Post say?" became the criterion for resolving any social dilemma.

Potemkin village   A cardboard facade with nothing behind it, as on certain B-movie sets; a showy exterior to hide real and embarrassingly poor conditions. From Prince Potemkin, a favorite of Catherine II of Russia, for whose visit to the Ukraine in 1787 he had cardboard villages constructed.

Use: With regard to rehabilitated housing for the homeless: "The question is whether the extent of the work approximates what needs to be done and whether the examples we're being shown represent a Potemkin village." (N.Y.C. Comptroller Harrison J. Goldin, quoted in *The New York Times*, October 17, 1988)

Potsdam   In Germany, site of July 1945 conference to iron out the emerging post-World War II disagreements among the victorious Allies vis-a-vis spheres of influence in Europe. Stalin represented the U.S.S.R.; President Harry Truman the United States and Clement Attlee, newly elected prime minister, Great Britain.

Often referred to as the place where the freedom of Eastern European countries such as Bulgaria, Rumania and Hungary, was sacrificed to communist control by the U.S.S.R.

preemptive strike   A nuclear attack in anticipation of an imminent nuclear attack by an enemy. First strike capacity was considered an absolute necessity in the nuclear age since that might be all it would take to destroy an enemy country. The Soviet Union unilaterally abjured first strike. The United States refused to follow suit. A preemptive strike may be launched with conventional weapons, as in 1967, in what was to become known as the Six-Day War, when Israel made a preemptive strike against the Arab armies poised to strike at its borders.

The term "preemptive strike" may be used in any highly competitive field, as in stock takeovers.

Presley, Elvis Aron   Dubbed the "King of Rock n' Roll," Elvis Presley (1935–1977), like all great popular singers, was an original. Of himself he once said, "I don't sound like nobody."

Elvis represented a fusion of various musical currents in America's subcultures: black and white gospel, country and western, rhythm and blues. Within two years of his appearance on the musical scene, he was easily its dominant figure despite the criticisms that were leveled at him for his "novocaine lips, hormone hair, pale poached face, his guitar a sort of phallic tommy gun...he seemed to be sneering with his lips—Elvis, the pelvis, virtuoso of the hootchy-kootchy—his undistinguished whine."

Elvis was a symbol of youth in revolt, providing an opportunity for a restless, irreverent generation to thumb its nose at society. His rendering of songs like Heartbreak Hotel, Love Me Tender, Love Me True, Jail House Rock, You Ain't Nothin' But A Hound Dog left an indelible mark on American popular singing style, sold millions of records—and won him faithful audiences that make their year-round pilgrimages to his home and shrine, Graceland, in Memphis, Tennessee.

priceless ingredient   The famous ad written by Raymond Rubicam for E.R. Squibb and Sons (1921). The essential point of what was to become a permanent part of Squibb advertising is made in the opening parable:

In the city of Bagdad lived Hakeem, the wise one, and many people went to him for counsel, which he gave freely to all, asking nothing in return.

There came to him a young man, who had spent much but got little, and said: "Tell me, wise one, what shall I do to receive the most for that which I spend?"

Hakeem answered, "A thing that is bought or sold has no value unless it contains that which cannot be sold. Look for *The Priceless Ingredient*."

"But, what is this *Priceless Ingredient?* " asked the young man.

Spoke then the wise one, "My son, the *Priceless Ingredient* of every product in the marketplace is the *Honor* and *Integrity* of him who makes it. Consider his name before you buy."

In common discourse, the concept of "The Priceless Ingredient" has been extended into social and professional relationships.

Protocols of Zion   *Protocols of the Wise Men of Zion,* a fake document purporting to reveal a Jewish plot for world domination. First appeared in Russia in the early part of the 20th century. Revived by Arabs to undermine plans for a Jewish state in Israel. Refers to spurious anti-Semitic documents or hate propaganda.

Proustian   Suggestive of the style and subject matter of Marcel Proust (1871–1922), French novelist who wrote but one novel (in many volumes) throughout his life: *A La Recherche du Temps Perdu (Remembrance of Things Past).* It has many autobiographical elements.

Proust is known for his exhaustive, almost mesmeric immersion in the past in order to retrieve it whole. His sentences are often a full-page long, convoluted, so that no nuance of feeling or observation is lost. The reader is taken by the narrator, Marcel, with the first taste of a madeleine dipped into tea, back to Marcel's childhood at his grandparents' house in Combray. He relives the sensitive boy's clinging dependence upon his mother. He meets the personages who are to play important rôles in Marcel's memory: Swann and his daughter Gilberte; the lady in pink, Odette, the demi-mondaine whom Swann unhappily marries; the opportunistic Verdurins; the Duchess of Guermantes and her aristocratic circle; the writer Bergotte; the musician Vinteuil; and the great painter Elstir; the insidious homosexual Baron de Charlus etc.

The novel is permeated with the memory of sickly jealousies and heartaches, which are essential to Proustian love. And overwhelmingly the novel depicts in infinite detail the life of the French bourgeoisie from the second half of the 19th century to the outbreak of World War I. Sadness pervades the book as Marcel notes the changes that Time, the villain, has wrought. He decides to recapture the past, to transmute the suffering into a great work of art.

Prufrock, J. Alfred   Persona assumed by T.S Eliot (1888–1965) in his early poem "The Love Song of J. Alfred Prufrock" (1910–1911), that of an aging, inhibited man who daydreams of erotic encounters but is too timid and too fastidious and too indecisive to bring them to fruition when real opportunities are offered.

public enemies   A term applied in the 1930s by J. Edgar Hoover, director of the United States Federal Bureau of Investigation, to a group of professional, career criminals. They were widely sought by local and federal police.

Now, generally used to describe individuals who are a constant threat to the peace, security, stability, of a society or a segment of a society.

public enemy number 1   See DILLINGER, JOHN.

pull a punch or punches   In boxing, to punch an opponent with less than one's full power, to hold back.

In informal use, to moderate one's speech or actions, to act with less force than one is capable of.

Use: In addressing the guilty man, the judge, usually severe and harsh in his speech, tended to pull his punches.

pumpkin papers   Microfilmed documents alleged to have been passed by Alger Hiss of the State Department to Whitaker Chambers, a member of a communist cell, and hidden in a hollowed-out pumpkin on Chambers' Pipe Creek Farm. When Chambers renounced his communist past, he implicated Hiss. Hiss pleaded innocence. When Chambers produced the pumpkin and its papers, Hiss was convicted of perjury and imprisoned for 44 months.

Now refers to hidden and farfetched evidence, evidence produced almost like a rabbit pulled out of a hat. (See also HISS, ALGER.)

punch drunk   In boxing, the characteristically slow speech, hand tremors and uncertain movements of a boxer who has been badly and frequently beaten about the head. His speech and gait indicate that he has suffered some brain damage.

Hence, by extension, any dazed, uncertain, unsteady, befuddled speech or behavior.

Use: "He looked and sounded punch drunk: speech slurred and slow, his hands trembling, weaving erratically in and out among the guests."

Purple Heart   U.S. medal awarded to a member of the Armed Forces for wounds inflicted by an enemy. Now used colloquially as in: "You should get the Purple Heart for what you have had to endure from your so-called best friend."

Quantum leap   Originally from the word quantum, meaning amount, and then from the phenomenon in physics where an electron jumps from one orbit in an atom to another.

Quantum leap is used in everyday language to mean simply a significant or very great jump from one dimension to another.

Use: In a *New York Times* article on Soviet emigré criminals in the United States (June 4, 1989): "'It is a quantum leap to jump to a statement that there is an organized Mafia,' said Mark Handelman, executive vice president of the New York Association for New Americans..."

Queeg, Captain Philip   Commander of the World War II minesweeper *Caine* in *The Caine Mutiny* (1951), a novel by Herman Wouk (1915–). Like his prototype, Captain Bligh in *Mutiny on the Bounty*, Queeg is tyrannical, cowardly and paranoid. He is forcibly relieved of his command. At the court-martial of the mutineers, Queeg is manipulated by a clever lawyer for the defense into exhibiting his extreme psychological instability. A neurotic idiosyncrasy of Queeg was to keep nervously rolling some steel ball-bearings in his fist.

quisling   From Vidkun Quisling, founder of the Fascist National Unity Party of Norway who collaborated with Hitler in the conquest and occupation of Norway. He was found guilty of high treason by a Norwegian court and executed in October 1945 at the end of World War II.

The term "quisling" was coined by Winston Churchill to signify traitor.

"Quiz Kids" A popular radio program of the 1940s. A kind of juvenile "Information, Please" featuring exceptionally bright kids answering questions that stump adults. Clifton Fadiman was the moderator.

"Quiz kid" has come to mean any unusually bright kid.

R

radar Acronym for *radio detection and ranging*. A device for ascertaining the position and speed of a moving object (an automobile or a plane, for example) by "bouncing a radio wave off it and analyzing the reflected wave." The American Stealth bomber is supposed to be able to fly so low that it escapes radar detection. "Radar" is used for any sensitive ability to detect, as if one had antennae.

Use: "The best that Mr. [Jesse] Jackson can do for his party is to turn out urban blacks without turning off resentful whites. That requires a low-flying campaign that slips under the radar of national television." (William Safire, *New York Times*, October 13, 1988)

radical chic Phrase coined in 1970 by Tom Wolfe, American journalist and novelist, in an essay of the same name. It referred to a party given by Leonard Bernstein, famous American composer and conductor, for the Black Panthers. Then the sponsorship of various radical causes and dinner invitations to members of radical leftist groups became fashionable in some sections of high society; hence, radical chic.

Raft, George American movie actor (1895–1980) who played with great authenticity the role of menacing gangster, the slicked-back dark-haired variety.

rain check When a baseball game or other outdoor sports event or concert has been postponed or interrupted by rain or other unforeseen circumstance, the spectators are given a ticket to be used at a future performance. This is called a rain check.

In general use "an invitation or requested postponement of an invitation" until a more convenient time: "Sorry you can't make it this Saturday. We'll give you a rain check."

Raisin in the Sun, A   Play (1959) by Lorraine Hansberry (1930–1965). The title was taken from a poem, "Harlem," by the black American poet, Langston Hughes (1902–1967), in which he asks:

> What happens to a dream deferred?
> Does it dry up
> Like a raisin in the sun?

A raisin in the sun stands for frustrated hopes and withered ambitions.

Rambo   Strongman hero of a series of global action films with Sylvester Stallone in the leading role. Rambo, as a mightily muscled, lone crusader, takes on the evils of the world—in Southeast Asia, in Afghanistan, and who knows where next.

Use: "Teen Murders His Family in Rambo Rage"—headline in *New York Post*, March 23, 1989)

Rand, Sally   Dancer, actress (1904–1979). Sally Rand's "act" was the sensation of the Chicago Century of Progress Exposition (1933–34). Her performance in the Streets of Paris concession was said to have made the fair a financial success. It was simplicity itself: Sally did a slow dance with two ostrich plumes to Debussy's "Clair de Lune." Lit by Lavender lights, she slowly rotated the plumes around her nude body—revealing absolutely nothing of what the frenzied audiences thought they would be vouchsafed at least a peek at.

Nudity, Sally maintained, was nothing new. She simply made it financially rewarding through her "sales methods." For 30 highly profitable years, Sally "presented" her act to virtually insatiable audiences.

Sally created a new genre—and helped pave the way for more kinds of "provocative" dancing.

Rashomon   Japanese film (1950) directed by Akira Kurosawa. The central event of the movie, the rape of a young bride and the murder of her noble husband as they are riding through a forest in 9th-century

Kyoto, is reenacted four times from four different points of view: the bride, her husband, the bandit and a woodcutter who witnessed the crime. The film suggests the unreliability of evidence and poses the question: What is truth?

Thus, Rashomon is an allusion to the flickering nature of truth, and perhaps to our inability ever to know the real truth.

Use: "[Russell] Baker, 63, grew disenchanted with reporting. 'It's almost impossible to get it right,' he said. 'The deadlines are too quick, and you don't have time to go into the background. It's Rashomon: you interview four different people, you get four different answers.'" (*Newsweek*, June 12, 1989)

Rasputin, Grigory Yefimovich   An illiterate, licentious Russian peasant mystic, Rasputin (1872–1916) was introduced into the Russian Court in 1908. Here, his reputation as a mystic and a healer brought him to the attention of the Czar, who soon became convinced that the destinies of his hemophiliac son, his family and his Court were irrevocably linked to Rasputin. This burgeoning influence with the Czar was seen as a sinister menace. A small group of conspirators, led by the Czar's cousin, decided to get rid of Rasputin. At a special dinner, held in the luxurious palace of Prince Yusupov, they poisoned Rasputin's wine, shot him twice, bound him hand and foot, and threw his body into the Neva River.

Rasputin exercised mysterious powers over others—especially women. Essentially, he was an evil man. Never hesitating to use his powers, Rasputin was always moved by deep, dark impulses.

real McCoy   Around 1890, Norman Selby (1873–1940) left his farm in Indiana. A year later he appeared as a boxer under the name of Kid McCoy. He was a phenomenal fighter, challenging anyone, anywhere. For years he averaged a fight a month and won most of them by knockouts. Quite naturally, many imitation Kid McCoys began to appear. On March 24, 1899, the Kid settled any possible confusion. In a brutal 20-round match, he knocked out the formidable Joe Choynski. In the words of the *San Francisco Examiner*'s boxing reporter "Now, you've seen The Real McCoy. There are other accounts of how this phrase came into being. Like this one, none of them has been authenticated.

In general use, what is promised, stated, or implied, usually preceded by "the" or "the real."

Use: "You were cheated. The dealer sold you a copy. The real McCoy is in the New York Gallery."

Rebel Without A Cause   Movie (1955) starring James Dean (1931–1955), a cult hero for disaffected youth. Dean played the part of Jim Stark, a confused, inarticulate teenager searching for the meaning of manhood, feeling betrayed by the hypocrisy and weakness of adults. He had a desperate need for love and understanding. Dean's death in an auto accident at the age of 24 turned him into a tragic symbol. He became, himself, the "rebel without a cause." He starred in only two other films, *East of Eden* and *Giant*.

Use: A headline in *Newsweek*, April 24, 1989, turns this phrase around into "A Lifelong Rebel With A Cause." The article is an obituary on Abbie Hoffman, one of the Chicago Seven defendants charged with and acquitted of inciting riots at the 1968 Democratic National Convention.

red neck   Originally an unlettered farm laborer, especially from the South, it has now taken on a number of related meanings: a person who is bigoted, reactionary, prejudiced, narrow-minded. Frequently used as an intensifier with HARD HAT.

Right Stuff, The   Book (1979) about the training of the first astronauts, written by Tom Wolfe and later adapted for the movies, with John Glenn, Sam Shepherd. Having the right stuff is having what it takes to complete a dangerous mission.

"The Road Not Taken"   A lyric poem by Robert Frost (1875–1963), the last three lines of which are:

> Two roads diverged in a wood, and I—
> I took the one less traveled by,
> And that has made all the difference

These lines refer to the choices we make at every step in our lives and to the consequences of our choices. We cannot help wondering how our lives would have differed had we taken other paths, and especially had we taken the less conventional road.

Use: "A man of high intellect, winning charm and puckish humor, Bukharin embodied the alternative to Stalinism, the road not taken." (From "The Limits of Glasnost," *Newsweek*, November 16, 1987)

Robbins, Jerome   New York-born dancer and choreographer (1918–) who together with GEORGE BALANCHINE codirected the New York City Ballet, where he created such ballets as *Dancers at a Gathering* and *The Goldberg Variations* among many others. He is most widely known, however, for his energetic, freewheeling American-style choreography and direction in such Broadway musicals as *On the Town* (1944) and *West Side Story* (1957), both of which were done to the music of Leonard Bernstein.

Robinson, Bill (Bojangles)   American tap dancer extraordinaire (1878–1949). At the peak of his phenomenal dancing career, he was the toast of Broadway night clubs and musical comedy. Bojangles was equally successful in Hollywood where he appeared in 14 films. Among the most memorable were *The Little Colonel* (1935), *The Little Rebel* (1935) and *Rebecca of Sunnybrook Farm* (1938), all with Shirley Temple.

Almost universally known as Bojangles, Robinson continued dancing until his mid-sixties. His versatility, endurance and inventiveness won him the title of "satrap of tap." His performances epitomized the spirit of tap dancing. It was said of Bojangles, that "his feet responded directly to the music—his head had nothing to do with it."

Use: "[Sammy] Davis was above all an entertainer...In the moments before a 1987 Vegas show...Davis warmed up backstage...then the curtain opened and it was...Mr. Bojangles." (Arthur Schwartz, *Newsweek*, May 28, 1990)

Robinson, Edward G.   Actor (1893–1973). Robinson was the personification of the gangster in films such as *Little Caesar* (1930).

Robinson, Jack (Jackie) Roosevelt   Black baseball player (1919–1972). While Robinson was playing in the Negro National League, Branch Rickey, president of the National League Brooklyn Dodgers, asked him to join the Dodgers as the first black major league player. Robinson accepted, breaking the color barrier and paving the way for many other black players into the Major Leagues.

In 1949, Robinson won the Most Valuable Player Award. In 1972, he was the first black man to be inducted into the National Baseball Hall of Fame.

In the long and troubled history of race relations in America, Jackie (as he was affectionately called by millions of fans) was a true pioneer.

Use: "There had not been a Jewish manager in the entire history of Boston and Northeastern [not quite our class, as they used to say on the Mayflower], and my father, with his eighth grade education wasn't exactly suited to be the Jackie Robinson of the insurance business." (Philip Roth, *Portnoy's Complaint* [1969])

Rockefeller   American business and philanthropic dynasty founded by John D. Rockefeller (1839–1937) on the basis of an oil fortune amassed by Standard Oil Company of New Jersey. In 1911 this corporation was ordered dissolved by the U.S. Supreme Court as a result of an antitrust suit. It owned three-fourths of the entire oil business in the United States and was a symbol of the concentration of business power in the hands of a few individuals.

John D. Rockefeller's only son was John D. Rockefeller Jr. (1874–1960) who devoted himself primarily to philanthropic and civic causes: the restoration of Colonial Williamsburg; development of Rockefeller Center in New York City; the purchase and building of the United Nations permanent headquarters in New York City; the management of the Rockefeller Foundation; and the development of the Rockefeller Institute for Medical Research, set up by his father in 1901. John D. and John D. Jr. are estimated to have given more than $750 million for philanthropic causes.

John D. Jr. and Abby Aldrich had five sons: John D. 3rd (1906–1978); Nelson (1908–1979); Laurance (1910–); Winthrop (1912–1973); and David (1915–).

The sons devoted themselves not only to business and philanthropy but to politics as well. Winthrop Rockefeller was twice elected Republican governor of Arkansas. Nelson Rockefeller was elected four times as governor of New York State and he served as vice president of the United States under President Gerald R. Ford. The fourth generation of Rockefellers continues to be active on all fronts.

In the modern world, to be rich as Croesus has been replaced by "to be rich as Rockefeller."

Rockettes   A long line of female dancers famous for their precision high-kicking in Radio City Music Hall shows in New York.

Rockwell, Norman   American illustrator and cartoonist (1894–1978) who between 1916 and 1963 painted 317 covers for the popular magazine, *The Saturday Evening Post*. Rockwell painted hundreds more for *Boy's Life*, a publication of the Boy Scouts of America. He seems to have captured, with humor and sentiment, the pleasant and homey spirit of American small-town characters and their everyday concerns: visits to the doctor, the dentist, the teacher; eating at luncheonette counters; dunking in the old swimming hole; expressions of puppy love.

A Norman Rockwell is truly as American as apple pie.

Use: In the *New York Times* (September 4, 1988) John Gross writes about the film *Tucker*, directed by Francis Ford Coppola: "The Tucker home is a comfortable frame house; there are lots of dogs, and a plump cook, and, when morale needs a fillip, collective trips to the local soda fountain. One way and another, it is all rather like a Norman Rockwell come to life."

Rocky   Main character in the 1976 Oscar winning film of the same name. SYLVESTER STALLONE stars as Rocky Balboa, a boxer who wins against formidable odds in fairy-tale endings. His street-smart cunning combined with true grit and a spaniel-eyed innocence turned him into a new popular hero.

Rogers, Will   Actor and humorist Will Rogers' (1879–1935) unique act in the *Ziegfeld Follies* (1916–1925) consisted of rope-twirling, chewing gum, telling jokes. Underneath his innocent-looking performance, Rogers was an unusually perceptive political commentator. His thrusts at shenanigans in high places, though delivered with a smile and a drawl, unerringly found their mark. He soon became known as America's "cowboy philosopher." In 1922, he conducted a daily syndicated column in the *New York Times* and 350 other newspapers.

Rogers reached a vast (40 million) and hugely appreciative audience. For his good-natured, homely satire, he found himself compared with "Mr. Dooley," Artemus Ward and Mark Twain.

Successful as he was on stage and in the news media, Rogers achieved even greater success in the movies: *The Connecticut Yankee* (1931), *State Fair (1933), David Harum* (1934).

On August 15, 1935, Rogers died with his pilot-friend Wiley Post in an airplane crash near Point Barrow, Alaska.

roller-coaster   A series of open cars connected into a train, which moves along the tracks of a high, sharply winding trestle, gathering momentum on the upward incline and then plunging down the steep-tilted decline to the accompaniment of screams from thrill-seeking passengers in amusement parks.

By extension, a roller-coaster has come to be any sharply swinging up and down movement, so that one may refer to the stock market's being on a roller-coaster or a person's being on an emotional roller-coaster.

Rolls-Royce   The aristocrat of expensive, hand-tooled cars, made in Great Britain. Generally driven by chauffeurs, for the very rich.

By extension, the symbol of the best, the most elegant, the most expensive, the classiest.

Use: "Congress is grabbing for a Cadillac salary, but it already has a Rolls-Royce pension." (*Palm Beach Post*, February 4, 1989)

roll with a punch   In boxing, to move one's head or body in the same direction of an opponent's punch in order to diminish its effect.

In general use: To deal successfully or vigorously with a downturn in one's fortunes.

Rommel, Erwin   German general (1891–1944) in World War II. Field marshal of the African Theater of War. Commander of the Afrika Korps. Known as the "Desert Fox" for outwitting and outflanking Allied forces in Egypt, Libya and Tunisia. Eventually beaten by Field Marshall Montgomery at El Alamein and sent to the Normandy area. Suspected of participating in the 1944 assassination attempt on Hitler, he was forced to commit suicide.

Rorschach test   Introduced by Hermann Rorschach, a Swiss psychiatrist, it is a psychological probe for personality traits based on an individual's interpretation of a series of random ink blots. What the subject sees is a configuration not in the inkblots but in his own mind. Many jokes have arisen out of patients' interpretations. Often the jokes are at the expense of the psychiatrist who, in the eyes of his patients, is a dirty man showing dirty pictures.

A person's interpretation of certain modern plays like *Waiting for Godot* is often a Rorschach test of his own obsessions and predilections rather than an understanding of what may have been the intention of the author.

Use: "The question proved a political Rorschach test, and the Governor [Dukakis] reinforced the sense that he is a public figure who does not care to, or does not know, how to touch the heart." (*New York Times*, October 13, 1988)

rosebud   Mystery word uttered with his last breath by the dying tycoon in the opening scene of Orson Welles' film CITIZEN KANE. The movie is a search for the real Kane behind the wealth, power, acquisitions, achievements. What makes him tick? "Rosebud" is thought to be the key. Who is Rosebud? In the closing scene, when workmen are throwing into the flames the accumulated junk in Kane's castle, they pick up a sled. On it we see the faded letters "Rosebud." It is the sled Kane played with when he was a poor boy, before he was thrust out of his home by his mother to live with a guardian in the style necessitated by his unexpected inheritance. "Rosebud" is a symbol of the unspoiled happiness of one's youth.

Rosie the riveter   Character in popular patriotic song and in a satirical poster by NORMAN ROCKWELL. She symbolized the women who took over men's jobs on the home front, especially in defense plants, during World War II under the government policy of "equal pay for equal work." Women, who no longer had to be traditionally "feminine," have been entering the work force in greater and greater numbers ever since.

rose is a rose is a rose, a   Quotation from the works of GERTRUDE STEIN (1874–1946), American writer who lived in Paris most of her life. The line is from "Sacred Emily" in *Geography and Plays* (1922). It illustrates Stein's theory of naming (use of nouns) in poetry. She wrote: "You can love a name and if you love a name then saying that name any number of times only makes you love it more" and poetry is "really loving the name of anything." Stylistically, Stein is famous for her experimentation with language and composition. She loved repetition, rhyme, automatic writing coming from the subconscious, and she hated punctuation.

The phrase is always quoted playfully to indicate the inadequacy of description; that is, what more can one say about something, since everything is subsumed in the one word "rose."

Use: Headline in *New York Times* (August 31, 1988) review of the play *The Man Who Mistook His Wife for a Hat*: "A Rose Is a Rose Is a 'Convoluted Form.'"

Roseland   The home of ballroom dancing at "ten cents a dance." The brain child of Louis J. Brecker, Roseland opened in New York City at 51st Street and Broadway on New Year's Eve, 1919. Mounted police had to control the crowds clamoring to get in. On a dais behind a silken rope sat 150 taxi dancers (hostesses) waiting to be summoned by gentlemen with tickets. It was all very proper, jacket and tie de rigueur, no dating the clients. Nevertheless, there is a record of 550 couples meeting at Roseland and subsequently marrying. Roseland was open seven nights a week, with music by the Big Bands of Glenn Miller, Benny Goodman, Artie Shaw et al.

With the advent of rock n' roll, disco dancing replaced traditional social dancing and Roseland went into decline, although it has never closed. In 1956, Roseland moved to 52nd Street between Broadway and 8th Avenue. The taxi dancers had been eliminated. In 1977, Albert Ginsberg bought Roseland, and brought back the taxi dancers, who now included men for female patrons. The price was now a dollar a dance, open Thursdays only.

Rothko, Mark   American artist (1903–1970) born in Russia; immigrated to the United States in 1913. An abstract expressionist, he covered huge canvases with horizontal bands of luminous color, suffused in focus and seemingly floating in air.

Rothko said that he was searching for the most simple means to express universal truths. He hoped that the effect of his paintings would be calm and contemplation.

In looking at certain dawns and sunsets one may say, "Look, a Rothko sky!"

Rouault, Georges   French expressionist (1871–1958) whose early training in the restoration of medieval stained glass carried over into the black-outlined jewel-like colors of his paintings of judges, clowns, outcasts, prostitutes, saints and kings. He wanted to create "the passion mirrored upon a human face" as in *The Old King*. Of deep religious faith, he was haunted by the image of the suffering Christ, e.g., in *Head of Christ* and in *Christ Mocked by Soldiers*. His slashing brush strokes as well as his mixture of rage and compassion mark him as heir to van Gogh.

round up the usual suspects   A line spoken by Police Prefect Captain Louis Renault (Claude Rains) at the end of the movie *Casablanca*, directed by Michael Curtiz in 1942 and starring HUMPHREY BOGART, INGRID BERGMAN and Paul Henreid. Bergman and Henreid (a leader of the underground movement against the Nazis) are racing to board a plane leaving Casablanca. Bogart has engineered their flight to safety. Bogart is holding Rains at gunpoint so that he will not prevent them from boarding the plane. At this moment the Nazi Major Strasser arrives in hot pursuit. He draws a gun to shoot Henreid. Bogart then shoots the Nazi. Covering up for Bogart, Claude Rains tells his men that Strasser has been shot and that they are to "round up the usual suspects." For Bogart and Rains, this is the beginning of a "beautiful friendship."

Use: In an article in *The New York Post* (March 27, 1989), headlined "Who's Gunnin' for Gotti?" we read of a wild-card suspect, Michael McCray, a Queens medical photographer who claimed he planted a dud to scare Mafia leader Gotti in a protest against drug-dealing. The article continues: "Should McCray's claim prove to be another dud, police will have to resume rounding up the usual suspects."

Rubashov, Nicolai Salmanovich   Hero of *Darkness at Noon* (1941), a novel by Arthur Koestler. A top-level Bolshevik, a brilliant intellectual with ideals who has hewn to Party discipline even when he has had to violate personal trust and friendship, he is arrested and accused of plotting against the life of Stalin and of being ambivalent about the regime. During his successive interrogations in a prison cell, he gradually allows himself to be brainwashed with the rationalization that by confessing to these false charges and accepting execution for them he will be performing a last act of selflessness for the revolutionary cause.

Rubashov stands for those who betray their own humanity, who are seduced into believing that the end justifies the means, only to discover that the ends themselves have been brutally tarnished.

Ruth, George Herman (Babe)   Baseball player (1895–1948). Starting as a left-handed pitcher, by 1919 Ruth was the best in the American League. When his Red Sox manager moved him to the outfield that season, Ruth took off like the proverbial rocket, piling up one home run record after another.

Following the White Sox scandal of 1919–1920, public interest in baseball fell to its lowest point. Ruth's spectacular playing literally arrested baseball's precipitous slide. He was widely hailed as the "savior of baseball."

Ruth's performance as a Yankee player was a major factor in attracting vast numbers of fans to the new Yankee Stadium, which some inspired writer called "the House that Ruth built."

In 1936, Ruth was inducted into the Baseball Hall of Fame.

A man of heroic, mythic proportions, he taxed the ingenuity of the writers of his time to capture, in words, his essential qualities. "The Bambino" and the "Sultan of Swat" seem to be the most promising contenders. The most durable—and the simplest—of all is probably "the greatest slugger of them all."

A measure of Ruth's worldwide fame and prestige turned up during World War II when the Japanese hurled at the Americans what they considered the supreme insult, "To Hell with Babe Ruth."

S

Sacco-Vanzetti   Political anarchists Nicola Sacco, a shoemaker, and Bartolomeo Vanzetti, a fish peddler, became the central figures in an international cause célèbre. Italian immigrants to the United States, they were convicted of murdering the paymaster and guard of a shoe factory in South Braintree, Massachusetts, during a payroll holdup in 1920. In spite of worldwide protests and demonstrations, they were finally executed on August 23, 1927. Many people still think of them as victims of a frame-up, punished for their political convictions and labor affiliations. Books continue to be written trying to prove either their guilt or innocence.

Sad Sack, The   Comic strip created by George Baker, an ex-Disney animator. *The Sad Sack* first appeared in 1942, in *Yank*, the U.S. Army enlisted man's weekly magazine. According to Baker, the Sad Sack was just "an average soldier" reflecting the soldier's way of looking at and responding to the world around him: "resigned, help-less, tired, and beaten."

The world, it seemed, had conspired to deprive the Sad Sack of the simple, expected joys. He never got the girl he wanted. Army regula-tions seemed especially set up to confuse and frustrate him. His superiors took advantage of him. In Army parlance, he was just "a sad sack of s - - t."

The Sad Sack was enormously popular. In a sense, he was, accord-ing to Maurice Horn, an authority on comics, the classic comic figure "reflecting the frustrations of the common man but at the same time…something for the common man to look down on." Hence a

Sad Sack is any ordinary mortal, helpless against the system that seems stacked against him. Also applied to anything lackluster, lacking in vitality or distinction, poor quality, below average.

Use: "The [Tony nominating] committee's task was not easy. It never is, but this *Sad Sack* season in particular must have given as much pause for prayer and thought." (Clive Barnes, in *New York Post,* May 8, 1989)

Sarajevo   City in Yugoslavia (then Austrian) where the Archduke Francis Ferdinand, heir to the Austrian throne, was assassinated by a Serbian nationalist, Gavrilo Princip, on June 28, 1914. Within days Austria-Hungary declared war on nearby Serbia. Soon all of Europe was involved and World War I began. By the end of the war the number of dead on both sides was nine million; the number of wounded 20 million. Sarajevo is associated with political assassination and its awesome consequences.

Use: "Assassination was a quaint idea when *The Manchurian Candidate* was first released in 1962, evoking places like Sarajevo..." (*New York Times,* May 23, 1988)

Saturday night massacre   President Richard Nixon's abrupt dismissal on Saturday night, October 20, 1973, of Archibald Cox, the special Watergate prosecutor who had insisted that Nixon release the tapes of Oval Office conversations. On the same night Attorney General Elliot Richardson resigned rather than fire Cox. Then Nixon fired William D. Ruckelshaus, the deputy attorney general, who also had refused to fire Cox. That left Solicitor General Robert H. Bork to do the actual firing of Cox.

The term is now used to connote the threat of arbitrary, wholesale firing.

Use: "Last month, executive editor (of the *New York Times*) Max Frankel told five of the (Washington) bureau's reporters that they were being relocated to New York. The move was seen by some as a way to 'clean house.' 'Shipler (David K. Shipler, chief diplomatic correspondent) wanted to stay on,' says a staffer. 'But after the massacre, he made it clear that his days at the paper were over.'" (From *New York Magazine,* March 1, 1988)

saved by the bell   When a boxer is knocked down by his opponent in a boxing match, he is allowed 10 referee counts to get on his feet without assistance. If he cannot arise unassisted at the count of 10, the bout is ended and he is declared "out"—the loser. If, however, the gong sounds before the referee has counted 10, the boxer is said to be "saved by the bell."

In general use, saved by the bell means to be rescued just in time from trouble or disaster by some unforeseen, unanticipated, lucky incident or interference.

say it ain't so, Joe   In the 1919 World Series, the Chicago White Sox were overwhelmingly favored to beat the Cincinnati Redlegs. But it was not to be. Eight Chicago players decided to throw the series by deliberately and uncharacteristically under-performing. The honest bettors lost heavily. The gamblers, who knew about the "fix" in advance, made the proverbial "mint." Most of the corrupt players got about $5,000 apiece.

A year-long investigation revealed who the players were in this sordid, corrupt transaction. The *Chicago White Sox* emerged with a stigma that remained with them for a long time. They were, unofficially of course, called the Chicago *Black* Sox.

When the players emerged from the grand jury room, a group of admiring young fans were waiting for them. One tearful small boy approached the Chicago centerfielder, Shoeless Joe Jackson:

"It ain't true, is it, Joe?"

"Yes, boys, I'm afraid it is," Jackson mournfully replied.

Crushed, the small boy plaintively looked up at his fallen idol: "Say it ain't so, Joe."

Never actually proved or disproved, this touching encounter has become an inseparable part of baseball folklore. It remains a moving account of youthful idealism tarnished or destroyed by its awareness of the harsh realities of the real world.

Use: When Pete Rose was charged with gambling and betting on baseball games in which his own team (Cincinnati Reds) was playing, the *Daily News* of June 28, 1989, carried this headline, reminiscent of an incident reported during the trial of the Chicago White Sox players: "Cincinnati Cries: 'Say It Ain't So, Rose!'"

Schweitzer, Albert   Scientist (1875–1965). An exemplary figure whose central precept was "reverence for life." He gave up very successful careers as an organist, a scholar and a theologian (he wrote *The Quest of the Historical Jesus* in 1906 as well as a biography of

J.S. Bach in 1905) to study medicine. He had determined that when he reached the age of 30 he would devote the rest of his life to serving mankind. He founded the Schweitzer Hospital in Lambarene, Gabon, Africa, to treat the native population. In matters of healing, he became a benevolent despot. The compound at Lambarene became a Mecca for all those inspired by Schweitzer's humanitarianism to follow his example in other parts of the world. In 1952 he was awarded the Nobel Peace Prize. His name has become a spiritual symbol, a symbol of dedication to the poor, the ill.

Use: "[Dr. Konner] argues that if you put a bunch of bright, competitive people into white coats and scrub suits, expect them to have memorized human genetics but skipped Homer and permit them to treat very sick people they've never met in street clothes, they are unlikely to present themselves as Dr. Albert Schweitzers. He may be right; but the European humanistic tradition also produced Dr. Mengele..." (Gerald Weissman, review of *Becoming a Doctor* by Melvin Konner, *New York Times* Book Review, July 26, 1987)

scorched earth   Military policy of a retreating army, to burn and destroy the land and its contents so that a pursuing enemy can make no use of it. This was a recurrent tactic of the Russian army, as it retreated from Napoleon in the 19th century and from the Nazi German divisions in the 20th century.

The term's use has been extended to difficult domestic battles, as in a particularly hostile divorce. You burn your bridges behind you almost out of spite.

Use: "The practice is 'hardball,' and the practitioners talk of 'scorched earth' or 'taking no prisoners' or 'giving no quarter' in advocating a client's cause: 'When I go into the courtroom, I come in to do battle—I'm not there to do a minuet,' was how the lawyer Gerry Spence explained his philosophy in the American Bar Association Journal." (*New York Times* August 5, 1988)

score   To accumulate "points" in a game or match. In football, the score is expressed as points for touchdown, field goal etc. In baseball, the score is given in runs.

In general usage, to score means to succeed, to win, to triumph.

Scottsboro Boys   One of the greatest civil rights battles of the 1930s centered on nine black youths accused of raping two prostitutes. It all started as a fight on a freight train between white and black men. The blacks won and tossed the whites off the train. The two prostitutes remained on the train.

At Scottsboro, Alabama, the authorities stopped the train and removed the black men and the two prostitutes: Victoria Price, 19, and Ruby Gates, 17. The women accused the men of gang rape.

The trial of the Scottsboro Boys (as they came to be known) was marked by widespread hysteria and threats of lynching. During the trial, the defense introduced evidence that the women showed no physical sign that they had been raped. Nonetheless, the all-white jury found the men guilty. Eight were sentenced to death. The ninth (a 13-year-old) was sentenced to life imprisonment.

The verdict was appealed to the Supreme Court, with Samuel Leibowitz, a brilliant New York City lawyer, heading the defense. The Court threw out the original Guilty verdict, holding that the defendants were not allowed adequate counsel. A later ruling held that the exclusion of blacks from the jury was unconstitutional. Under pressure, the state eventually dropped charges against four of the Scottsboro Boys—and later placed the remaining four on probation.

The case of the Scottsboro Boys stands as a complex symbol of justice denied/justice triumphant.

SDI   Strategic Defense Initiative, also referred to as Star Wars. A comprehensive laser cover over the United States to knock out any incoming Soviet atomic missiles before they can land. This massive military project was ardently sponsored by President Ronald Reagan. It threatened to upset the existing balance of terror called Mutual Assured Destruction (MAD), which was credited by many as having prevented nuclear war. The Soviet Union understandably balked at this so-called "peace" program.

Use: "Now that spring is upon us, every gardener should develop his or her own Strategic Defense Initiative. Here's a list of non-lethal safe guards." (Article on animal destruction of gardens, *Metropolitan Home*, April 1989)

search-and-destroy   Refers to the mission of U.S. patrol units in the Vietnam War to search for pockets of Viet Cong resistance in the jungle and to wipe them out. Now used for any such mission, as in fighting drugs or, comically, even in fighting cockroaches and other pests.

second front   "Open up that second front" became a rallying cry in 1943–1944 for a propaganda campaign in Great Britain and the United States to take the pressure off the Russian armies on the fiercely contested Eastern front. Finally, on June 6, 1944, the Allies launched an amphibious attack on German-occupied western Europe and established a beachhead in Normandy.

A second front is a strategy for dividing an enemy's resources by attacking on more than one front.

send someone to the showers   In baseball and football, removing a player from the game for poor playing or engaging in illegal plays on the field.

In general use, someone who has been dismissed from his position is said to have been sent to the showers.

Sennett, Mack   (1880–1960) Silent film pioneer in the field of slapstick comedy. Founded the Keystone Company using zany actors recruited from vaudeville and the circus: Slim Summerville, Fatty Arbuckle, Mabel Normand, Ben Turpin, Buster Keaton, Chester Conklin, Louise Fazenda and Charlie Chaplin.

A Mack Sennett comedy situation is any sequence of events that is illogical, irreverent, farcical, extravagantly slapstick. Pratfalls, pie-throwing, grotesque physical types and bathing beauties are some of the ingredients. (See also KEYSTONE KOPS.)

separate but equal   The notion that no discrimination existed if separate but approximately equal facilities were provided for Negroes and whites; enunciated by the Supreme Court of the United States in *Plessy v. Ferguson* (1896). This doctrine in effect condoned segregation in schools, restaurants, theaters and transportation. In 1954, the Court reversed itself and unanimously ruled in *Brown v. Board of Education* in Topeka, Kansas that the doctrine of separate but equal was discriminatory and damaging to the educational development of black children. It ruled that all children were entitled to the equal protection of the laws guaranteed by the 14th Amendment. Therefore, state laws requiring segregation in public schools were unconstitutional.

September Morn   Early 20th-century painting by Paul Chabas, a portrait of a young woman bathing nude in a pond. Not a great work of art, it was made into a lithograph designed for a calendar. It achieved international fame as the most famous "pornographic" painting because it was attacked by ANTHONY COMSTOCK, "The great American Blue Nose" and head of the New York City Society for the Suppression of Vice.

When *September Morn* was brought to his attention, Comstock ordered the dealer to remove the "filthy" picture from the window. The dealer refused. Comstock brought suit. He lost the case. Ironically, in the years following the trial, over 7,000,000 copies of *September Morn* were sold. It still sells.

Sergeant Bilko   Leading character of a highly popular television SITCOM, zestfully played for belly laughs by Phil Silvers (1912–1965). TOP BANANA on the burlesque circuit, Silvers brightened television with his high-spirited antics. Working with a superb supporting cast from scripts by the not yet famous Neil Simon, Silvers and his company created one of television's zestier comedy classics.

The action of "You'll Never Get Rich" (later known as "The Phil Silvers Show") takes place on an army base presumably run by Colonel John Hall, played by Paul Ford, whose looks alone produced wild laughter. Actually, however, the scheming, money-hungry, motor pool Sergeant Ernie Bilko (Phil Silvers) runs the base. His mind teems with endless harebrained schemes for bilking everyone he meets.

Bilko is the archetypical con man: fast-talking, endlessly inventive, thoroughly, incurably manipulative.

"Sesame Street"   Pioneering educational television program for children. Begun in the late 1960s.

"Sesame Street" makes children aware of letters and numbers by using a variety of dramatic and musical techniques, including animation, and an unusual combination of live actors and puppets.

Many of the MUPPETS who appear on "Sesame Street" are cherished by millions of adults and children all over the world: Kermit, the Frog, those inseparable companions Bert and Ernie, the insatiable Cookie Monster and, of course, Big Bird, who towers over the whole cast.

Settembrini   See MAGIC MOUNTAIN, THE.

Seven Dwarfs   Animated cartoon characters in WALT DISNEY's full-length movie *Snow White and the Seven Dwarfs* (1937) The seven dwarfs were named Happy, Sneezy, Bashful, Grumpy, Doc, Dopey and Sleepy, an assortment of types, but all friendly. They made famous the songs "Whistle While You Work" and "Heigh Ho, Heigh Ho."

Use: In the 1988 Democratic primaries for President of the U.S. the original contenders were called "the seven dwarfs." They did not seem to have presidential stature and they seemed to be all alike in their programs. "The people are not exactly helpless. They can at least make their wishes known on T-shirts and bumper stickers. But of course if they stuck around joking about 'Snow White and the Seven Dwarfs' and if only 52 percent of the eligible voters go to the polls...they'll get what they deserve." (James Reston, *New York Times*, October 12, 1987)

Shangri-la   A fictional lamasery situated on a remote and hidden plateau high up in the mountains of Tibet. This tranquil place, isolated from the tensions of the world below, is the setting for *Lost Horizon* (1933), a novel by the British writer James Hilton (1900–1954), which was made into a Hollywood movie starring Ronald Colman. Shangri-La is a utopian refuge where nobody grows old.

Sharpeville   Town in South Africa where police fired submachine guns into a crowd of thousands of black Africans demonstrating against the government requirement that black Africans carry identification passes. In what has become known as the Sharpeville massacre, 56 black Africans were killed and 234 protesters against apartheid were arrested. The government declared a state of emergency.

Sharpeville has become a symbol of South African oppression of blacks.

Shavian   Witty and iconoclastic, in the style of George Bernard Shaw (1856–1950), Irish playwright, novelist, critic, essayist, lecturer, reformer. In literature, an admirer of Ibsen; in politics, a Fabian Socialist; in language, a would-be reformer of the English alphabet and spelling. He wrote over 50 plays, in which dramatic tension comes from the brilliant clash of ideas via sparkling dialogue; from paradoxical reversals of conventional opinions rather than from the conflict of passions or wills. Among his best plays are *Man and Superman* (1903), *Major Barbara* (1907), *Pygmalion* (1913), which was adapted for the stage as *My Fair Lady*, and *Saint Joan* (1924). The published plays are valued as much for their pungent introductory essays as for themselves. A vegetarian who never drank alcohol, coffee or tea, Shaw lived to the age of 94, a delightful, acerbic curmudgeon to the end.

Use: "He writes with insight, humor and a firm grasp of human and Shavian perversity!" (*New York Times*, September 27, 1988)

Sheen, Bishop Fulton J.   An auxiliary Roman Catholic bishop of New York who became a radio and TV personality (1895–1979). He was the first evangelist to preach regularly on a radio program, "The Catholic Hour," in 1930. In 1951 he started a TV ministry with the show "Life Is Worth Living." His orotund voice, his passionate eloquence, his mannered and dramatic gestures attracted an audience of twenty million. His views were anti-communist, anti-liberal, anti-Freudian, anti-monopolistic. He converted many well-known people to Roman Catholicism, including Clare Boothe Luce, Fritz Kreisler and Henry Ford II. He wrote a regular newspaper column as well as almost 50 books.

He became a target of satire because of his over-dramatic, elocutionary manner.

shopping mall   An area in which a large number of diverse retail stores, restaurants and entertainments is concentrated. Often, these are connected within an enclosed, protected-from-the-weather structure with a central promenade. The shopping mall started as a suburban phenomenon that displaced colorful "Main Street" mom-and-pop shops, but it has gradually invaded the cities as well.

Use: *The Shopping-Mall High School*—title of a book that criticizes schools that offer anything the students want in the way of easy courses, as if they could shop around for the least expensive bargain in credits.

silent majority   Term applied approvingly first by Vice President Spiro Agnew and then by President Richard Nixon to the vast majority of Americans who did not express their opposition to the Vietnam War in mass demonstrations, draft card burning, marches on Washington, D.C., etc. The question is: What does the silent majority think?

Silicon Valley   The name comes from silicon wafers used in semi-conductor devices. Silicon Valley itself is an area in northern California, south of San Francisco, which has become famous for its concentration of high technology design and manufacturing companies in the semi-conductor industry. Here young geniuses almost overnight built great empires and great fortunes.

Use: "Like other nations, the Emerald Isle is betting its economic future on high technology. but rather than grow its own Silicon Valley, the Dublin government has put money into people, building one of Europe's most computer-literate work forces and attracting foreign electronics firms by the score." (*U.S. News & World Report*, July 10, 1989)

Silvers, Phil   See SERGEANT BILKO.

Simple   A folk character—a humorous Everyman—who spoke his mind to generations of black readers through Langston Hughes' weekly newspaper column in *The Chicago Defender*. These pieces were gathered into a book called *Simple Speaks His Mind* in 1950.

Simple exemplifies a common man speaking in everyday street language the wisdom that comes from fresh perceptions.

Sinatra, Frank   American popular singer (1917–). At the height of his popularity, Sinatra attracted hordes of hysterical, Sinatra-smitten teenagers. The "Sinatrance" that came over the female adolescents in the 1940s at the sound of his warm, tender, vulnerable-sounding voice turned Sinatra into one of the sociological phenomena of the century—much like the BEATLES.

There is a misguided tendency to dismiss Sinatra as "just the 'voice' or 'the crooner.'" He is an accomplished jazz singer as well as a movie and television star.

Sister Carrie   In Theodore Dreiser's realistic novel of the same name (1900), an innocent country girl who goes to Chicago to find work but who discovers that it is much more pleasant to be somebody's mistress. After her first affair with Charles Drouet, a traveling salesman, she forms a liaison with George Hurstwood, an affluent manager of a fashionable bar and a married man with a family. She is tricked into running away with Hurstwood, who has stolen $10,000 from the bar. In New York, her star rises as she embarks on a stage career, while Hurstwood sinks lower and lower until he becomes a Bowery bum and eventually commits suicide.

Sister Carrie belongs to the genre of novels concerned with "the young man from the provinces," as Lionel Trilling has called them. Only this time it is the young girl from the provinces who makes her fortune in the big city. Carrie is a prototype of the shallow, pretty young woman caught up in materialistic dreams of success and quite willing to sacrifice virtue to attain it. But she never feels fulfilled.

sitcom   Short for "situation-comedy" the simplistic, fabulously profitable staple of television programming. Each episode puts its characters into a crisis or series of crises, from which they try to extricate themselves in a half hour, the usual length of a sitcom episode. The actors and actresses play familiar, recognizable stock characters to which TV audiences relate quickly and easily. The humor is usually basic and obvious, crafted to evoke a predictable, satisfying audience response. The serious, tragic scenes are similarly constructed.

Recent sitcoms have involved the characters in more mature, more real-life problems and solutions, with more complications extending over several episodes—this to build and sustain suspense and interest.

Use: "...the natural tendency of television news to turn public figures into *sit-com* characters. The punchy reports, often ending with punch lines at the expense of the subject...and the sharply edited pictures chosen for instant impact..." (Walter Goodman, *New York Times*, May 1, 1989)

Six-Day War   In only six days (June 5–June 11, 1967) the tiny nation of Israel won a great victory over the massed armies and air forces of Egypt and its Arab allies, Syria and Jordan. Israeli forces under the command of General Moshe Dayan and Chief of Staff Itzhak Rabin took the holy city of Jerusalem, rolled over the Golan Heights on the north, and swept through Gaza and the Sinai Desert all the way to the Suez Canal. The Israelis found themselves occupying territories four times as large as Israel itself.

The Six-Day War has attained mythical status: David once more defeated the giant Goliath in a stunning reversal of expectations.

"$64,000 Question, The"   The most-watched of the big-money television quiz shows of the 1950s. Each contestant (a self-declared expert) appeared in an "isolation booth" to sweat out the answers to the questions prepared by the Columbia Broadcasting System's staff. The top prize: $64,000. Successful contestants were allowed to go beyond $64,000 until they were stumped.

For years, the quiz shows ran very successfully until a Tennessee preacher on "Lotto," another quiz show, revealed that he had been fed an answer before he appeared on the show. At a congressional investigation that followed, some contestants testified that they had been given answers before they entered the booth and faked their emotions in the booth. Dan Enright, CBS producer of six quiz shows, admitted on the stand that his quiz shows had been rigged and that some of the contestants had been coached.

These and other scandalous revelations drove the quiz shows off the air.

The players in this sordid drama suffered public and private degradation. Prominent among them was Charles Van Doren, an instructor at Columbia University and son of Mark Van Doren, a member of the Columbia University faculty. For participating in the rigged quiz show "Twenty-One", Van Doren lost his jobs at Columbia and at the National Broadcasting System. Ironically, the corporate sponsors who polluted the media and perverted the contestants got off scot-free.

Use: The $64,000 question (sometimes shortened to the $64 question) is any fundamental, vital question the answer to which is crucial to the solution of a problem or the successful execution of a project or enterprise.

skid row   From skid road or skidway, a logger's slippery decline for rolling heavy logs. By extension, an area frequented by loggers, and then an area of cheap hotels, flophouses and saloons for those on the skids (those who are down and out): alcoholics, vagrants, derelicts.

Use: "Toward the end, there was an unmistakable whiff of Skid Row con artistry about him, even though he made two hundred thousand dollars his last year." (Pauline Kael, reviewing *Let's Get Lost*, a movie about jazz trumpeter Chet Baker; *New Yorker*, May 1, 1989) (See also the BOWERY.)

skin you love to touch   One of the most famous advertising slogans, it first appeared in the *Ladies Home Journal* for May 1911, touting the cosmetic and romantic virtues of Woodbury Soap.

Skokie   Suburb of Chicago, Illinois, and the home of hundreds of survivors of the Nazi concentration camps. The Supreme Court ruled on June 12, 1978, that the National Socialist Party of America (American Nazis) had the right to march through the town. At the last moment, the Nazis, defended by the American Civil Liberties Union, called off the parade in Skokie and held a demonstration in Chicago's Marquette Park instead.

Skokie has become a symbol of the stretching of principles by which freedom of assembly and freedom of speech may be protected under the U.S. Constitution. It has become for many the low-water-mark of the ACLU's defense of civil liberties for those who would destroy our civil liberties if they ever came to power.

slouching toward Bethlehem   Phrase from "The Second Coming," a poem by William Butler Yeats (1865–1939). Yeats believed in the cyclical progression of history. We are approaching the end of Christ's 2,000-year-old ideal of compassion and forgiveness, and Yeats sees in 20th-century events an adumbration of the evil to come. He has a vision of the Second Coming and asks at the end of the poem:

> And what rough beast its hour come round at last,
> Slouches toward Bethlehem to be born?

Use: "I write the way I do because I am a Catholic. There is nothing harder or less sentimental than Christian realism. I believe that there are many rough beasts now slouching toward Bethlehem to be born and I have reported the progress of a few of them." (Flannery O'Connor, as quoted by Brian Moore in *New York Times* Book Review, August 21, 1988)

smoking gun   Indisputable proof of evidence of a crime. In the WATERGATE scandal (1972–1974) Nixon's tapes of Oval Office Room conversations turned out to be the smoking gun, the absolute evidence that he had been a coconspirator in the Watergate break-in and in the cover-up of the crime. During the Iran-Contra hearings, no "smoking gun" was discovered to implicate President Reagan in the diversion of funds from Iranian arms sales to the Nicaraguan Contras.

Use: "'Smoking gun or not, North's testimony further damages a president who is aging rapidly, losing political clout and fresh out of initiatives." (*Newsweek*, July 13, 1987)

Snake-Pit, The   Novel (1946) by Mary Jane Ward about a girl who becomes mentally deranged and is placed in an insane asylum where she experiences horrifying conditions. It was made into a movie in 1948 starring Olivia de Havilland. The book was a muckraking piece and aroused people to seek more sympathetic treatment of the mentally ill.

The term snake-pit is used to describe a mental institution or any place or situation that is chaotic, unfeeling, squalid, where people are treated with cruelty or indifference.

Snopes   See FAULKNERIAN.

"Snows of Kilimanjaro, The"   Short story (1936) by ERNEST HEMINGWAY about Harry, a writer who has wasted his talent. Together with the woman who has been keeping him, he goes on safari in Africa, hoping to recapture the discipline of his vocation. But he develops gangrene, and in his delirium, he sees on the summit of Kilimanjaro the legendary frozen leopard, a symbol of death.

soap operas   Radio or television serials (also known as soaps) dramatizing the everyday problems of one-dimensional, stock characters. Generally quite sentimental and melodramatic. The "soap opera" name for these programs derives from the soap manufacturers who were their original sponsors.

Use: In general usage, soap opera is applied to a melodramatic situation. "She lost her job and her husband left her. Her life is a regular soap opera."

Son of Sam   David Richard Berkowitz (1953–). From July 1976 to August 1977, David Berkowitz terrorized New York City. Berkowitz who signed his letters to the newspapers "Son of Sam," shot 13 young women and men— girls alone or couples parked in cars at night. Six died, seven were wounded. On August 10, 1977, 11 days after he killed Stacy Moskowitz and blinded her escort Robert Violante, Berkowitz was caught.

Sentenced to a long prison term, Berkowitz announced his plans to sell his "memoirs," which he would write while in prison. The New York State Legislature put an end to Berkowitz's plans. It passed a law forbidding convicted killers from capitalizing on their crimes. Subsequently, 42 states passed similar "Son of Sam" laws.

Use: "Convicted killer Jean Harris must fork over the profits ($90,000) from her autobiography to crime victims, a state court has ruled—under the so-called "Son of Sam" law which mandates that criminals give their victims the profits they make from their crimes." (*New York Post*, April 28, 1989)

South Bronx   Neighborhood in New York City that has become a symbol of urban blight in the form of: poverty, abandoned buildings, drugs and crime.

Use: "entropy—things going from a state of relative order to one of disorder—is the upshot of all natural actions...It's what happens when you move into a nice neighborhood and within a few years it turns into the South Bronx." (Judy Jones and William Wilson, *An Incomplete Education*)

Spade, Sam   Famous hard-boiled detective who made his first appearance in THE MALTESE FALCON (1930), a novel by Dashiell Hammett (1894–1961). The book was adapted for the movies three times. The third version, with Humphrey Bogart as the private eye, became a film classic. Sam Spade's milieu is the world of cops and hoods in San Francisco, where he wins the admiration of both sides. He is a man who can take care of himself in any situation. He is tough, tight-lipped, seemingly cynical, but, oddly, he does not carry a gun.

spark plug   A device for producing the electrical spark in each cylinder, which starts up a gasoline-powered internal combustion engine.

By analogy, a spark plug came to be in the 1930s an enthusiastic leader who supplies vital energy and inspiration to any undertaking.

Spenglerian   See DECLINE OF THE WEST, THE.

Spielbergian   Having the qualities associated with the films produced, directed or written by Steven Spielberg (1947–), the director of such action pictures as *Jaws* (1975) and *Raiders of the Lost Ark* (1981), as well as fantasies like *Close Encounters of the Third Kind* (1977) and *E.T.* (1982), a film about a lovable creature from outer space. His films have been blockbusters at the box office.

Use: "The high point is Cymbeline with its Spielbergian supernatural touches (ghosts appearing in dreams, Jupiter descending from the heavens) and robust battles." (Wm. A. Henry III, "London's Dry Season," *Time*, July 18, 1988)

Spillane, Mickey   Creator (1918–) of the fictional private eye, MIKE HAMMER. He belongs to the tough, realistic school of detective fiction, using abrasive diction, violent action and steamy sex. His detective often seems brutally sadistic.

Spock, Benjamin (Dr.)   American pediatrician (1903–). One of the most influential mass market books ever published, Spock's *Common Sense Book of Baby and Child Care* (1946), has sold over 30 million copies. Spock liberated parents from the rigid child-rearing "advice" of the time. He encouraged them to be kinder, more flexible, and to rely on their good judgment and common sense.

Many people blamed Spock and his permissive theories of child-training for the rebellious behavior of youth in the 1960s. Despite these criticisms, Spock still remains a standard guide in the field—the mother's bible on bringing up baby.

As a political activist, Spock was involved in opposing America's role in the Vietnam War.

In the mid-1930s, American mothers were "massively" under the influence of the dogmatic-teachings of Dr. Luther Emmett Holt Jr., professor of pediatrics at Columbia University. Dr. Holt was the author of *The Care and Feeding of Children*, then the unchallenged household authority on the subject. The *New York Times* called the book "the Dr. Spock" of its time.

Spoon River   A small fictional village modeled on Petersburg, Illinois and Lewistown, Illinois, in *The Spoon River Anthology* (1915) by Edgar Lee Masters (1868–1950). The anthology contains about 250 free-verse poems in the form of epitaphs or, more precisely, monologues, spoken from the grave with the utmost candor. Sometimes they contradict each other as we read of the same series of events from different points of view. All in all, these life summations reveal the "buried" secrets, the hopes, the frustrations, the pettiness and boredom, the crimes, as well as the satisfactions and even epiphanies of the inhabitants of a small midwestern town. (See also WINESBURG, OHIO.)

SS (Schutzstaffel)   Protective echelon, in German. Originally consisted of a few dozen fanatical Nazi Party members who acted as black-shirted personal guards to Hitler and other Nazis. By the end of the Third Reich, they numbered five million and, under Heinrich Himmler, controlled every department of government. A law unto themselves, they were brutal and ruthless "storm troopers," an apparatus for terrorizing the population into submission to Hitler. They later manned the concentration camps and the death camps. Synonymous with brutal, inhuman oppressors.

Stakhanovite   From Aleksei Grigorevich Stakhanov (1906–1977), a Soviet coal miner who became a hero in 1935 because of his prodigious productivity on the job.

Any person who regularly exceeds production quotas and is used as an example to be emulated by the rest of the workers.

Stallone, Sylvester   American film actor and producer, (1946–) who created the immensely popular roles of ROCKY (1976), a prizefighter, and RAMBO (1982), a tough soldier. Stallone's name has become synonymous with the kind of role he plays.

Use: In an article on summer restaurant-discos: "On a drizzly Tuesday evening, we pull up to the unmarked portals and confront the Stallone Twins poised behind a velvet rope. They are unsubtly informing a couple of casually clad beach combers that they have about as much chance of getting inside as piloting the next space shuttle." (*New York Times*, August 12, 1988)

Star Wars   Epic space movie (1977) about the interplanetary struggle of the forces of good against the forces of evil. At the end, the hero, young Luke Skywalker, blows the Death Star space station, commanded by the Grand Moff Tarkin (and DARTH VADER), into smithereens.

Use: When President Ronald Reagan announced his plans for the development of an ambitious Strategic Defense Initiative (SDI), a laser shield to protect the United States against all enemy nuclear missiles, skeptics derisively dubbed the plan "Star Wars."

Stein, Gertrude   American expatriate writer (1874–1946) whose salon in the Rue de Fleurus in Paris became a meeting place for many of the young writers and artists of the "LOST GENERATION," a term she coined. She lived with her friend and factotum, whose name she used for her own *Autobiography of Alice B. Toklas* (1933). An eccentric in her own person and in her work, she stamped her name upon the general consciousness, and not only among the literati. Few people have ever read her work, but everybody supposedly knows her cinematic quirks of style. Sherwood Anderson said of her: "She may be, just may be, the greatest word-slinger of our generation." Her portrait by Picasso is known to all. Picasso's retort to Stein, who upon first viewing the painting complained that it didn't look like her, was prophetic. "It will," he said. And it does! She was opinionated, egotistical, thoroughly convinced of her genius.

In common parlance, Gertrude Stein stands for crazy, incomprehensible, repetitious, disconnected use of language, as well as for eccentricity of manners. (See also ROSE IS A ROSE IS A ROSE.)

strategic bombing   Saturation bombing of an enemy target, not only to knock out a military or industrial installation, but also to strike terror into and cause demoralization of the civilian population, as in the bombings of Schweinfurt, Dresden, Rotterdam. Saturation bombing was used by the U.S. Air Force against North Vietnam, devastating entire areas but without the intended effect of reducing morale.

strike out   In baseball, a player strikes out (or is struck out) when he swings at and misses three pitched balls—or he does not swing at three pitched balls that pass through the "strike zone"—or hits a foul ball for the first and/or second strike and then misses for the second and third pitch.

Thus, to strike out means "to fail" in baseball, and in informal usage, too.

Use: "Were you able to get any concessions from Abernathy?" "Not a thing," replied the negotiator. "I struck out."

Stroheim, Eric Von   Film actor, director (1885–1957). Born in Austria, Von Stroheim immigrated to the United States in 1913 and moved to Hollywood where he became "the man you love to hate" in war films. As an actor he played the stereotypical Prussian general, with a German accent, straight spine, bald head, monocle, high polished boots and clipped, barking speech.

As a director he made films exposing the decadence of the pre-World War I Austro-Hungarian Empire.

Sturges, Preston   Movie writer-director who revived the slapstick tradition and coupled it with satire. Among his films are *Hail the Conquering Hero* (1944) about a 4F army reject (Eddie Bracken) who is mistaken for a war hero and becomes the object of hero worship in his home town and *The Great McGinty* (1940), the tale of a crooked politician who meets his Waterloo in the performance of a single honest deed.

Use: "Like the characters in a Preston Sturges movie, his people are a collection of corrupt politians, bumbling bachelors, feckless con men, and other assorted boobs, smart alecks, and dreamers; and as in these movies there is an air of rambunctious confusion." (*New York Times*, August 1987)

Stutz-Bearcat   Named after Harry Clayton Stutz (1876–1930), a U.S. car manufacturer, it was the sports car of the Roaring Twenties, the Jazz Age.

Sullivan, Edward (Ed) Vincent   (1902–1974) A sports reporter for the racy, sensation-mongering *New York Graphic* in the 1920s, Sullivan signed on with the *Daily News* (1932) as a Broadway "gossip"—the *News'* answer to the unique Walter Winchell.

In 1948, Sullivan started a weekly TV show, eventually called "Ed Sullivan Show." It ran for 23 years. Rather awkward and nervous in speech and manner, not especially telegenic, full of mannerisms and malapropisms—by all standards *not* a showman—Sullivan managed to produce and to present the most popular variety show on TV. The acts ran the gamut from Shakespeare to the Beatles, from trained dogs and cats and ventriloquists to Elvis Presley and grand opera stars.

Sunday, Billy   William Ashley Sunday (1863–1935). American evangelist born in Iowa who turned the old-time revivalist camp meetings into a three-ring circus with parades, marching bands, large choirs and audience participation. Having sown his wild oats in his youth and having started out as a professional baseball player with the Chicago White Stockings (1883–90) before he got religion, he was able to pepper his fiery sermons with colorful colloquialisms. He inveighed against drinking, gambling, whoring in a "degenerate,

God-forsaken gang you call society." His revivals were attended by millions of Americans who enjoyed his ranting and clowning. Naturally, he made a fortune. After 1920 his popularity waned as more sophisticated fundamentalists entered the field.

Superman   *Superman,* "the quintessential comic strip," first appeared in June 1938. Superman is now part of American Mythology, embodying three major themes or clichés. First, he is a visitor from another planet, the doomed Krypton. Threatened with death in infancy, he is launched to earth by his wise and powerful father. Second, he is a superhuman being. He can fly limitless distances. He can leap tall buildings. No bullet can penetrate him. In time, he acquires X-ray vision. Third, he has dual identity. Superman's alter ego is Clark Kent, a humble reporter on *The Daily Planet* devoting his life to fighting for "truth, justice, and the American way." When evil "rears its ugly head," Clark changes into his Superman costume and sallies forth to subdue or eradicate it. After each such mission, Superman again becomes Clark Kent, "mild-mannered reporter."

Superman is a symbol of extraordinary physical strength and power. He decides what is good and what is evil. He acts on his judgment, recognizing no higher authority. Superman is omnipresent and omnipotent.

The character of Superman has appeared in all the major media: radio, movies, animated cartoons, TV, a Broadway play.

Use: "A crack team was brought in and the result was a January 16 story comparing Mr. [President] Bush to a most un-Bushlike character—Superman." (*New York Times,* January 28, 1989)

Susann, Jacqueline   American author (1921–1974) of the best-selling, blockbuster novels *Valley of the Dolls* and *The Love Machine,* each of which sold millions of copies. Susann offers an escape for the average housewife into the glamorous worlds of show business and the media where sex, money and power are the driving forces. These spun-out novels, akin to gossip columns, are easily accessible to the reader because of their easy, fast-paced narrative style and their ample use of dialogue.

A Jacqueline Susann type of novel is essentially a phenomenally successful soap opera between covers.

T

take the Fifth   To seek the protection of the Fifth Amendment to the Constitution of the United States. (The first 10 amendments are known as the Bill of Rights.) The Fifth Amendment reads in part: No person "shall be compelled in any criminal case to be a witness against himself."

The phrase "to take the Fifth" was often invoked by witnesses called to testify in 1954 before the House Un-American Activities Committee, presided over by Senator Joseph McCarthy. The hearings were held to investigate communist infiltration into government and the media. Witnesses often refused to testify on the grounds that they might be incriminating themselves.

More recently, in 1987, Lt. Col. Oliver North took the Fifth. He refused to testify about his activities as a member of President Reagan's National Security Council until the Senate and House panel on Iran-gate granted him limited immunity from prosecution.

Although taking the Fifth is a perfectly legal, constitutional right, invoking it suggests, perhaps erroneously, that the witness has something to hide.

In popular or jocular use: to refuse to answer a question for fear of self-incrimination.

taken for a ride   Standard criminal underworld euphemism for being murdered. Coined in the Chicago bootleg wars of the early 1920s. The victim was usually taken in a car driven by the individual who was charged with "rubbing" him out. The actual murder was committed by the "hit" or "trigger" man hidden in the back of the car. It was he who shot the victim in the back of the head or neck.

The Chicago gangster Hymie Weiss is alleged to have called this method of disposing of one's enemies as a "one-way" ride. Now, when someone is taken for a ride, he is tricked into something, cheated or swindled.

Tallulah   Tallulah Bankhead, (1903–1968), flamboyant American actress famous for her low, husky voice and racy language. A beauty from an aristocratic Alabama family, she starred in many Broadway plays, including *Dark Victory* (1934), *Rain* (1935), *The Little Foxes* (1939) and *The Skin of Our Teeth* (1942). She was one of the wits at the Algonquin Round Table.

When one calls a woman "Tallulah," it is because of the woman's unusually deep voice and her salty stevedore's vocabulary.

Tarzan   The hero of the jungle in a series of stories by Edgar Rice Burroughs (1875–1950). The son of an English noble, he is abandoned in the jungle and reared by apes. He learns the language of the animals, marries an American girl named Jane, and has a son. Burroughs' stories were translated into 56 languages, adapted into a comic strip, and used in many movies.

"Me Tarzan, You Jane" is a phrase derived from a movie version and is often used to connote inarticulate, primitive reactions.

Teapot Dome   Political scandal during President Warren G. Harding's administration (1921–23), over the leasing of Navy oil reserves to private oil companies; it was not exposed until after Harding's sudden death in 1923. One of the reserves was called Teapot Dome, in Wyoming; another, Elk Hills in California. Secretary of the Navy Denby resigned from office. Secretary of the Interior Albert B. Fall was convicted of accepting a bribe of $223,000 and was sentenced to jail for a year. The Supreme Court voided the leases.

Teapot Dome has become synonymous with scandal in high government office, equaled only by Watergate and Iran-Contra.

Teddy Boy   Post-World War II, rebellious British teenagers who affected Edwardian costume. By the 1960s the Teddy Boys were in competition for disaffectedness with the "Mods," the "Rockers" and the "Punks." Gang fights along the King's Road in London were not uncommon.

teflon   A thin plastic coating of tetrafluoroethylene applied to industrial machine surfaces to reduce stress. Later applied to cooking utensils to render them non-stick. Called the slipperiest substance on earth. Discovered by the DuPont chemist Dr. Roy Plunkett in 1938.

Has come to mean slippery, immune to blame or responsibility.

Use: "The Teflon presidency is ending with President Reagan at the top of the greased pole and his critics politically and legally in a frustrated heap at the bottom." (John Hall, *Richmond Times Dispatch*, January 8, 1989)

Temple, Shirley   Blond, curly-haired, appealing little girl (1928–) who sang and danced her way into the hearts of moviegoers all over the world. She was one of the most popular stars of the 1930s, outranking even Greta Garbo. *Little Miss Marker* (1934) was one of her best known films.

Terry and the Pirates   Milton Caniff's exotic adventure comic strip first appeared on October 22, 1934. It had a long and highly successful run, lasting until February 25, 1973.

A zesty version of the usual adventure strip, drawn and scripted with panache, it nonetheless did not reach its peak popularity until the female characters—Dragon Lady, Burma, and Normandie Sandhurst (neé Drake)—appeared, all vying for Pat Ryan's affection.

Upon America's entrance into World War II, Terry, emerging from his adolescence, joined the Air Force in China and from this point became and remained the strip's central character.

Theater of the Absurd   A revolutionary departure from the well-made play, which seeks by new forms to express the sense of absurdity, the meaninglessness of the human condition. Theater of the Absurd rejects the conventions of traditional drama: plot, resolution of crisis, developing characters, a well-defined theme and rational dialogue. It does not hold the mirror up to nature but creates, instead, the atmosphere that dreams, or rather nightmares, are made of. It is not a self-conscious school of drama with a manifesto or purpose. It happened that at a certain time in 20th-century history individual playwrights began to express their sense of isolation, their sense of loss of all integrating values. They perceived that we are all strangers in a strange land where God is dead and reason is dead. In their anguish they wrote savage, bitter, often mordantly funny plays attacking hypocrisy, conformity and spiritual sterility.

Among the playwrights associated with Theater of the Absurd are: Samuel Beckett (Irish), Eugene Ionesco (Romanian), Jean Genet (French), Harold Pinter (English) and Edward Albee (American). They wrote, respectively: *Waiting for Godot* (1952), *Rhinoceros* (1959), *The Balcony* (1956), *The Caretaker* (1960) and *The American Dream* 1961).

Use: In an article about Oprah Winfrey's TV talk show: "Sometimes one feels as if one were watching Theater of the Absurd, or Saturday Night Live." (*New York Times Magazine*, June 11, 1989)

there is no joy in Mudville   "There is no joy in Mudville—mighty Casey has struck out" is the wrenching last line of that immortal baseball ballad "Casey at the Bat," by Ernest L. Thayer.

Here, in brief, is how it happened on that unforgettable day:

> The outlook wasn't brilliant for
> the Mudville nine that day.
> The score stood four to two
> with but one inning more to play.
> So when Cooney died at second
> and Burrows did the same,
> A pallor wreathed the features of
> The patrons of the game.
>
> With defeat almost a certainty:
> Flynn lets drive a single
> to the wonderment of all
> And Blake the much despis-ed
> tore the cover off the ball.
> There was Jimmy safe at second
> and Flynn a-hugging third.

Radiating confidence, the mighty Casey stepped up to the plate, to the delighted roar of thousands in the stands: Casey would save the day. But the dirge-like mood of the last line tells it all:

> There is no joy in Mudville—Mighty Casey has struck out.

Use: The day after the New York Yankees lost the 1963 World Series (October 7, 1963), the *New York Herald Tribune* carried the following headline: "The Mighty Yankees Have Struck Out."

Thimble Theater   See POPEYE.

third degree   Police use of torture, brute force, psychological manipulation, intense and prolonged questioning, to extract confessions from suspects. Subjected to the "third degree," many suspects confessed to crimes they hadn't committed, or implicated innocent people. The rich and influential were rarely, if ever, subjected to the third degree. That was reserved for the poor, the friendless, the ignorant.

Within recent times, the Supreme Court's MIRANDA DECISION has sharply reduced the use of the third degree.

Now, "third degree" has acquired broad meanings such as: a severe rebuke from one's superiors, a "bawling out" or "chewing out," a searching interview full of sharp, probing questions.

third world   Underdeveloped, usually poverty-stricken nations of Africa, Asia and South America; sometimes refers to those nations unaligned with either of the two superpowers, the United States and the U.S.S.R.

Now often used to describe the poor, the uneducated and the unemployed minorities within a developed society.

Use: "We have a *third world* nation inside America, growing radically poorer, more violent and more hopeless as the rest of America gets its BMW's." (*New York Times*, Op-Ed page, April 4, 1988)

Three Mile Island   Nuclear power plant in Middletown, Pennsylvania, where on March 28, 1979, an accident exposed some 36,000 people living within five miles of the plant to a slight increase of radiation (two to eight millirems). The facility, owned by General Public Utilities Corporation, was closed down. Widespread fear led to an investigation of the rules and procedures governing nuclear power plants and of the Nuclear Regulatory Commission in charge of them.

Three Mile Island has become a code word for all those opposed to the construction and operation of nuclear power plants. These people fear a recurrence of accidents and claim that no orderly evacuation of nearby residents is possible. (See CHERNOBYL)

three-ring circus   The term originated with the merger of P.T. Barnum's "Greatest Show on Earth" and James Anthony Bailey's Circus. The Barnum and Bailey Circus boasted three rings in which three separate acts appeared simultaneously. Colloquially, a three-ring circus means confusion and noise arising from too many activities going on at the same time, as in a farce.

Throttlebottom   From Alexander Throttlebottom, the ineffectual vice president in *Of Thee I Sing*, a 1932 political satire in the form of a musical comedy by George S. Kaufman, Morrie Ryskind and George Gershwin. A Throttlebottom is any inept public servant. When George Bush chose the inexperienced Dan Quayle to be his Republican running mate for the vice presidency in 1988, many thought he was opting for a nonentity, a Throttlebottom.

throw a curveball   In baseball, a pitch thrown in such a way that the ball will spin to the right, the left or downward. The curveball is usually more difficult for the batter to hit than is the straight ball.

In general parlance, being thrown a curveball is being given something difficult to deal with, something unexpected, something embarrassing, being caught off guard.

throw in the towel   In boxing, a boxer's trainer or seconds may concede that he is beaten by throwing a towel into the ring. This is done to keep the badly hurt boxer from suffering further injury. In practice, the referee usually stops the match when he feels that the boxer has been decisively beaten and can no longer safely absorb his opponent's blows. He names the opponent as winner by a technical knockout.

In general usage, to throw in the towel is to admit one is beaten, defeated.

Use: The day after Representative Jim Wright (Democrat from Texas) resigned from his job as Speaker of the United States House of Representatives, the following caption appeared under his picture on the front page of the *New York Daily News* (June 1, 1989): "Speaker Jim Wright brushes tear away as he throws in towel yesterday in D.C."

Thurber, James   American writer and cartoonist (1894–1961). It is in the latter role that he caught the popular imagination. He created a series of misogynous cartoons called "The Battle of the Sexes" for *The New Yorker.* The woman, gigantic, always loomed over her timid, self-effacing husband in a menacing way. Somewhere in the picture was a big dog, also dwarfing the husband. No captions were really necessary.

Use: The bride and groom were the embodiment of a Thurber cartoon: she Amazonian, he shrunken. Only the ubiquitous dog was missing. (See also WALTER MITTY.)

Tiananmen Square   Huge plaza in Beijing, China, where, in the early morning hours of June 4, 1989, the 27th People's Army massacred hundreds of unarmed students who had been demonstrating since April 18 for democratic political reforms like freedom of speech and freedom of the press.

The students' marches into the square, their hunger strikes, which evoked sympathy from the workers, their heroism in the face of tanks and troops who at first disobeyed orders to fire at them, brought the government to the brink of civil war. Zhao Ziyang, the Communist Party General Secretary who wanted to negotiate with the students, was forced out. Hardliners Li Peng and Deng Xiaoping won out. Martial law was declared on May 20. Army units from the provinces rolled into the capital to clear the square.

After the carnage, student leaders were hunted down, arrested and executed as "counter-revolutionaries." The government propaganda machine tried to mask its brutality, but the Big Lie did not work, since millions of people all over the world had watched on TV the events in Tiananmen Square.

Tiananmen Square has become a term associated with a totalitarian government's savage massacre of unarmed demonstrators for democracy.

Use: "Decades before Tiananmen Square, the Chinese Communists showed in Tibet that their answer to nonviolence was slaughter." (Abe Rosenthal, Op-Ed, *New York Times*, July 25, 1989)

Tiffany   Ultra-swank Fifth Avenue store in New York City. Tiffany stands for luxury, the highest quality, the best.

Times Square   The crossroads of Manhattan at 42nd Street and BROADWAY, the hub of the theater district, site of huge neon advertisements, center of prostitution, pornography and crime, the square where throngs gather every December 31st to welcome in the New Year.

Synonymous with the bustle and activity of great crowds.

Tinker to Evers to Chance   In the early 1900s, Joe Tinker, Johnny Evers and Frank Chance were known as the "peerless trio" of the Chicago Cubs baseball team. They were all superb infielders and great hitters. But they won their place in Baseball's Hall of Fame for their legendary ability to execute double plays. The frequent appearance of DP (double play) in the box scores of the day made "Tinker to Evers to Chance" a part of the American language. It has now come to mean any successful maneuver or operation involving the deft, highly coordinated effort of several individuals.

Tinker toy   A child's toy consisting of detachable wooden wheels and spokes that can be easily assembled into various shapes.

It has come to mean something with interchangeable parts that can be readily disassembled and reconstructed.

Use: "Nations are not Tinker toys to be pulled apart and reassembled casually." (George Will, *Newsweek*, January 29, 1990)

tin lizzie   Generally, the nickname for a Model T Ford. The name seems to derive from Lizzie, "the common name for a Black maid who, like the car, worked hard all week and prettied up on Sundays." Now, any broken-down, shabby but still serviceable car.

Tin Man   Character in L. Frank Baum's *The Wonderful Wizard of Oz* (1900).

Dorothy discovers the Tin Man as she travels along the YELLOW BRICK ROAD on her way to see the wizard. She persuades him to accompany her. He is stiff and rusted but some squirts of oil from an oil can enable him to move. He is hollow and has no heart. As played by Jack Haley in the movie, he sings, "I could be human if I only had a heart." At the end he discovers that he does indeed have a heart when he sheds tears because of Dorothy's imminent return to Kansas.

Tobacco Road   Novel (1932) by the American writer Erskine Caldwell, dramatized in 1933 by Jack Kirkland (3,182 performances on Broadway) and made into a film in 1941. Jeeter Lester, the main character, and his family are sharecroppers and what used to be called "poor white trash." They live in squalor and degradation on Tobacco Road in Georgia. Their degenerate antics shocked, amused and titillated wide audiences.

Tobacco Road has become synonymous with squalid and morally obnoxious conditions among the rural poor, especially in the South.

toe–to–toe   In boxing, when the boxers face each other and continue to exchange punches, making no effort to defend themselves. The purpose of this apparently unplanned exchange is to land as many damaging blows as possible on each other.

In general use, hostile, unyielding confrontation or opposition.

Use: The meeting started out peacefully enough. But before long, the participants discarded the rules of civilized discourse and went at each other toe-to-toe.

Tokyo Rose   Alias for Iva Togori, born in Los Angeles, who broadcast daily appeals from a radio station in Tokyo to GIs in the Pacific theater of war to desert the Armed Forces. She was arrested on September 8, 1945, in Yokohama and tried for treason.

The term Tokyo Rose is applied rather sneeringly to subversives because Tokyo Rose was so ineffectual.

Tombs   Built in 1838, this New York City prison has been rocked by scandals from its very beginning: mistreatment of prisoners; unsanitary, crowded conditions; inadequate security; escapes. A second Tombs was built in 1905. It shortly acquired the same kind of bad name as the first Tombs.

To compare any prison facility to the Tombs is to place it in the lowest possible category.

Use: "I wouldn't send any prisoner to the Huddleston Prison," said the judge. "It's as bad as the Tombs."

Tonio Kröger   Main character in *Tonio Kröger* (1903), a novella by the German writer Thomas Mann. Within him we find personified a recurrent theme in Mann's works and in his personal life: the conflicting claims of his artistic and bourgeois heritage. The sensitive

Tonio Kröger, a writer who has always felt isolated and set apart, longs for the vitality, the animal spirits, the everyday commonplaceness and the comradeship enjoyed by the burger types around him. Kröger realizes that *they* are the true inspiration for his writing.

Toonerville Trolley   The most famous "character" in Fontaine Fox's comic strip, *Toonerville Folks* (1915). The Toonerville Trolley was unforgettable: tall, angular, equipped with an interior stove and a smokestack and a twisted antenna, traversing miles and miles of twisted country track.

The colorful, irascible skipper—with cap, spectacles and beard as unruly as his temper—is the "living adjunct" of the Toonerville Trolley.

Until fairly recently, Americans relied heavily on the trolley for surface transportation within cities and towns. When a trolley or trolley line went to its final rest, the residents frequently mourned its demise as "the passing of our Toonerville Trolley."

In the 1950s, Fox folded the real Toonerville Trolley with all its colorful passengers and villagers.

Fox's Toonerville Trolley has entered our language as any aging, aged, broken-down, erratic, uncomfortable, yet fondly regarded public transportation.

top banana   The leading comedian in musical comedy, vaudeville, burlesque. By extension, the chief executive officer, the most important individual in a group, a business or any undertaking.

Use: It didn't take Farrell too long to become top banana in the newly-organized steel company.

touch base   In baseball, the player who has hit the ball must touch each base in sequence: 1st, 2nd, 3rd, home plate. If he touches each base and home with one hit, he has hit a home run. If he doesn't hit a home run, he must either physically touch the base his hit has taken him to or be in a position to touch base when he is approached by a member of the opposing team. If he is tagged by an opposing player while he is not touching the base, he is "off base" and hence "out"—and must leave the field.

In general use, to touch base means to make contact with or keep in touch with, confer with.

Use: During the campaign, Matlock touched base with every voter group in town.

Tracy, Spencer   U.S. movie actor (1900–1967). Projected the craggy, strong, upright, self-sufficient man with natural good humor, as in *Captains Courageous* (1937), *Boys' Town* (1938), *Bad Day at Black Rock* (1954) and *The Old Man and the Sea* (1958). Tracy made memorable film comedies with KATHARINE HEPBURN.

trench warfare   From 1915 on, both Allied and opposing German forces dug in on the Western Front. World War I was in many ways a war of attrition with both sides fighting bloody battles for patches of land, advancing and retreating to their trench positions. Between the opposing lines of trenches was a NO-MAN'S LAND, the land of crossfire.

Use: In connection with corruption in procurement procedures at the Pentagon, the *New York Times*, (July 13, 1988), suggesting possible solutions, wrote: "Changes like these cannot be legislated from above...It will be a tough job, though, requiring protracted trench warfare throughout the bureaucracy..."

Triangle Fire   On Saturday, March 25, 1911, fire raged through the top three floors of a 10-story building at the corner of Washington Place and Greene Street in New York City. Within half an hour, 146 workers of the Triangle Shirtwaist Company (mostly young Jewish and Italian immigrant girls) died in the flames or died leaping from windows, their clothes and hair ablaze. Charred bodies littered the pavement below.

This traumatic disaster galvanized the movement for reform of sweatshop conditions in the garment industry. The Triangle Fire remains a symbolic warning against indifference to sweatshop violations that threaten the lives of exploited workers.

trickle-down theory   President Ronald Reagan's economic policy in the 1980s of encouraging production by cutting taxes was ironically referred to as the trickle-down theory. Supposedly the flood of advantages to the rich would trickle down to the poor in the form of more jobs and more income. But Reagan balanced decreased revenues from the rich with decreased social expenditures on housing, hospitals and education for the poor. Thus, the rich became richer and the poor became poorer.

triple threat   In sports, a player who is efficient or outstanding in three skills as, for example, a football player who can run, kick and pass—or, in baseball, a pitcher who can pitch, hit and steal bases.

In general, a triple-threat person is master of three disciplines in the same or separate fields.

Use: Thornton was a triple threat. He could sing, act and play the piano.

Typhoid Mary   Mary Mallon (1870–1938), an Irish-born cook employed in a home in Oyster Bay, Long Island, New York, was suspected of being a typhoid carrier as early as 1904. She ran away from the authorities and was not captured until 1907. She spent almost all of the rest of her life confined in Riverside Hospital on North Brother Island, New York City. She herself was immune to typhoid but she transmitted the disease (through her handling of food) to at least 50 people.

Today, a "Typhoid Mary" is anyone who is suspected of being a carrier of anything unpleasant, harmful or even disastrous; therefore, someone who is to be shunned. Most often used jocularly, as when one pretends to shrink from a person who may have been employed by two companies that went bankrupt.

U

United Nations An international peacekeeping organization founded after World War II, with headquarters now in New York City. Its charter was drafted at Dumbarton Oaks in 1944 and ratified on October 24, 1945. By 1988 the number of member countries was 159.

In colloquial use, the United Nations connotes variety and heterogeneity, more in its composition than in its peacekeeping function. Looking at a schoolroom containing black, white, Asian and Hispanic children, one might say, "Why, it's a regular United Nations."

Untouchables Nine incorruptible, unbribable agents assembled by Eliot Ness (1920–1957), head of a special Prohibition unit, to fight the Al Capone gang of bootleggers in Chicago in the 1920s. Dubbed "The Untouchables" by the underworld itself, their adventures formed the basis of a TV series and then of a 1987 movie, *The Untouchables*, with Robert De Niro.

Up the Down Staircase On November 11, 1962, the *Saturday Review of Literature* published a modest little story, *Up the Down Staircase*. The author, Bel Kaufman, granddaughter of Sholem Aleichem, after some difficulties had finally landed a job as teacher of English in a New York City high school.

The story was composed of scraps of paper found in a teacher's wastebasket. Ironically, those papers told a story of "chaos, confusion, cries for help, bureaucratic gobbledygook, and one teacher's attempt to make a difference in one child's life."

In 1963, Prentice Hall published an expanded version of the story as a novel under the same title. An instant, international success, it brought fame and fortune to its author. It was translated into many languages.

The "Up" and "Down" in the title refer to stairwell signs designed to facilitate the orderly movement of students throughout the school day. The title, now a part of the language, has become a metaphor for "going against traffic, bucking the system."

upper   A drug (e.g., amphetamines) that stimulates and provides a temporary feeling of exhilaration or elation.

By extension, "upper" has come to mean a pleasant, stimulating experience, condition or set of circumstances or events.

Use: The last meeting of the staff was an upper for everyone.

"Upstairs, Downstairs"   Enormously popular British TV series which traces the fortunes of an upper-class family and their servants through the first few decades of the 20th century. Lord and Lady Bellamy and their son and daughter represent the upstairs contingent; the butler, the cook, assorted maids, chauffeurs and governesses represent the downstairs contingent. All inhabit the same town house on Eaton Place in London. Both groups are bound by the respective privileges, duties, responsibilities, manners and even linguistic differences of the British class system. Both groups are affected not only by domestic affairs but also by such public events as the sinking of the *Titanic*, the suffragette movement and World War I. The entire series is marked by consummate acting, riveting plot development and absolutely authentic settings.

Weekly episodes ran for four years on Masterpiece Theatre (Public Broadcasting System in the United States). Eventually the series was seen by about one billion people in 50 countries.

"Upstairs, Downstairs" has come to be shorthand for class differences.

Use: "The upstairs-downstairs relationship between Jews and Arabs is conspicuous in Nazareth. The run-down biblical town, where 60,000 Arabs live, has overcrowded schools and streets full of potholes. The 20,000 Jews live in upper Nazareth, where the schools are spacious and the streets are well maintained." (*Newsweek*, January 4, 1988)

V

Valentino, Rudolph   Silent screen star. Sinuous, dark and sleek, the heart-throb of millions of women, Valentino played the lover in exotic movies like *The Sheik, Blood and Sand, The Young Rajah, Cobra* and *The Son of the Sheik.* Valentino became a cult figure for whom women swooned. He died on August 23, 1926, at the age of 31.

A "Valentino" is a parody of the romantic, exotic, passionate lover, one who exhibits these qualities in excess.

Valium   Trademark for *diazepam,* one of the most widely prescribed medications for stress and anxiety. Now past its 25th anniversary, it has become part of our culture—a sort of metaphor of our high-strung, agitated, hard-driving age. Thus, mellow, popular music has been described as "audio-valium" and columnist John Leonard, refers to the women of New York City's East Side as "the Valium Girls."

Vance, Philo   Aristocratic young amateur detective created by S.S. Van Dine (1888–1939), a pseudonym for Willard Huntington Wright. A graduate of Harvard and several European universities, Philo Vance has knowledge of all kinds of esoteric subjects, which helps him in his criminal investigations. He is not above lecturing on these subjects in a rather pedantic way. He is an intellectual detective, a sophisticated poseur with a British accent. There are 12 Philo Vance cases, among them *The Benson Murder Case* (1926), *The Canary Murder Case* (1927) and *The Bishop Murder Case* (1929).

V-E Day   Victory in Europe, May 8, 1945.

The allies accepted the unconditional surrender of Germany, signed in Rheims and in Berlin. World War II was over in Europe, but not yet in Japan.

Use: "The election of 1984 was a kind of V-E Day: one last frolic." (Daniel Patrick Moynihan, *New York Times Magazine*, June 19, 1988)

Verdun   City in France where the longest single battle in history was fought in 1916 during World War I. In the 10 months the battle lasted, the front line moved less than four miles. Almost a million men were killed, wounded and shell-shocked. Verdun symbolizes the horror and brutality of war.

V-For-Victory   Hand sign using the index and middle finger to form the letter V. It was made popular by Winston Churchill during World War II. Actually, the use of "V" was introduced by a Belgian exile in a radio broadcast from London to his native land in 1941. His V stood for "Vrieherd" (freedom), but all the allies adopted the V for "victory" over the Nazis. It was ubiquitous all during the war, appearing in posters, slogans, V-mail.

The V-for-Victory hand sign is still used today to anticipate or to celebrate winning, whether in a football game, a political campaign or a personal triumph over adversity.

Vichy   Collaborationist, fascist government formed by Marshal Henri Philippe Petain in that part of France not occupied by German troops after Petain signed an armistice with Germany on June 22, 1940. Vichy became a puppet government of the Third Reich in the south of France. It rounded up thousands of Jews and German refugees and handed them over to the Nazis for deportation to the concentration camps. Petain was followed by Pierre Laval, who was executed for treason at the end of World War II.

Vichy has become a symbol of betrayal, of easy surrender to and collaboration with a detested enemy.

Vietnam   Refers to the U.S. involvement in the Vietnam War, an undeclared war to oppose communist expansion in Southeast Asia. It was the most divisive war in modern American history. From 1965 to 1973 almost 55,000 Americans died in the conflict in Vietnam and although the U.S. Air Force dropped more bombs on North Vietnam than in all of World War II, the United States was unable to achieve a victory. Vietnam has become a symbol of U.S. defeat abroad and of disunity at home. Vietnam taught the United States that it could not win an unpopular war. Many refer to Vietnam as the American agony, which has resulted in the paralysis of the American will in foreign affairs.

The Vietnam War Memorial wall, with the names of all the dead carved into its polished granite surface, attracts more visitors than any other memorial in Washington, D.C.

Vladimir (Didi)   One of the two tattered tramps in Samuel Beckett's *Waiting for Godot* who while away the time in poignant antics as they wait and wait. "At this place, at this moment, all mankind is us, whether we like it or not," says Vladimir. (See GODOT.)

W

Wallenberg, Raoul   Swedish attaché (1912–?) in Hungary during World War II. He made it his mission to save as many Hungarian Jews as he could during the Nazi occupation. By giving them Swedish identification papers, by hiding them in safe houses flying the Swedish flag, he literally snatched Jews from SS round-ups and deportation lines. On January 17, 1945, Wallenberg went to a meeting with Soviet officers whose troops had entered Budapest just a few days before. He disappeared on that day and has never been heard from since. It is known that he was taken prisoner by the Russians and sent to a camp in the GULAG. But why? The Russians say that he has died; other prisoners claim that he still lives on in a prison camp. The mystery has never been solved.

Wallenberg has become a heroic symbol of what a single individual can achieve against evil.

Wall Street   A street in lower Manhattan that has come to be known as the financial center of the world. It is the location of the Stock Exchange. The term is also used as an indicator of economic trends.

Wall Street has become the symbol for mammoth financial dealing, for insider trading, for greed and ruthlessness.

Walter Mitty   The henpecked, ineffectual husband in "The Secret Life of Walter Mitty," a 1939 short story by JAMES THURBER (1894–1961). Mitty escapes the indignities of a humdrum life in daydreams of glamorous adventures in which he plays the hero—as an intrepid commander-pilot; as a famous surgeon; as a tough gunman on the witness stand.

A Walter Mitty is an inconsequential person who compensates for the pettiness of daily life in self-dramatizing daydreams.

Use: "Sometimes it seems that for every lawyer happy with his or her lot, there are five others wishing they were somewhere else, like off writing novels or Broadway musicals. The fictional counterpart of these unhappy lawyers isn't Perry Mason; it's Walter Mitty." *New York Times*, October 21, 1988)

Warhol, Andy   Painter (1930–1987) associated with POP ART, maker of experimental and outrageous films, man-about-town and member of café society.

Warhol stands for the most avant of the avant-garde.

Warsaw Ghetto   On November 26, 1940, German troops began herding the Jewish population of Warsaw, Poland into a ghetto enclosed by an eight-foot-high wall. The Jews were systematically forced into labor for the German war machine, starved, beaten and finally decimated by mass deportations to concentration camps. By April 1943 only 60,000 of more than half a million Jews remained. A handful of Jewish resistance fighters made a last-ditch stand against heavily armored SS troops commanded by General Jurgen Stroop. With a meager supply of arms, they fought the Nazi troops from house to house and in the sewers in a desperately heroic but losing battle. By May 16 there were no Jews left. They'd all been killed or had committed suicide. Symbol of Jewish resistance to the Nazis.

By extension, Warsaw Ghetto is a symbol of heroic resistance.

war to end all wars   The war that came cynically to be called World War I, when it became obvious that the terms of the peace were inevitably leading to a World War II. The "war to end all wars" was a World War I slogan to make the slaughter seem palatable, as were other shibboleths like "making the world safe for democracy."

war to make the world safe for democracy   World War I, in President Woodrow Wilson's phrase. The phrase is now used cynically in view of the spread of totalitarian governments all over the world during the 20th century, especially in Fascist Italy, Nazi Germany, and Communist Russia.

Waste Land, The   A poem (1922) of 434 lines, in five sections, written by T.S. Eliot. By means of symbols and myths, especially that of the impotent Fisher King, it deals with the fragmentation and sterility of modern civilization. It contrasts the splendor and richness of the past with the sordidness and decadence of the present. We live in a spiritual wasteland.

Use: Newton Minow, head of the FCC (Federal Communications Commission), caused a national stir when he declared that American television was a "vast waste land."

Watergate   An apartment-office complex in Washington, D.C., which gave its name to one of the biggest political scandals in American history, a scandal that culminated on August 8, 1974, in the resignation of President Richard M. Nixon, two years into his second term.

On June 17, 1972, five men were arrested for breaking into the executive quarters of the Democratic National Committee in Watergate. Through the investigative reporting of two young journalists for *The Washington Post*, Carl Bernstein and Bob Woodward, what appeared at first to be a simple robbery turned out to be a conspiracy involving a Republican Party espionage network with a secret fund at its disposal. Top White House aides (H.R. Haldeman, John D. Ehrlichman, John W. Dean etc.) as well as former Attorney General John N. Mitchell were implicated. President Nixon was forced to turn over tapes of conversations in the Oval Office, which proved conclusively his own involvement in the conspiracy and the cover-up. On July 30, 1974, the House Judiciary Committee recommended impeachment proceedings against Nixon for "obstruction of justice, abuse of power, and contempt of Congress." Ten days later Nixon resigned.

Watergate stands for political scandal involving abuse of power, corruption and cover-up on the part of high government officials. (See also DEEP THROAT; SATURDAY NIGHT MASSACRE.)

Use: "Branch, like his fellow new historians, has the insatiable curiosity of a post-Watergate investigative reporter." (Jim Miller reviewing a biography of Martin Luther King Jr., *Newsweek*, November 28, 1988)

Watson, Dr.   Constant companion and admiring audience to Sherlock Holmes in the detective stories of Sir Arthur Conan Doyle.

Steady, deliberate, loyal, often amazed, he acts as a foil to the nervous and erratic energy of Holmes.

"Elementary, my dear Watson" are the words purportedly used by Sherlock Holmes to the openmouthed Dr. Watson as he launched into an explanation of his solution to a crime.

The phrase has become a popular opening to any explanation.

Watts   Black ghetto in Los Angeles, California, which erupted in rioting, looting and arson in August 1965. The violence raged for five days before 20,000 National Guardsmen, called by Governor Edmund Brown, restored order to the ravaged area. Results: 30 dead; hundreds injured; 22,000 arrested; property worth millions destroyed. Watts established a pattern for riots in other depressed Negro ghettos, like Newark and Detroit in 1967.

Watts has become synonymous with racial rioting during "the long hot summer," when people tend to gather in the streets and the heat makes tempers flare.

Wave of the Future, The   Originally the title of a book by Anne Morrow Lindbergh (1940) whose argument was the inevitable triumph of fascism over democracy.

Wayne, John   Born Marion Morrison, (1907–1979) renamed by movie director John Ford; nicknamed the "Duke." Archetypal western hero: strong, silent, stoic, incorruptible. One of his many starring roles was the hero in *Stagecoach* (1939).

Use: "Bush is Jimmy Stewart after Reagan's John Wayne." *(Newsweek*, February 20, 1989)

we have met the enemy and they are us   See POGO.

Welk, Lawrence   The band leader (1903–) of a popular, all-musical TV program appealing to older Americans, sometimes uncharitably referred to as the "geriatric set." For them, Welk and his attractive company provided unabashedly sentimental music—danceable, singable, listenable.

Use: "In all of American entertainment there is no real equivalent to what the Red Army Chorus offers, unless you put a bit of Lawrence Welk together with a half-time show and add a touch of vaudeville." (Laura Shapero, *Newsweek*, October 23, 1989).

"We Shall Overcome"   Signature song of hope and resolution during the Civil Rights movement, sung at innumerable rallies, demonstrations and marches throughout the United States. It was adapted by Pete Seeger in 1955 from a Baptist hymn. Now the phrase is used to express faith in the ability to overcome any obstacle, not only the obdurate obstacle of bigotry or discrimination.

West, Mae   Movie star comedienne (1893–1980) whose special variety of femme fatale was that of a bordello madame: openly, brazenly, vulgarly sexual. Her ample hourglass bulk swaddled in sequined silk or satin, swaying her indolent hips and batting her false eyelashes, she could insinuatingly greet a male visitor to her suite with a drawled: "Is that a gun you've got in your pocket, or are you just glad to see me?" Some of her famous lines were "Come up and see me sometime"; "Beulah, peel me a grape"; and the song "I Like a Man Who Takes His Time." She opened in *Night after Night* (1932), then made *She Done Him Wrong* (1933), *Goin' to Town* (1935) and many other films.

A Mae West is: (1) a large-bosomed parody of unabashed sexuality; (2) an inflatable life-preserver, suggesting the shape of Mae West.

What Makes Sammy Run?   Satirical novel (1941) by Budd Schulberg (1914–) about Sammy Glick, a tough young New York City Jew whose ambition and unscrupulous opportunism take him to a position of power in the movie industry. The title refers to the ambitious drives that make people trample each other to get to the top.

What Price Glory?   Title of a 1924 play by Laurence Stallings and Maxwell Anderson about the stupidity and cynicism of war. At the end of the play, when the main characters, weary soldiers, are once more deprived of furlough and ordered to the front, Sergeant Quirt says: "What a lot of God damn fools it takes to make a war!"

The phrase is now generally used ironically to question the sacrifices or compromises one makes for fame or even ephemeral recognition.

"What's It All About, Alfie?"   Song from the 1966 British film *Alfie*, about a philandering cockney playboy (Michael Caine) who can't make up his mind whether his "freedom" is really better than marriage. The phrase is used to express puzzlement about the purpose of life itself.

When you call me that, smile!   Phrase spoken by the hero of *The Virginian: A Horseman of the Plains*, an early Western (1902) by Owen Wister (1860–1938). It is a tale set in Wyoming cattle country and has to do with the hero's adventures among cowpunchers as well as with his courtship of Molly Wood, a schoolteacher from Vermont.

The phrase is now used banteringly to counter any derogatory remark.

"Where Have All the Flowers Gone?"   Antiwar song written and popularized by Pete Seeger in 1961. It is an elegiac lament for the young boys gone to war, "gone to graveyards everywhere" and for the women they left behind. It was inspired by a passage from Mikhail Sholokhov's novel, *And Quiet Flows the Don* (tr. 1934). It became a hit record done by the Kingston Trio under the Capitol label. The phrase has a dying cadence and is used to bemoan the disappearance of fragile things and people, somewhat akin to the refrain of Villon: "Where are the snows of yesteryear?"

Use: "Where Have All the Nurses Gone?"—title of an article in *Columbia* magazine (October 1988) about the shortage of nurses in U.S. hospitals.

Where the Wild Things Are   Title of a 1963 children's picture book written and illustrated by Maurice Sendak. It tells the story of Max, a little boy who is sent to his room without supper. He imagines himself in the forest where the wild things are. These are frighteningly grotesque creatures with beaks and claws and prominent eyes, but they make him their king and obey him. Nevertheless, Max decides that he wants to be back where he is loved. He goes home to his room, where supper is waiting for him.

The phrase "where the wild things are" has come to represent our subconscious fears and imaginings and our desire to master them.

Use: "More than two decades have passed since my paralysis at the top of the stairs. Like all of us, I have since crossed other dark landings where the wild things are. But each time when I reached the other side, I found my supper waiting for me, and it was still hot." (*New York Times* Op-Ed page, May 10, 1988)

whistle stop   Any town too small or too insignificant for a regularly scheduled train stop. When a passenger wishes to descend at such a place, the conductor notifies the engineer by pulling the signal cord and the engineer responds with two toots of the whistle. President Harry Truman confounded the prognosticators when he campaigned successfully against Thomas Dewey for the presidency in 1948 by speaking from his train at innumerable whistle stops.

Whitman Sampler   Box of assorted chocolates with the familiar cover designed like a cross-stitched, early American sampler. It has the convenience of easy accessibility since it can be bought in any candy shop, stationer's or drug store.

Use: "I started my lessons at a dance school in an introductory course, the Whitman Sampler approach to ballroom dancing. In the short span of one month, my teacher at the Sandra Cameron dance center taught a little swing, fox-trot, waltz, tango, rumba, and cha-cha." (Alice J. Kelvin, in *The Smithsonian*, March 1989)

Wicked Witch of the West   One of four (two of them good, two of them wicked) witches in the Land of Oz in *The Wonderful Wizard of Oz* by L. Frank Baum. This formidable, evil witch melted away when Dorothy threw a pail of water at her.

Use: "The teamsters leadership fears losing control like the Wicked Witch of the West feared water." (*New York Times*, September 4, 1988) (See also OZ; YELLOW BRICK ROAD; WIZARD OF OZ.)

Wiesel, Elie   A survivor of the concentration camps at AUSCHWITZ and BUCHENWALD, where his whole family was murdered, Wiesel (1928–) has dedicated his life to bearing witness against the Nazi atrocities against the Jewish people. To this end, he has written several autobiographical novels which have caught the attention of the world: *Night* (1958), *Dawn* (1960) and *The Gates of the Forest* (1966). He has written many other books about the Jewish experience, both contemporary and historical. He has taught and lectured and insisted upon remembrance. Yet he has inveighed against all attempts to commercialize, vulgarize or sentimentalize the Holocaust.

Wiesel became the conscience of the world when he pleaded eloquently but unavailingly with President Ronald Reagan to cancel a state visit to Bitburg cemetery in Germany, where a group of SS officers were buried beside regular army troops. In 1986 he received the Nobel Peace Prize.

Wiesenthal, Simon   Having lost 89 relatives in the Holocaust and being, himself, a survivor of Nazi concentration camps, he has become the chief hunter of Nazi war criminals in the world. Wiesenthal (1908–) has located over a thousand of them. He stalked Adolf Eichmann, notorious former chief of the Gestapo's anti-Jewish operations, and was instrumental in having Eichmann spirited out of Argentina to be tried, convicted and hanged in Israel. He wrote *I Hunted Eichmann* (1961) and *The Murderers Among Us* (1967). Wiesenthal is head of the Jewish Documentation Center in Vienna.

Wiesenthal is a modern-day nemesis, hunting down and bringing to justice those responsible for the murder of six million Jews in the Holocaust.

Wild Bunch, The   A small group of outlaws put together and held together by BUTCH CASSIDY circa 1890. They were absolutely loyal to Cassidy and to each other. By 1902, their bank and train robberies, their assaults on guards and police officers were over and most of the gang members were dead or imprisoned.

Wimsey, Lord Peter   Aristocratic amateur detective in the novels of Dorothy L. Sayers (1893–1957). Witty, sophisticated, eccentric, epicurean, he has a wide range of interests, such as rare books, history, classical music (he is an accomplished pianist) and criminology. His character was played by the British actor Ian Carmichael in TV versions of *Clouds of Witness, The Unpleasantness at the Bellona Club, The Nine Tailors* and *Murder Must Advertise.*

Winesburg, Ohio   Written by Sherwood Anderson (1876–1941), this 1919 work contains 23 stories about characters who live in a small midwestern town with limited horizons. Each is seen through the eyes of a young reporter, George Willard. Anderson tears the veil from the idealized, sentimentalized picture of American small-town life and shows the loneliness, the cruelty, the boredom beneath the calm exterior. Winesburg became the prototype of a whole series of novels (*Main Street* by Sinclair Lewis) and poetry (*Spoon River Anthology* by Edgar Lee Masters), that expose the steamy, inbred, passionate entanglements of a town's inhabitants.

Winnie-the-Pooh   The lovable, ostensibly stupid but strangely wise, honey-eating bear who is the hero of A.A. Milne's Christopher Robin books for children, *Winnie the Pooh* (1926) and *The House at Pooh Corner.*

"Pooh's way is amazingly consistent with the principles of living envisaged long ago by the Chinese founders of Taoism." (Benjamin Hoff, "The Tao of Pooh")

with all deliberate speed   In 1954 in *Brown* v. *The Board of Education*, the United States Supreme Court struck down the concept of separate but equal and ordered the desegregation of public schools. Many states in the South were loath to comply. In *Brown II* (1955) the Supreme Court ordered recalcitrant school districts to integrate the schools "with all deliberate speed."

without redeeming social value   For years the courts have had to adjudicate cases in which charges of obscenity leveled against printed material have been countered by charges of First Amendment violations of freedom of the press. One of the most famous cases involved the government's attempt to ban James Joyce's *Ulysses.* Judge John M. Woolsey in 1933 concluded: "I am quite aware that owing to some of its scenes, 'Ulysses' is a rather strong draught to ask some sensitive, though normal, persons to take. But my considered opinion after long reflection, is that whilst in many places the effect of 'Ulysses' on the reader undoubtedly is somewhat emetic, nowhere does it tend to be aphrodisiac. 'Ulysses' may, therefore, be admitted to the U.S."

In 1966 the Supreme Court, in a case involving the banning of John Cleland's *Fanny Hill: Memoirs of a Woman of Pleasure* (1748–49) ruled that henceforth the burden of proof of obscenity rested squarely on the censors. They would have to prove that the material (1) appealed to prurient interest, (2) was patently offensive and (3) was utterly without redeeming social value.

Wizard of Oz, The   Film musical (1939) made from the popular children's book of the same name written by L. Frank Baum.

Dorothy (Judy Garland), a young girl, lives with her aunt on a farm in Kansas. During a tornado, Dorothy is hit on the head by flying debris and knocked unconscious. She and her dog Toto are borne away to the Land of Oz, ruled by a wizard known only by his dreaded stentorian voice. Dorothy follows the YELLOW BRICK ROAD to meet the wizard and enlist his help finding her way home. Along her path she encounters a host of strange characters whose names have become metaphors: the Tin Man, who has no heart (Jack Haley); the Cowardly Lion (Bert Lahr); the Scarecrow, without a brain (Ray Bolger); the wicked Witch of the West; and the diminutive Munchkins.

At the end of the road, Dorothy is brought before the Wizard's (Frank Morgan) hidden presence and tearfully begs him to help her and Toto home. The Wizard's voice is fierce, but Dorothy pulls the curtain aside and unmasks the Wizard as a genial, bumbling fraud. Armed with a pair of ruby slippers and counseled by the Good Witch Glinda, Dorothy has but to will herself home to get her wish. All ends happily in Kansas.

Wolfe, Nero　Fictional detective created by Rex Stout (1886–1975). Wolfe has been called a "corpulent recluse." Weighing "a seventh of a ton," he abhors all unnecessary physical activity and relegates all leg work to his assistant, Archie Goodwin. He is a gourmand with a Swiss chef, lives luxuriously in a brownstone on West 35th Street in New York City, grows orchids on his roof, speaks seven languages and has an extraordinary command of English.

woman I love, the　Phrase used in his abdication speech of December 11, 1936, by Edward VIII, king of Great Britain, to describe Wallis Warfield Simpson, a divorcee from Baltimore, Maryland whom he afterwards married. The context of the phrase runs: "You must believe me when I tell you that I have found it impossible to carry the heavy burden of responsibility and to discharge my duties as King as I would wish to do without the help and the support of the woman I love." Edward was succeeded by his brother, the duke of York, who became George VI.

Every man feels himself a tragic king of romance when he points to his wife and says, "the woman I love," for whom he is mockingly willing to sacrifice his all.

Wonder Woman　When it appeared on the comic book scene in 1942, *Wonder Woman* was hailed by feminists as an embodiment of some of its tenets. It was sharply condemned by such critics as Dr.

Frederic Wertham who, in his *Seduction of the Innocent*, (1954), took it to task for being one of the most harmful crime comics.

Originally, Wonder Woman was an Amazon princess who lived on Paradise Island. No men were permitted on the island. Wonder Woman came to America to help win World War II. Clad in a flashy red, white, blue and yellow costume, she performed her fantastic feats. She was virtually all-powerful—unless a man linked together her "bracelets of submission."

Female readers simply identified with *Wonder Woman*, the super-heroine, just as the male readers were drawn to Superman. Psychological experts of all sorts, however, had a field day with *Wonder Woman*, claiming to find in the comic book evidences of lesbianism and sadomasochism, among other aberrations.

Use: "...less an overt *Wonder Woman* than a walking platonic ideal"—description of Jackie Joyner-Kersee, Olympic Gold Medalist. (*New York Times Magazine*, July 31, 1988)

Woodstock   Town in New York State where in August 1969 thousands of counterculture young people sprawled on a field to listen to rock music or ballads by performers like Joan Baez, Arlo Guthrie, Jimi Hendrix, Richie Havens, the Jefferson Airplane, the Who. Anti-establishment dress and behavior and the longing for peace marked the attitudes of youth in the 1960s at Woodstock. A documentary of the same name about the festival won an Academy Award in 1970.

Wright, Frank Lloyd   Controversial American architect (1869–1959) who pleaded for an end to America's "lust for ugliness." Although in his youth he studied with Louis Sullivan, "the father of the skyscraper," Wright came to detest steel and stone cities. He rejected box-like structures, saying "a box is more of a coffin for the human spirit than an inspiration." He promoted organic architecture, that is, architecture that uses poured reinforced concrete, takes its shape from organic forms of nature and looks as if it has "grown" upon its site rather than been imposed upon it. He is famous for his dramatic prairie homes in which interiors merge with the landscape, e.g., the Robie House with its low, horizontal planes (1908); the Kaufman House cantilevered over a waterfall (1936); and the various Taliesins (1911, 1914, 1925), which housed his school for architects.

Wyeth, Andrew   American painter (1917–) whose canvases depict with photographic realism lonely people against a rural background of wide skies, open fields and poor farmhouses. His painting *Christina's World* (1948), showing an isolated girl half sprawled upon an upland pasture and looking toward a gaunt farmhouse on the horizon, has become almost a cliché, because it is so popular. Wyeth succeeds in evoking the girl's mood: a mixture of desolation and yearning. A Wyeth is synonymous with pictorial realism.

X

X-rated   For adults only, according to the self-regulatory Code of the Motion Picture Industry. X-rated films carry the warning: "This movie contains scenes of explicit sex, not suitable for children's viewing."

The term X-rated may be applied to any verbal or graphic material: language, magazines, newspapers, comics, as well as movies and theater.

Y

Yalta   Russian seaport on the Black Sea where American President Roosevelt, British Prime Minister Winston Churchill and Soviet leader Joseph Stalin met from February 4 to 12, 1945, to carve out their separate spheres of influence following the end of World War II. History has accused Roosevelt of giving the store away to Stalin, with concessions that led to the domination of Poland, Romania, Bulgaria, Hungary, Czechoslovakia and Eastern Germany by the U.S.S.R.

Yalta has come to stand for a betrayal of Western democratic entities to communist domination; a cynical or perhaps pragmatic bargaining away of freedom in a quid pro quo.

Yellow Brick Road   The golden paved road along which Dorothy, Toto, the Tin Man, the Scarecrow and the Cowardly Lion travel in search of the wizard in *The Wonderful Wizard of Oz*. The wizard supposedly has the power to grant each one of them what he or she desires, but he turns out to be a fraud. In the 1939 MGM musical made from L. Frank Baum's 1900 fantasy, the characters sing a happy song, "Follow the Yellow Brick Road."

The Yellow Brick Road suggests a quest, a journey in a fantasy land to find one's heart's desire.

Use: An ad by Mobil in the *New York Times*, July 14, 1988, reads: "Follow Your Own Yellow Brick Road." (See also WIZARD OF OZ, THE.)

Yippies   Self-styled, tongue-in-cheek acronym for Youth International Party; coined by leaders of the student demonstrators against the Vietnam War at the Democratic National Convention in Chicago

284

in August 1968. Riots started by Mayor Daley's police against the demonstrators led to the arrest and trial of the "Chicago seven," including Abbie Hoffman and Jerry Rubin; all seven were acquitted.

Yoknapatawpha   See FAULKNERIAN.

York, Sergeant Alvin C.   Originally a conscientious objector from Tennessee (1887–1964), he became a World War I hero in the U.S. infantry. In the battle of the Argonne on October 8, 1918, he charged a German machine-gun emplacement and captured 90 Germans almost single-handedly, then repeated the exploit, capturing 42 more.

young Turk   Expression derives from a reformist Turkish political party, which took control from 1908 to 1918. Now a young Turk is any insurgent, usually of a liberal persuasion, who tries to take control of an organization by political maneuver.

Yo-yo   A toy invented in 1920 by an American named Donald Duncan, although similar toys were in use in China as early as 1000 B.C. The toy consists of two wooden disks and a string wound around the connecting dowel. When let out, the yo- yo returns to the hand.

A yo-yo may be a stupid person who can be wound around one's fingers and manipulated up and down. Or something or someone that fluctuates repeatedly, e.g., one's emotions, stock market prices, foreign policy.

Yuppie   An acronym for young urban professional. Yuppie carries a slightly derogatory connotation since it implies an inordinate interest in upward mobility through materialistic goals: money, clothes, fashionable addresses, physical fitness, social climbing.

Use: Headline for John Simon's review of the play *Waiting for Godot, New York Magazine* (November 21, 1988): "Yuppie 'Godot'"—suggesting that stars Robin Williams and Steve Martin were too young, too well-fed and too successful to suggest the pathetic tramps Estragon and Vladimir.

Z

Zelda   Zelda Sayre (1899–1948), beautiful, madcap, reckless wife of writer F. SCOTT FITZGERALD, the model for his heroines. A JAZZ AGE flapper, she drank, smoked, danced the days and nights away and eventually died in a hospital for the mentally ill.

Ziegfeld, Florenz   American theatrical producer (1869–1932) famous for his Ziegfeld Follies (1907–1931), "glorifying the American Girl." He chose the music for his productions, approved the lavish costumes and stage effects, directed every scene and musical number. His taste and judgment brought the musical show to heights it had never attained before. Ziegfeld left his mark on the American musical revue.

Among the famous composers who wrote scores for the Follies were Irving Berlin, Rudolf Friml, Victor Herbert, Jerome Kern. Various stars contributed their own material: Eddie Cantor, Fannie Brice, W.C. Fields, Will Rogers, Ann Pennington. Among the enduring songs that were first heard in the Follies: "Shine on, Harvest Moon," sung by Nora Bayes (1908); "A Pretty Girl Is Like a Melody," composed by Irving Berlin and used as a theme song for the Follies; "My Man," sung by Fannie Brice (1921). (See also ZIEGFELD GIRLS.)

Ziegfeld Girls   They were "the most beautiful girls ever to walk across an American stage." And they were all personally selected by the legendary *Florenz Ziegfeld* (1869–1932) for his fabulously successful Ziegfeld Follies, which, with only a few interruptions, ran from 1907 to 1931.

Just as Charles Dana Gibson created the *Gibson Girl*, so did Ziegfeld create the Ziegfeld Girl. Tall, slender and elegant, she displaced the more amply endowed female as the "ideal" woman.

From this point on slenderness was in, plumpness out. Any tall, statuesque woman might find herself, not unhappily, labeled as a Ziegfeld Girl.